By the same author

CANADA'S CENTURY

THE RT. HON. VINCENT MASSEY, C.H.
GOVERNOR-GENERAL OF CANADA

Nation of the North

CANADA SINCE CONFEDERATION

by

D. M. LeBOURDAIS

*With Four Portraits
and Three Maps*

FREDERICK A. PRAEGER
NEW YORK

PRINTED IN GREAT BRITAIN
BY BUTLER AND TANNER LTD., FROME AND LONDON

8439

TO
JULIEN

PREFACE

CANADIAN history falls naturally into three parts. The first consists of the French regime which, except for Cartier's voyages, begins with Champlain at Port Royal in 1604 and at Quebec in 1608, and concludes with the Peace of Paris in 1763, when the dream of a French North American empire came to an inglorious end. The second period, covering about 100 years, from the Conquest to Confederation, was a time of struggle between British conquerors and the conquered French, the latter striving to retain their ancient culture, the former determined to dominate, culminating in their joint struggle for the right to govern themselves, free from dictation by governors sent out from England. The third, with which this book is chiefly concerned, begins with the failure of French-Canadians in Lower Canada (Quebec) and British-Canadians in Upper Canada (Ontario) to carry on a government acceptable to both. This led to the union of the British North American colonies, beginning with Nova Scotia, New Brunswick and Canada (Quebec and Ontario) in 1867, extending to the Pacific when British Columbia joined in 1871.

Most writers of Canadian history are attracted by the colour and romance of the French regime; and certainly across the history-pages of few other countries does such a procession of heroic figures pass. One does not need to possess French blood to appreciate the steadfast devotion of a Champlain, a Maisonneuve, a Jeanne Mance or a Laval; to thrill to the heroism of a Dollard, or the audacity of a d'Iberville, complaining to the French king that he was 'tired of conquering the Bay of Hudson'. Who would not follow the gallant La Salle to the mouth of the Mississippi, or cross the plains with La Verendrye and his sons, to gaze with the latter upon the snow-capped Rockies? History must borrow from fiction to find another pair the equal of Medard des Groseilliers and his brother-in-law, Pierre Esprit Radisson.

Except, perhaps, to explain the subsequent appearance of such figures as Louis La Fontaine, Wilfrid Laurier and Ernest Lapointe; of François Garneau, Philippe Hebert, Gabrielle Roy and Gratien

Gelinas (Fridolin), a knowledge of the French regime is not essential to an understanding of modern Canada any more than it is necessary to know the antecedents of those of British or other ancestry. A knowledge of the second period is undoubtedly desirable because of its bearing on what comes later, and therefore a summarized account is given of that tumultuous century.

Although the period chiefly covered by this book is relatively short, it is equalled in significance only by that during which Canada's neighbour was occupied with the development of the southern half of the continent. Aside from Confederation itself, the most important events in the era under consideration have occurred since World War I, a period during which the writer has been a close observer of Canadian affairs. In addition, he has had the benefit of association with students of affairs whose memories reached back to Confederation times. This chronicle may therefore, in a sense, be considered a first-hand account.

It is not, however, a book of memoirs or reminiscences; and nothing has been set down that cannot be documented. The author belongs to no school; and although he has read most of what has been written concerning the period, is indebted only in a very general way to other writers. He would like to acknowledge, however, his indebtedness to the Public Archives, the reference library of the Toronto Public Libraries, the library of the University of Toronto, and the Ontario Legislative Library, and to their staffs for courteous and efficient co-operation.

Many persons, some in official positions, have been consulted, and the manuscript has been read, wholly or in part, by men and women with special knowledge of some part of the subject. To these the author is indebted for many suggestions, for which he is grateful, even though he may not always have been able to accept them. In the circumstances, it would be invidious to name any particular person or persons.

Photographs of Macdonald, Laurier, and Mackenzie King were supplied by the National Film Board and that of the Rt. Hon. Vincent Massey by Karsh.

TORONTO   D. M. LeB.
April 25, 1953

CONTENTS

ILLUSTRATIONS

Photos: National Film Board of Canada

Prologue

CHAPTER I

A CENTURY OF STRUGGLE

WHEN the history of our times comes to be written, the emergence of Canada as a nation will rank as a most significant event. Such a statement needs qualification. What is a 'significant' event, and for whom? We assume that the aims of every people is to get along together without undue dissension, attaining for all as full a life as possible; and to live peaceably with its neighbours. Every intelligent people will also desire to improve the lot of less-fortunate ones elsewhere. By this standard, Canada's record is exceptional.

It is not contended that Canadians are an exceptional people, for they are not; but they are fortunate. They are fortunate in possessing half a continent, endowed with everything needed for successful living in a modern state; they are fortunate in their neighbours, against whom they require no defence; and they are fortunate in belonging to that group of people who first evolved the principles of self-government and have steadily and tenaciously held by them.

It would not be right to assume from this that Canadians have not had many problems to face and obstacles to overcome. In the first place, they have had to contend with what is probably the most difficult of all human problems—the union of two peoples in one nation, conquerors and conquered, with different languages, religions and backgrounds, while attempting to retain the individuality and the culture of each. There has been friction, of course; but the extent to which they have succeeded, as will become evident in the following pages, is a remarkable achievement.

A concurrent problem resulted from the attempt to secure, on the part of those of French as well as of British ancestry, an increasing share in the control of their own government. This was particularly difficult because no precedent existed for the extension to a colony, especially one so largely composed of a conquered people, of what eventually amounted to equality of status with the Imperial authority. Many, who in the United Kingdom would have insisted on their right to the fullest possible political freedom, were not only

3

content in Canada with an inferior status, but strongly opposed those who sought a higher one.

These problems, with others that have developed from time to time, run like threads throughout the course of Canada's struggle for nationhood; and while this book is concerned chiefly with the period since Confederation, these threads must be examined at a much earlier period in order to determine the influence they have had upon the course of later events.

When Wolfe, the 'Conquering Hero', scaled the heights at Quebec and defeated Montcalm's regulars and colonial militia on the Plains of Abraham, the prospects of the 65,000 people of New France could not have been more dreary. Abandoned by their mother country, whose interest in them had never been very keen, they were now at the mercy of their traditional enemies, who hated their religion, and whose language and ways were strange to them; a handful of people amid ever-increasing numbers of their one-time enemies, their chance of survival seemed indeed very slim.

The reality, however, was in many ways less terrible than their fear-induced anticipations assumed. Military control is never pleasant; but in General James Murray, the first governor, the *Canadiens* [1] had a friend who somewhat extravagantly referred to them as 'perhaps the bravest and best race upon the globe'. His view seems to have been reflected by the British government, increasingly harassed by the American colonists, and perhaps already having premonitions of the conflict soon to begin.

At any rate, the government, when it thought of them at all, was disposed to be conciliatory, and shortly after offered the *Canadiens* a voice in their own affairs, which they had never had under French rule. Although no statutory authority yet existed for it, Roman Catholics had not generally been subjected in the colonies to the restrictions against them current in the United Kingdom. Consequently, Murray allowed the *Canadiens* to sit on juries, granted them commissions in the army and appointed them to judicial positions, over the protests of the camp-followers and carpetbaggers who considered themselves entitled to the spoils of war. Murray's rule was, of course, that of an autocrat, but he has been warmly remembered by generations of *Canadiens*.

Since, in New France, the fur trade and the effort to Christianize the Indians had been the major objectives, two tendencies were constantly at war with one another: the allurement of the forest, giving

[1] This spelling will be used to denote French-speaking Canadians.

rise to the numerous *coureur-de-bois* class, whose freedom from control annoyed the clergy; and the pleasant intercourse of the settlements, each gathered about its church, especially along the St. Lawrence, the Great Highway. The seigniorial system had never greatly resembled the feudal system of France, upon which it was patterned, for the reason that the gap between *seigneur* and *habitant* had never been great. A life of leisure on his rents was never possible for the *seigneur*; while it was even possible for a *habitant* with energy and ambition to attain seigniorial rank.

The *habitant*, in most cases unschooled, was a capable, independent person, skilful in the construction of his buildings, furniture, tools and equipment; he produced all his food, cured his own meat and boiled maple sap for sugar, still an expensive luxury in other countries; his wife spun yarn and wove cloth for the family's clothing, bedding and household draperies. From the standpoint of relative wealth, the *habitants* of New France constituted one of the most prosperous agricultural classes in the world.

With the Conquest, the fur trade and every other form of business, except small-scale retailing, passed into the hands of the British—chiefly Scottish—to be monopolized by that class for many years; but the *habitant* changed his way of life very little. The artisan in the village continued to ply his trade. Most of the officials returned to France, but the clergy, especially those Canadian-born, remained. Since the people had always been accustomed to look to the *curé* for guidance, they continued to do so; and the clergy, concerned only with the preservation of that culture which to them ranked next to their hope of salvation, counselled submission to the victors so long as the use of their language, continuance of their familiar laws and customs and the freedom to practise their religion were assured.

It is sometimes asserted that the *Canadiens* were an ignorant lot, but that is not correct. While the educational range of even the best educated was somewhat narrow, the proportion of illiteracy was probably no greater than in any other country at the time. The *habitants*, with little or no schooling, formed the base of the educational pyramid. Next came people in the villages, where schools of some sort had existed from an early period. Forming the apex, were the more prosperous city-dwellers, including officials, army officers, physicians and surgeons, surveyors, notaries (lawyers were barred from the colony) and the clergy, for whom the seminaries and classical colleges were available.

Although the *Canadiens* were content to be left alone, the little group of English-speaking colonists complained bitterly that they, not the vanquished, were the oppressed. Nevertheless, the Quebec Act, passed in 1774, assured to the *Canadiens* the right to their religion, customs and civil laws, privileges with respect to religion denied—and for many years to come—to their co-religionists in Ireland.

The Quebec Act more than justified the expectations of its framers; for when, a short time later, the American colonists rebelled, the *Canadiens* resisted even the blandishments of Benjamin Franklin, who tried to induce them to revolt. The clergy, with some exceptions, took the view that they had nothing to gain, and perhaps much to lose, by joining the disaffected colonists, whose depredations they had had to bear for generations. And when the Revolutionary War was over, the only North American subjects of King George III were the *Canadiens*—and a straggling host, since known as United Empire Loyalists, who, either voluntarily or otherwise, had left their former homes to begin life anew in the only territory still flying the British flag.

Increasing numbers of Loyalists in what is now Ontario made necessary further legislation on the part of the British government. The Constitutional Act of 1791 provided for two separate provinces, Lower Canada, inhabited chiefly by *Canadiens*, and Upper Canada, preponderantly Loyalist in origin. The government was to consist of a governor-general (who resided in Quebec), with a lieutenant-governor in Upper Canada, an appointed executive council, an appointed legislative council (or upper House), and an assembly, elected, as in England, on a property franchise. The governor, however, was under no obligation to accept the advice of either the executive council or the legislature.

The new arrangement might have succeeded after a fashion if Canada had consisted only of conquered people, for the conquered could not be choosers, but in Upper Canada many had been reared in the tradition of the New England town meeting; and some, come directly from Great Britain, objected to the lowering of political status involved in the westward crossing of the Atlantic: they desired the same degree of freedom that they had formerly enjoyed.

Yet, in England, there were few, if any, who did not draw a distinction between the rights of British subjects at home, and colonial subjects. John Morley tells of Gladstone that 'when he had been only four years in the House he took a firm stand against pretensions in Canada to set their assembly on an equal footing with the imperial parliament at home'.

The chief settlements in Upper Canada were on the St. Lawrence above the mouth of the Ottawa and along Lake Ontario, near the western end of which was York (Toronto), selected as the capital in 1793. The settlements extended westward in the peculiar arrow-shaped peninsula lying between Lakes Ontario, Erie and Huron, where, however, the practice of awarding large grants to favoured persons or organizations tended to thwart quick and easy settlement, although grants to John Galt's Canada Company and to Colonel Thomas Talbot did result in many needed settlers.

These newcomers, attracted by the promise of cheap, fertile land, found they must wrest that land from the forest which, for many years, was the chief concern of everyone; and it is possible that the indifference of Canadians in later years to the wanton exploitation and destruction of the forests had its origin in those days when the bush was an ever-present enemy.

Although, while under French rule, the *Canadiens* had enjoyed no political advantages, they were not slow to appreciate the advantages of the British system, and many of them protested vigorously against being excluded from its benefits; in fact, some of them displayed remarkable proficiency in the use of parliamentary procedure. Upper Canadian reformers demanded responsible government as it had been evolved in England, and their counterparts in Lower Canada would be content with no less; if Upper Canada had its William Lyon Mackenzie, Lower Canada had its Louis Joseph Papineau.

Baulked in their efforts to win legislative liberty, the reformers turned to rebellion, but in this they were baulked even more effectively. The risings were suppressed in both provinces, but they had at least one result: they convinced the British government that something must be done. The Earl of Durham, a liberal aristocrat, was sent to Canada with power to deal with the situation as he saw fit, and to make recommendations for the government of the country thereafter.

In many respects, a man of advanced political ideas, Durham nevertheless seems to have been incapable of appreciating the *Canadien* character or point of view. In his report, he declared that it must be 'the first and steady purpose of the British government to establish an English population, with English laws and language, in this province, and to trust its government to none but a decidedly

2

English legislature'. This, of course, meant minority rule, since there were then 650,000 *Canadiens* and only about 450,000 English-speaking subjects; but Durham was convinced that the 'nationality of the French-Canadians' must be 'obliterated'.

Lord Durham's chief recommendations were that the two Canadas should be united under a single legislature, and that the executive should be responsible to a majority of the assembly. These recommendations were duly implemented by the Act of Union passed by the British parliament in 1840. Though Lower Canada had the greater population, both provinces were given equal representation in parliament.

Looking back on the event, after more than a century, it is evident that Durham erred in his diagnosis and also in his suggested remedy. Time was to prove that English- and French-speaking Canadians are not essentially different; in each province, despite differences of language and religion, men found themselves in accord on political questions with those of like mind in the opposite province; differences of opinion cut across linguistic lines. Durham's chief remedy, legislative union of the provinces, was ultimately found to be unworkable, not entirely because Canadians were divided into two opposing national groups ('two nations warring in the bosom of a single state'), but also because, in both sections, but especially in Upper Canada, varying political views were held.

As the struggle for responsible government (Durham's recommendation was ignored by the governors who followed him) grew more intense, the two leading protagonists were Robert Baldwin, in Upper Canada, and Louis H. La Fontaine, in Lower Canada, leaders of the Reform party. As evidence of how well men of similar views could work together, despite differing language and religion, it is interesting to note that once when La Fontaine had lost his seat, Baldwin sponsored him in an Upper Canadian constituency in which he was elected, while La Fontaine later came to Baldwin's rescue in a similar situation by arranging for his election in a friendly Lower Canadian constituency.

Eventually, there came a governor (Sir Charles Bagot) who, although no Liberal, was willing to accept the inevitable when confronted with it, and he invited La Fontaine to join with Baldwin in an executive council which should have the support of a majority of the assembly. Thus, within five years of Durham's predictions concerning French political incapacity, a *Canadien* leader was actually recognized as Prime Minister of Canada.

Bagot's successor, Sir Charles Metcalfe, was of different metal. He attempted to turn back the clock and refused to recognize the right of colonials to responsible government, which to him was the 'virtual surrender into the hands of the council of the prerogatives of the Crown'. Baldwin and La Fontaine resigned.

The governor himself took a hand in the elections that followed (1844); the issue, unfortunately not for the last time, was 'loyalty'. Those who opposed the governor and his satellites were disloyal, rebels, annexationists; and, as a result, the Reformers found themselves in a minority. Metcalfe selected his advisers from among the Tories, who, as Stephen Leacock observed of Simcoe, wanted what they conceived to be British government, and 'wanted it all; its established church, its hereditary titles, its form, its feathers, its venerable humbugs; and nothing newer than Queen Anne'.

When the next elections were held, however, Canada had a new governor, the Earl of Elgin, who believed in responsible government. This time the Reformers won by a large majority and again La Fontaine and Baldwin headed what for the first time was referred to by some as a ministry. Much still remained to be done before the Canadian people had achieved their full political independence, but the great fight for responsible government was over. It was a fight that was to affect many more than the people of Canada, and many who now enjoy the right to govern themselves owe a debt to Louis La Fontaine and Robert Baldwin.

The La Fontaine-Baldwin ministry initiated much useful legislation, a good deal of which was long overdue. In the second session of parliament, no less than 195 laws were passed. Neither of the leaders was a radical, and as time went on opposition developed on the left as well as on the right. The leaders had expected opposition from the right, but were inclined to resent it from within their own ranks. These left-wing dissidents, who called themselves 'Clear Grits', became increasingly critical of the government, and, among other things (in which they were supported by many other Reformers), were in favour of an elective legislative council, to which La Fontaine and Baldwin were opposed.

In 1851, Baldwin resigned and went into complete retirement; La Fontaine's resignation soon followed. Two years later, La Fontaine was appointed Chief Justice of the Court of Queen's Bench for Lower Canada, and in the following year was created a baronet in recognition of his conspicuous services to his country.

The Reform administration was continued under Francis Hincks and A. N. Morin. By now the railway era had burst upon the country, thereby introducing a new major thread into the warp and woof of Canadian life, one which was to persist until far into the twentieth century; and for a time constitutional issues gave way to problems associated with the rapid spread of railways. In 1850, only 66 miles of railway existed in the whole country, but by 1860 the mileage had increased to 2,000, which included the Grand Trunk and a number of lines later absorbed by it.

Hincks was essentially a financier, and soon the government was deeply involved in a maze of railway promotion and speculation; and, as is often the case when promoters of large enterprises wait, cap in hand, upon governments, corruption followed. The charge has been made that sometimes it was hard to tell when those in high places were acting as members of the government or as officers of a railway company, since many ministers of the Crown were also railway directors. Only the vigilance of rival promoters and politicians, themselves intent upon securing charters, subsidies, and even outright gifts for their own schemes, prevented the public treasury from being looted much oftener than it was.

Except for resistance to armed invasion (1812–14), and except for a growing trade, Canadians hitherto had very little official relations with the United States. Not for many years yet was it possible for Canada to deal directly with its neighbour; but in 1854, Lord Elgin, on behalf of all the British North American colonies, negotiated a treaty with the United States for the free exchange of natural products which, in the twelve years it covered, was a boon to the colonies.

Both in Upper and Lower Canada, the electorate was nominally divided into Reformers and Conservatives; but in Upper Canada the Reformers now became definitely split, a large section swinging to the Clear Grits.[1] When, in due course, the Hincks-Morin ministry was defeated (1854), Sir Allan MacNab, a leader of the Tory section of the Conservatives, as well as a leading railway promoter, joined the Reformer Morin in an attempt to form a stable government, but stability was not in its nature. In fact, stable government had by now become almost impossible.

The little city of Kingston, at the eastern end of Lake Ontario, where, in 1673, Frontenac had built a fort, was the first capital after the Act of Union. There, in a structure built for a hospital, members

[1] See Underhill, F. H. *Some Aspects of Upper Canadian Radical Opinion in the Decade Before Confederation.* Canadian Historical Association, Annual Report, 1927.

from the two Canadas met in parliament for the first time. Kingston, however, soon proved too cramped, and in 1844, the capital was moved to Montreal, where it remained till 1849, when the parliament building was burned, not by recalcitrant *Canadiens*, but by a Tory mob intent upon demonstrating its loyalty. Need for a capital which should be dominated neither by French nor English was recognized, but agreement could not be reached on a suitable place. In the meantime it was decided that parliament should meet for four years alternately at Toronto and Quebec, beginning with Toronto. The choice of a permanent capital was left to Queen Victoria who, not entirely unassisted, chose Bytown, renamed Ottawa, which, while in Ontario, is only half the width of the Ottawa river from Quebec, but not till 1866, the year before a greater Canada came into being, were government and parliament established at the new capital.

Meantime, Canadian governments were becoming even less permanent than the site of the capital; between 1854 and 1864, ten ministries held office. John A. Macdonald, first elected to parliament as member for Kingston in the Metcalfe election of 1844, who had accepted the fact that Canada was a country consisting of two distinct national groups, and that no government could exist for very long which did not represent both groups, eventually attained the chief position of influence in Upper Canada. Conservative in politics as well as by conviction, Macdonald yet possessed the faculty, amounting almost to genius, of working with others, although they might not be entirely of his own way of thinking; but even he was unable to compose a combination that could command a continuing majority of the legislature.

The principal Reform leader in Upper Canada during this time was George Brown, a Scot who had come to Canada in 1843 and had shortly after founded the Toronto *Globe*, which, due to his vigorous writing, was soon to attain a position unique in Canadian journalism. He hated Macdonald, to whom he had not spoken for a number of years, and was often also at odds with his fellow-Reformers. Because of his strong antipathies toward the Roman Catholic religion, he had difficulty in finding allies in Lower Canada. The time had not yet come when Conservatives or Reformers were willing to follow a single leader, either English or French, for Canada as a whole.

When it was evident that stalemate had been reached, George Brown did a magnanimous thing; despite his hatred of Macdonald, he offered to join him in a coalition for the purpose of bringing about a federal union of all the British North American colonies.

CHAPTER II

PRELUDE TO UNION

UNION of the North American colonies was not entirely a new idea when George Brown offered to join Macdonald in a coalition government for that purpose; he himself had spoken and written on the subject many times before, especially in relation to the vast Northwest Territories still under the control of the Hudson's Bay Company. In this westward extension of Canada he not only saw a possible barrier to further aggression by the United States, but also a means of countering the influence of the French-Canadians, for whom he did not have much love.

Durham, too, had envisaged a wider union, but finding the time inopportune had proposed, as a preliminary step, the union of the two Canadas. In 1858, Alexander T. Galt, an English-speaking member of parliament from Lower Canada, had moved a series of resolutions calling for a committee to sound out the people of the Maritime colonies and the British government on the question of union.

The resolutions did not get to a vote; but Georges E. Cartier, leader of the French-Conservative group in Lower Canada, who headed the next ephemeral government, announced that his government was prepared to proceed with the proposal; and at the close of the session appointed a committee consisting of himself, Galt and John Ross (President of the Executive Council) to discuss the matter with the British government. Arrived in England, the committee endeavoured to secure the concurrence of the government, requesting its authority to call a meeting of delegates from all the colonies to consider the next step; but the government declined the request, giving as its reason that only one colony (Nova Scotia) had so far expressed a desire for union, and that it was not advisable, in the circumstances, to authorize the meeting.

So much for the Canadas; but the possibilities of union had been discussed in Nova Scotia as early as 1826, when Richard Uniacke had proposed such a scheme in a memorial to the British government. Joseph Howe also had visions of a broader British North

America. He had visited England in 1850, and with characteristic
vigour and imagination had attempted to interest the British people
and government in a scheme to unite the colonies by means of a
railway.

It was perhaps natural that such ideas should take root in Nova
Scotia. Although, in a sense, Newfoundland had a longer history of
British ownership, and despite the fact that for the greater part of
the time most of its people were French, Nova Scotia, which became
British in 1713, had had half a century of British rule before the
conquest of New France. Not till after the founding of Halifax in
1749, and the expulsion of the Acadians six years later, did the
population become preponderantly English-speaking (even though
spoken in different parts of the province with Irish, Scottish or
German accents!).

The coming of the Loyalists following the Revolutionary War
swelled the numbers of English-speaking people, marking also the
beginning of the inevitable struggle for representative government.
While the governors did not have, as in Canada, to contend with a
majority descended from a recently conquered people, they were no
less determined to preserve intact that which they were pleased to
term the prerogative of the Crown. Nevertheless the governors of
Nova Scotia—and their masters in the Colonial Office in London—
were, at length, also to admit the right of colonials to govern themselves. If Canada had its Sydenhams and Metcalfes, so did Nova
Scotia have its Campbells and Falklands; but in 1848—the same year
as in Canada—Joseph Howe and his associates won the fight for
responsible government.

New Brunswick, until 1784 part of Nova Scotia, was sparsely
settled till the coming of the Loyalists. Despite their background of
self-government in the American colonies, the Loyalists were not so
eager for it as their fellow-colonists in other provinces: they were
inclined to associate all such ideas with the republicanism from which
they had but recently fled. Consequently, New Brunswick has in its
history no Howes, no La Fontaines, or Baldwins; and the boon of
responsible government came to its people without much effort on
their part.

Isle Saint Jean, with an area of 2,184 square miles, lying off the
Acadian coast, was retained by France in 1713 when the rest of
Acadia, except Isle Royale (Cape Breton), was finally ceded to
Britain; but following the next war, it, too, was lost to France, and
the new owners called it Prince Edward Island. The few French

who had made their homes on the island were either killed or driven off, and, aside from a few Loyalists, not many of British stock arrived until 1804, when the Earl of Selkirk, whom we shall meet again, assisted some 800 dispossessed Scottish Highlanders to settle there and become the ancestors of most present-day Islanders.

Like New Brunswick, Prince Edward Island achieved responsible government through the efforts of others, but its people have been as tenacious in maintaining their political rights as those of any other province. With the population of a small city, the island lacks none of the governmental trappings of its more populous sisters. Even after its neighbours, Nova Scotia and New Brunswick, with whom its intercourse has always been close, had become part of a larger scheme, sturdy little Prince Edward Island for a time held aloof.

The same considerations—and a few additional ones—that finally drew Prince Edward Island into the fold, brought the others together earlier. Questions of trade probably carried most weight. Each colony had its own customs tariffs against the products of its neighbours and the colonies or states to the south, but these did not prevent a considerable interchange of goods. Most of their trade, however, was with the United Kingdom, in whose markets they were given a preference. Moreover, they were largely prevented by the British Navigation Acts from trading with foreign countries.

This was considered quite natural.

When, indeed, the colonies were first planted [says Spencer Walpole, in his *History of England*], no restrictions were placed on their commerce. It was only when their progress made their custom desirable that the legislature undertook to secure it for the mother-country. The Navigation Act virtually declared that the colonies should buy everything they wanted in England, and sell everything they had to sell in England.

For the sake of securing a monopoly for the British manufacturer, the colonists were forbidden to engage in any manufacture; they were even prohibited from refining their own sugars. They were regarded as mere dependencies of the mother-country—as useful in promoting British trade.

Thus, when the United Kingdom adopted free trade in 1846, this preferential market was lost, and the colonies were thrown to a much larger extent into the orbit of the United States, more especially so after the Reciprocity Treaty of 1854 became effective. This gave further impetus to the already strong tendency in some quarters for annexation. In 1849, a group of men in Montreal, previously and subsequently noted for their ultra-imperialist views, signed a Manifesto in which it was stated

That it is the resolve of England to invest us with the attributes, and compel us to assume the burdens of independence, is no longer problematical . . . An overruling conviction then, of its necessity, and a high sense of the duty we owe to our country, a duty we can neither disregard nor postpone, impel us to the idea of separation; and whatever negotiations may eventuate with Great Britain, a grateful liberality on the part of Canada should mark every proceeding.

Allied to questions of trade was the matter of communications, especially railways. These required the investment of large sums of money—larger than any previously required for anything. Practically all of this money must come from outside sources, chiefly Great Britain, and investors were chary of small pioneer communities with questionable credit. For twenty years previous to Confederation, the people of Nova Scotia and New Brunswick, led by Howe, had been attempting to build an intercolonial railway connecting them one with the other and with Canada, but their efforts had been frustrated by the difficulty of getting the financial support of the imperial government. This difficulty was increased by the machinations of influential British railway contractors eager to share in the spoils of this new Eldorado. Up to the time of Confederation, only short sections of railway had been completed in those provinces; while, in Canada, the chief railway, the Grand Trunk, built to connect Montreal with Toronto, Collingwood and Sarnia; Portland, Maine; and Riviere du Loup, was still an aggregation of disconnected pieces. Controlled in England and managed from there, it already had a sordid record of financial legerdemain and political corruption.

Third in importance from the standpoint of impelling forces, but of paramount influence, was the attitude of British governments. As we have seen, when the commerce of the colonies was closely controlled, the relationship, from the standpoint of the United Kingdom, was based directly upon profit. Then British policy consisted in keeping the colonies in leading-strings, and the weaker and more divided they were the better for that purpose.

When free trade had opened their markets to the world, the attitude of British statesmen changed. In 1850, a member of Lord Palmerston's government, and leader in the House of Commons, said:

I anticipate with others that some of the colonies may so grow in population and wealth that they may say 'Our strength is sufficient to enable us to be independent of England. The link is now become onerous to us. The time is come when we think we can, in amity and alliance with England, maintain our independence.' I do not think that time is yet approaching.

But let us make them, as far as possible, fit to govern themselves; let us give them, as far as we can, the capacity of ruling their own affairs; let them increase in wealth and population, and whatever may happen, we of this great empire shall have the consolation of saying that we have contributed to the happiness of the world.

The final factor, by no means of least importance, especially with respect to the Canadas, was fear of the United States. When the Civil War ended in 1865, the northern states swarmed with demobilized soldiers ripe for any emprise, and the regular armies were still strong. Great Britain had been sympathetic toward the Confederacy, and there was also a strong feeling in Canada in favour of the South, which caused considerable irritation in the northern states. General Grant had declared that Sheridan's cavalry could conquer Canada in a month, which was probably a correct estimate: the situation had changed appreciably since the days of 1812–14.

The greatest cause for concern, however, lay in the territories under the jurisdiction of the Hudson's Bay Company, and which, in conformity to that company's desire to keep the country a vast fur-preserve, were still almost empty. In 1777, Captain James Cook had sailed northward along the Pacific coast, charting the shoreline, and establishing for the United Kingdom a claim to lands beyond. By an irony of fate, he missed the mouth of the great Columbia, into which, in 1792, Captain Robert Gray of Boston sailed in the ship from which the river got its name. President Jefferson sent Lewis and Clark overland to the Columbia in 1803, and John Jacob Astor planted a trading post at Astoria, near its mouth, in 1811. David Thompson, between the years of 1807 and 1811, explored the river from its source to its mouth; and in 1812, the Hudson's Bay Company bought the Astoria post from Astor, which helped to bolster the British claim to what was becoming known as the 'Oregon Country'.

So confused was the title to this great country that the British and United States governments, unable to agree on a boundary, signed a treaty in 1818 providing for ten years' joint occupation, later extended indefinitely. But a vital difference existed between American occupation and the manner in which the British, represented by the Hudson's Bay Company, occupied the country. The former, with their women and children, their household effects, their cattle and horses, their pigs and chickens, moved inexorably into the fertile valleys of the Pacific Northwest, sending word to friends and relatives in New England, in the South, in Missouri and

Kentucky, of the fabulous paradise they had found. And other caravans set out on the long trek across plains and desert, over snow-filled mountain passes, fording or swimming foaming rivers in wave after wave of land-hungry adventurers.

The Hudson's Bay Company, on the other hand, planted its palisaded posts where the rivers joined so that the natives might come with the least inconvenience to trade their furs for the company's wares, as they had done for a century and a half, discouraging in every way possible anyone who might wish to settle in the territory. As evidence of the Company's attitude in this connection, the testimony given by Sir George Simpson, governor-in-chief, at an enquiry held in London in 1857, may be cited. Asked if he was acquainted with the coast near Vancouver Island and farther north, he replied: 'Yes, I have gone along that coast from Puget's Sound to the Russian principal settlement at Sitka'; and he replied when asked: 'Do you believe that coast to be altogether unfit for colonization?'— 'I believe it to be quite unfit for colonization.'

Doubtless, if asked concerning the coast south of Puget Sound, his answer would have been the same.

Russian North America (Alaska) reached as far south as latitude 54° 40′ N., and Americans were demanding all the intervening country. In the presidential election of 1844, the Democrats' slogan was 'Fifty-four, forty, or fight!' For a time there was danger of war, but James K. Polk, the successful candidate, despite his party's slogan, with a war on his hands with Mexico, was prevailed upon to take a conciliatory line with the United Kingdom, and in 1846 the 49th parallel was accepted as the boundary, except for a swing to the south to allow all of Vancouver Island to remain British.

This settlement still allowed room for the inrushing Americans; and the discovery of gold in California in 1848 diverted for a time the tide of immigration in that direction. But not for long. In 1858, when the California diggings had passed their peak, gold was found in British Columbia on the lower Fraser River, and later in Cariboo, some 400 miles inland, causing one of the world's most picturesque gold rushes. While Cariboo drew the adventurous from all the world, the majority were Americans.

Under the spur of gold, California's population rose from 92,000 in 1850 to 380,000 in 1860; and if any comparable influx of Americans had occurred in British Columbia, it would have been impossible for a few thousand British people to hold so large a region against the wishes of the vast majority. But most of those who swarmed to

California were not goldseekers; they were men and women bent on finding homes for themselves; and since there was still plenty of land south of the 49th parallel, they did not have the urge to move northward.

Nevertheless, to British statesmen in London and a few far-seeing Canadians the danger of an American state occupying the Pacific coast from the 49th parallel to the southern limits of Russian America was very real. That there were good grounds for fear was shown a few months after the union of the British North American colonies when the United States bought Alaska.

If British Columbia had lost the first part of its name and gone the way of Texas and California, Canada's subsequent dreams of greatness could never have been anything but dreams.

Macdonald

CHAPTER III

CONFEDERATION

ALTHOUGH, in the Maritime provinces, the need for action was not so desperate as in Canada, the first steps toward union were taken there. Early in 1864, the legislature of Nova Scotia adopted a resolution endorsing a legislative union of the Maritime provinces. In moving the resolution, the Premier, Dr. Charles Tupper, explained that this was a step preliminary to a wider union, then unfortunately impossible of accomplishment. New Brunswick and Prince Edward Island were invited to appoint delegates to meet those from Nova Scotia at Charlottetown, on September 1 of that year, to discuss the subject.

Learning that the conference was being held, the government of Canada asked if it might send delegates, and upon receiving a cordial invitation eight members of the ministry, including Macdonald, Brown and Cartier, hurried to Charlottetown, where they were made welcome. Their presence greatly enlarged the original purpose of the meeting, and it was therefore decided to adjourn to a further meeting to be held at Quebec, when the question of a wider union could be discussed.

The Quebec conference met on October 10, with thirty-three delegates in attendance. As at the Charlottetown conference, the delegates from the Maritime provinces consisted of both government and opposition members. The Canadian delegation consisted of the entire cabinet of twelve members, already bipartisan, of whom the Prime Minister, Sir Etienne Taché, was elected chairman of the conference. The purpose of the meeting was set forth in a resolution moved by Macdonald that 'the best interests and present and future prosperity of British North America will be promoted by a federal union under the Crown of Great Britain, provided such union can be effected on principles just to the several provinces'.

In speaking to the motion, Macdonald said that if union did not result from the meeting, the Canadas would so need to reorganize the basis of their government that a larger union might be postponed indefinitely. In discussing the most desirable form of union, he admitted his preference for a legislative union, but should the federal principle prevail,

Care should be taken to avoid the mistakes and weaknesses of the United States' system, the primary error of which was the reservation to the different States of all powers not delegated to the general government. We must reverse this process by establishing a strong central government, to which shall belong all powers not especially conferred on the provinces.

In the light of subsequent events, Macdonald's views on this point are full of interest.

The discussion that followed was heated at times, but the desire for agreement was strong, and a way was found out of every difficulty. The Canadian constitution was conceived in a spirit of compromise, and its cornerstone is compromise. When the sessions ended on September 28, seventy-two resolutions were unanimously adopted, and the delegates were pledged to recommend that their respective legislatures should adopt them without amendment.

There is a tendency to glorify the men known as the 'Fathers of Confederation', but there is no doubt that, in the main, they were an exceptional group of people. Macdonald, Cartier, Brown, Tupper, Tilley, were statesmen in the fullest sense of the term. Macdonald would have been outstanding in any company, and the success of the conference was, in large measure, due to his peculiar qualifications. While not the first to entertain the idea of a federal union—in fact, he was at first rather averse to it—once he was convinced that no better solution could be secured, he never wavered; his capacious mind immediately grasped the essential requirements; and he held to them with great tenacity. His uncanny intuition concerning other men's minds enabled him to hold out on points on which he felt eventual agreement was possible, and to give way when necessary to meet the convictions of others.

History has not been kind to the 'indispensable man'; too often its verdict reverses the views of his contemporaries. In Macdonald's case, however, time has served to establish him as the supreme architect of Confederation. Some writers give Brown the chief credit, and undoubtedly he played an important, even vital, part; yet, despite his farsightedness and occasional magnanimity, his intolerance of opposing opinion largely nullified his effectiveness. First place has been given by writers to Cartier, and his claim, too, is great; without the concurrence of the 1,200,000 *Canadiens* for whom he spoke, Confederation would have been impossible. It was largely due to Cartier's ability to see both sides of a question that agreement was reached, and the faith of his compatriots in his integrity prevented opposition in Quebec which might have been fatal to union. Thus, to Brown's forbearance; to Cartier's spirit of compromise; to Tupper's aggressive steadfastness; to Tilley's self-effacing sincerity; to McGee's imagination and fervour; and to Galt's level-headed business acumen, credit must be given; but the contributions of these, great as they were, would have been unavailing without Macdonald's consummate tact, his constant awareness of the ultimate goal, and his untiring perseverance.

Macdonald is one of the most contradictory characters in Canadian history. Excelled by Brown as an expounder of ideas; by Mowat and Cartier, and probably others, as a lawyer; as an orator, by McGee, and even as a public speaker by many; from the standpoint of formal education, inferior to most of his colleagues; lacking in principles passionately held; opposed to universal suffrage, believing 'that classes and property should be represented as well as numbers'; in an age and community steeped in puritanism, a man of salty and almost bawdy humour; at times a heavy drinker, it is hard to reconcile all these negative characteristics with the man's total greatness. His success was probably due, in addition to other great qualities, to the fact that he, more than anyone of his time, was a reflection of the coming Canadian. In this, but in this only, he resembles another of Scottish ancestry who succeeded him in a later generation.

John Alexander Macdonald was born in Glasgow, Scotland, on January 11, 1815, but his father emigrated to Canada when he was five years of age, and settled at Kingston, Upper Canada. The father had left Scotland because of business reverses and was no more successful in Canada; consequently, at the age of 15, after but five years' schooling in the Kingston Grammar School, young John began the study of law in a local lawyer's office. He did so well that within two years he was given charge of a branch office in nearby Napanee, and a year later took over the management of an office at Picton. At the age of 21, he was called to the bar of Upper Canada, immediately opening a law office in Kingston, and soon was doing very well. His innate capacity, plus a fondness for reading, undoubtedly compensated for his lack of formal education, which in a less-gifted person might have been a serious obstacle. To the end of his life he was conscious of this lack; but there is nothing in his career to suggest that he was otherwise inconvenienced by it.

Of medium height, slight build, he was distinguished by a shock of wavy, black hair; his features were mobile, set off by a large nose.

As a speaker, he was slow and halting until he warmed to his subject; rarely eloquent, but often witty and quick in rejoinder, he marshalled his ideas well, presenting them in a convincing manner. His accent is best described as North American and, especially to English ears, seemed harsh.

Macdonald's public life began with his election in 1844 as Conservative member for Kingston. Although paying close attention to the affairs of the House, he at first took very little part in its debates. His ability was soon recognized, however, and in 1847 he was asked to become a member of the government. This was in the days when the great issue was responsible government. Macdonald does not seem to have had very strong views on the subject at that time, none at any rate that interfered with his accepting office in a government responsible to the governor rather than to parliament. With the victory of Baldwin and La Fontaine in the following year, although re-elected for Kingston, Macdonald entered into a long period of opposition, which also played an important part in his political development. Nothing had yet occurred, however, to mark him as a man of destiny.

After the break-up of the Reform administration in 1854, Macdonald had a hand in most of the ten administrations that came and went during the succeeding decade of political instability. Gradually, he came to be recognized as the leader of the Conservatives in Upper Canada, when his ability to co-operate with others, even though not always in agreement with them on every point, was an important factor in his success. He had come to realize that, short of absolutist rule, no government could succeed for long without the support of a considerable portion of the Lower Canadian electorate; and it is not surprising that during his long career he could always count on the support of a majority of voters in that province.

Now that, apparently, the colonies were so amicably agreed on union, it was necessary that the British government should also agree; for, without its concurrence, no alteration in the existing status could be made. The governor-general, Lord Monck, therefore transmitted the Quebec resolutions to the government, and George Brown hastened to London to make sure the scheme was favourably received. Writing to Macdonald from London on December 22, 1864, he expressed surprise mixed with alarm at the complacency with which British government and public alike had begun to view the possible independence of the colonies.

I saw all the members of the government who were in town [Brown wrote], and received much kindness from them. Indeed from all classes of people you hear nothing but high praise of 'Canadian statesmanship', and loud anticipations of the great future before us. I am much concerned to observe, however, and I write it to you as a thing that must seriously be considered by all men taking a lead hereafter in Canadian public matters —that there is a manifest desire in almost every quarter that, ere long, the British American colonies should shift for themselves, and in some quarters evident regret that we did not declare at once for independence. I am very sorry to observe this, but it arises, I hope, from the fear of invasion of Canada by the United States, and will soon pass away with the cause that excites it.

Except for such Liberals as Brown was unable to influence, and a very few others, public opinion in Canada was generally favourable to Confederation. Parliament met on January 19, 1865; and on February 3, Macdonald introduced the Quebec resolutions, moving an address to the Queen based on them, which, after a long and spirited debate, was adopted by a vote of ninety-one to thirty-three.

Things did not go so smoothly down by the sea. In Nova Scotia, Tupper had not been so successful as Macdonald in warding off possible opposition. While the Quebec conference had endorsed the intercolonial railway, no guarantees had been forthcoming. This was seized upon by Tupper's political opponents and others, including a number of Halifax bankers and many business men whose fears and prejudices were easily played upon. Joseph Howe, temporarily out of politics, driven by the bitterness of defeat, and despite his previous views, required little persuasion to take the lead against Confederation. In the circumstances, Tupper decided to play a waiting game and postpone reference of the resolutions to the legislature until public clamour had subsided, and consequently, although union was later endorsed, the resolutions never were.

In New Brunswick, where opposition was largely due to dissatisfaction over lack of action in connection with the intercolonial railway, and also disagreement concerning its route, Premier Tilley did not follow the example of either Macdonald or Tupper, but decided to submit the question to the electorate. In addition to the above obstacles, the government had to contend with the power and prestige of the governor, Hon. Arthur Gordon, son of the Earl of Aberdeen, who openly opposed Confederation, with the result that the government was badly beaten, and an anti-union government under Albert Smith was formed.

This was not pleasing to the British government, now convinced of the desirability of union, and the governor was induced to change his tactics. Soon after, a quarrel developed between Governor

Gordon and Premier Smith, bringing about the government's resignation. Tilley again formed a government, and in the elections that followed, with the aid of much Canadian money, the union forces won.

The wisdom of Tupper's policy of watchful waiting was shown when, although by no means ended, the agitation had so far subsided that he was able, in April 1866, to pass through the legislature, not the Quebec resolutions, but a motion authorizing the appointment of delegates to a conference in London to negotiate the final terms of union. The New Brunswick legislature followed suit; but Prince Edward Island and Newfoundland both decided to stay out of Confederation.

Despite the unsatisfactory situation in the Maritimes, the Canadian government had proceeded with its plans. In April 1865, a delegation consisting of Macdonald, Brown, Cartier and Galt sailed for England. In London, they met a committee of the cabinet, including Prime Minister Gladstone and Colonial Secretary Cardwell, with whom the following points were discussed: (1) The proposed union of the British North American provinces; (2) arrangements necessary for the defence of Canada in the event of war with the United States, and the extent to which the cost should be shared between Great Britain and Canada; (3) steps to be taken in connection with the Reciprocity Treaty; and (4) arrangements necessary for the settlement of the North-Western Territory and the Hudson's Bay Company's claims. On all of these points, the discussions were satisfactory; but nothing could be done concerning union, pending a decision in the Maritimes.

Shortly after the return of the delegation to Canada, Prime Minister Taché died; and a few days later, Lord Monck asked Macdonald to form a government. Macdonald wished to retain the existing cabinet with as few changes as possible, but George Brown refused to serve under him, refusing also to serve under Cartier when Macdonald offered to step aside. Finally, it was agreed that Sir Narcisse Belleau, a member of the legislative council, should become Prime Minister. Brown then consented to remain because he and Macdonald would still be on an equal footing in the cabinet, although it was generally recognised that Macdonald was in reality the head of the government. This, Brown could not fail to realize, and before long he handed in his resignation, which was accepted on December 21, 1865.

The session of 1865 was the last at Quebec; and in the autumn of that year the seat of government was transferred to Ottawa, where parliament next convened on June 8, 1866. In the meantime, the government, and particularly Macdonald, were busy drafting the constitutions for Ontario and Quebec, as they were now called. One of the points of contention was whether there should be one or two chambers. Sentiment in favour of two was strong in Quebec and consequently Quebec was given its legislative council, while Ontario wisely dispensed with it. (Subsequently, both New Brunswick and Nova Scotia continued their previous bicameral legislatures when they became provinces of Canada, the former to abolish its upper house shortly after, and Nova Scotia eventually to do likewise.) Provision was made also for the protection of religious minorities in both provinces, and, in Quebec, for special safeguards concerning language for the *Canadiens*.

While Canadian ministers were engrossed with these matters, Tupper and Archibald arrived from Nova Scotia to urge that a Canadian delegation join them in a trip to London. Irish Fenians had already made an attack upon Canada and threats of other raids had been made, rendering Macdonald reluctant to leave the country, especially since Lord Monck had received word from Mr. Cardwell that the passing of an act at the session of parliament then in progress was unlikely. Shortly after, news came of the Gladstone government's defeat, and that the new government had been formed by the Earl of Derby, with Lord Carnarvon as Colonial Secretary.

It must have seemed to those striving to bring about a union of the colonies that everything was conspiring against them. The Earl of Derby was the man who, as Lord Stanley, had looked with a jaundiced eye upon the efforts of colonials to achieve responsible government. Neither the Nova Scotia nor the New Brunswick government had endorsed the Quebec resolutions; in fact, both had repudiated them. On the other hand, the parliament of Canada had adopted them, which meant that Macdonald and his colleagues would be bound by their provisions, while the Maritime delegates were pledged to their modification. It might even be necessary to begin negotiations anew; and, if this happened, the Quebec delegates could object to the re-opening of a compact already agreed upon.

The Maritime delegates had a long wait in London; but in December, Macdonald, Cartier, Howland, McDougall, Langevin and Galt, three from Ontario and three from Quebec, joined them. The conference got under way on December 4 in the Westminster Palace Hotel, and, on motion of Dr. Tupper, Macdonald was elected chairman. Lord Monck had also arrived, and with Lord Carnarvon, 'sat at the cradle', as Macdonald put it, of the new state. Despite the interest which both Lord Monck and Lord Carnarvon displayed, Macdonald complained that they were quite 'unable, from the constitution of their minds, to rise to the occasion. The union was treated by them as if the B.N.A. Act were a private Bill uniting two or three English parishes.'

Macdonald, whose conception of the new state was on a much higher plane than British officialdom could evisage, wanted to call it 'The Kingdom of Canada'. This would have implied a status equal to that of the United Kingdom itself. A long time was to elapse before such a position was achieved by Canada; but it is typical of Macdonald's prescience and of his belief in the inherent greatness of the nation he was helping to create that he suggested such a title. Lord Derby, however, lacking Macdonald's faith and imagination, ruled that 'Kingdom' would not do because it might offend the Yankees! Consequently 'Dominion' was substituted. In recent years, use of this term has been eliminated where possible, but Macdonald's suggested designation, though now in every way applicable, has not yet been adopted.

Lord Carnarvon introduced the British North America Act in the House of Lords on February 7, and after a brief debate in both Houses it was passed and received the royal assent. The act, which was proclaimed in Ottawa on July 1, 1867, prescribed the form of government which should thenceforth control the affairs of the four provinces constituting the union, with provision for the admission later of Prince Edward Island, Newfoundland, the North-Western Territory and British Columbia. It provided for a Senate and House of Commons, fixing the representation of each, the term of parliament at a maximum of five years unless dissolved by the governor-general; and provided for redistribution of the House of Commons seats after every decennial census.

The federal government was given power (Section 91) to make laws for the 'peace, order, and good government of Canada in relation to all matters not coming within the classes of subjects by this Act assigned exclusively to the legislatures of the provinces'; and then follows a list of twenty-nine specified subjects. It might be noted that the phrase 'peace, order, and good government' was changed from the 'peace, *welfare*, and good government' of the Quebec resolutions.

The powers of the provincial legislatures were defined in Section 92 (sixteen sections). Clause 7 of the Quebec resolutions dealt with education, but in the British North America Act a separate section (93), consisting of four subsections, is devoted to that subject, specifically assigned to the provinces. Under that section, rights or privileges with respect to denominational schools existing in any province at the union are continued; and 'all powers, privileges and duties' in force or existing at the union with respect to Catholic separate schools in Upper Canada are extended to dissentient Protestant or Catholic schools in Quebec. Provision is also made in the section for an appeal to the governor-general-in-council from any act of any province affecting rights or privileges of Protestant or Catholic minorities with respect to education.

The act did not hand over to the colonies complete control of their own affairs—that they still had to achieve. The supreme authority in military matters, external relations, and diplomacy was retained in British hands. The governor-general had the right on his own initiative to reserve bills. The final court of appeal in the Canadian judicial system was the Judicial Committee of the British Privy Council.

Lord Monck returned to Canada as govenor-general of the Dominion, having previously written to Macdonald that he should call upon him to form the first government. It was decided that the cabinet should consist of thirteen members, five from Ontario, four from Quebec, and two each from Nova Scotia and New Brunswick. Their selection involved a great many factors and much discussion, not to say intrigue. Finally the choice fell upon the following: From Ontario: John A. Macdonald (Minister of Justice and Attorney-General), Alexander Campbell (Postmaster-General), William McDougall (Minister of Public Works), William P. Howland (Minister of Internal Revenue), A. J. Fergusson Blair (President of the Privy Council); Quebec: Georges Etienne Cartier (Minister of Militia and Defence), Alexander T. Galt (Minister of Finance), Jean C. Chapais (Minister of Agriculture), Hector L. Langevin (Secretary of State); Nova Scotia: Adams G. Archibald (Secretary of State for the Provinces), Edward Kenny (Receiver-General); New Brunswick: Samuel L. Tilley (Minister of Customs), Peter Mitchell (Minister of Marine and Fisheries).

Tupper should, of course, have been in the cabinet, and Thomas D'Arcy McGee also. Cartier, however, had strenuously insisted on the inclusion of three *Canadiens*, and it was therefore necessary that either McGee or Galt should be left out. In addition to his other claims, McGee was looked upon as the representative of the Irish

Catholics, while Galt represented the Protestant minority in Quebec. So serious was the deadlock that Macdonald actually considered advising the governor-general to ask George Brown to try his hand at forming a government, when the situation was saved by Tupper, who very generously offered to stand aside and allow the appointment of Edward Kenny, an Irish Catholic from Nova Scotia—and a Liberal, as well—if McGee would do likewise. After some soul-searching, McGee accepted the situation.

Thus was established the practice of having sectional, religious and other interests represented in the cabinet which has plagued successive Prime Ministers ever since, and has been responsible for the inclusion in every cabinet of mediocrities, and the exclusion of much more competent members.

In addition, Macdonald was required to recognize the fact that his was a coalition government. Of the thirteen cabinet members, seven were one-time Liberals or Reformers—McDougall, Howland and Blair from Ontario; Tilley and Mitchell from New Brunswick; and Archibald and Kenny from Nova Scotia. And although Liberals constituted the official opposition in parliament and in the country, the party of which Macdonald was the head, despite the obvious contradiction in terms and the fact that its membership consisted almost entirely of Conservatives, called itself the Liberal-Conservative party.

After having himself been sworn in on July 1, Lord Monck, who received a viscountcy in honour of the occasion, announced that the Queen had been pleased to confer upon the new Prime Minister the dignity of Knight Commander of the Bath, and that Cartier, Galt, Tilley, Tupper, Howland and McDougall had been created Companions of the same Order. Since the latter is a distinction of lower rank, and does not carry a title, Cartier and Galt felt they had been discriminated against, Cartier particularly objecting that through him the French people had been slighted. In order to mollify ruffled feelings, Cartier was later made a baronet and Galt a G.C.M.G., and both could add 'Sir' to their names. This incident lifts the veil on one of the less-pleasing aspects of politics.

The agitation in the Maritimes against Confederation continued, especially in Nova Scotia, where the issue was kept alive by Joseph Howe. Even after the union was proclaimed, the opposition did not cease. Armed with petitions, Howe went to England, but failed to influence the British government. He did succeed, however, in gaining from the Canadian government better financial terms for Nova

Scotia; and, eventually, through the persuasiveness of Macdonald and Tupper, he not only ceased his opposition, but joined the government as President of the Privy Council. In the meantime, the Macdonald ministry had been sustained by a comfortable majority in the first elections held under the act, but of the nineteen members in Nova Scotia, Tupper alone was a supporter of the government; as Stephen Leacock summed it up, the others went to Ottawa only to protest against being there.

CHAPTER IV

CANADIANS ALL

A LEGISLATURE 3,000 miles away had passed an act bringing four communities into a political union, combining in a single entity the ancient French provinces of Acadia and New France. The latter, after the Conquest called Quebec, was divided in 1791 into Upper Canada (Canada West after 1841), and Lower Canada (Canada East); and New Brunswick had been carved out of Nova Scotia (Acadia) in 1784. Now all were to come together in what it was hoped would be a permanent union.

Canada, at Confederation, contained few who thought of themselves as citizens of a single country. In the Maritimes, where large numbers of people still looked to New England as their most logical affiliation, dissatisfaction was rampant at being merged with Canada. Those who thought otherwise wished mostly for closer ties with the United Kingdom, which they feared this new alignment might jeopardize.

In Canada West, soon to become Ontario, many thousands of recent immigrants looked back with mixed feelings upon the Ireland, the Scotland, or the England from whose shores they had sailed, while the spiritual home of many others was south of the border.

Although the people of Canada East had fond thoughts for no other country, it cannot be said that they exhibited much enthusiasm for their newly-attained citizenship. Hitched in double harness since 1841 with an alien people, they had chafed at the union. Now they were asked to extend the hand of brotherhood to another group of aliens to the eastward; as in the past, they would cling to that which they knew, and hope for the best.

Ontario, the most populous of the four provinces, had then about 1,525,000 people; Quebec was next with 1,123,000; Nova Scotia had 364,000; and New Brunswick, 271,000, making a total of 3,283,000. These are estimates; no census had been taken since 1861.

What sort of people were these slightly more than three million men, women and children scattered over so large an area of territory? If one include all whose ancestors came, either directly or by way of

32

the United States, from the British Isles, the largest group was British. They were chiefly in Ontario, Nova Scotia and New Brunswick, with a small number in the Eastern Townships of Quebec and in Montreal. The next principal group consisted of the descendants of the original French colonists, living mostly in Quebec, but with increasing numbers in each of the other provinces.

Scots made up a large portion of the British settlers, and were scattered pretty generally throughout the English-speaking provinces, here and there in fairly solid communities, one of which was in eastern Nova Scotia, fronting on Northumberland Strait. Originally farmers, these Scots, after clearing land for their new homes, had taken to the sea, as sailors and fishermen.

Later, when coal measures were discovered nearby, many became miners, spreading across the eastern end of the province, with centres at Pictou, New Glasgow and Antigonish. Some crossed into Cape Breton where they found work in the coal mines, took up land or followed the sea; generally, those in the southern part of the island were farmers, while farther north they were fishermen.

Scots were also widely distributed throughout Ontario; some sections, especially along the St. Lawrence, such as Glengary County, and in the northwestern parts of what later became known as Old Ontario, were almost exclusively Scottish. In some of these regions, as in Cape Breton, the Gaelic tongue survived well into the twentieth century.

Irish immigrants flocked to Canada to escape famine and persecution in their homeland during the early decades of the nineteenth century, a considerable percentage settling in Quebec, but there were also extensive Irish communities in the other provinces. Truro, Nova Scotia and Peterborough County, Ontario, had large numbers of Irish people. For many years Ulsterites constituted a local Tammany in Toronto.

Among non-British stocks, next to the French, the most important consisted of Germans. Among the first to settle in British North America were a colony of Hanoverians, established in Nova Scotia in 1750–52 at a place they called Lunenburg, on the south coast. Farmers at first, they soon succumbed to the lure of the sea, and by Confederation had become fishermen and shipbuilders; and it is largely due to these Germanic people of Lunenburg that the Bluenose sea tradition has so consistently been maintained.

Considerable numbers of Germans also settled in Ontario, some direct from Germany, but the majority were Mennonites from

Pennsylvania. They settled chiefly in the central part of the Ontario peninsula, in Waterloo County, but also spread into counties to the north and east. Those from Pennsylvania were mostly farmers, but the European Germans consisted largely of masons, metal-workers, carpenters, handloom weavers, potters, and other skilled tradesmen. The census of 1871 showed 158,000 persons of German extraction in Ontario, which was almost 10 per cent of the population.

In most cases the immigrant groups brought with them ways of living to which they were accustomed, and thus contributed colour and variety to the Canadian strain. Among other things, the rival Irish groups introduced the Hibernian Society and the Orange Order, both of which have thrived on Canadian soil. The former had branches in each province; but the Orange Order sent its roots deepest in Canada West. The Grand Orange Lodge of North America was founded in 1830 at Brockville, and by Confederation had upward of 2,000 lodges in the province.

Confederation had come at an opportune moment. Expansion was in the air. The telegraph, the Atlantic cable, the railway, promised to bring an end to isolation. Places hitherto far-distant were brought up close; and the first steps were taken along a course which, in the end, would make neighbours of everyone on earth.

It was a time for optimism. In fact, without optimism the prospect of a Dominion stretching from sea to sea was unthinkable. Men planned enterprises appropriate to a great nation in the making, and a surprising number of these survive to this day.

The optimists would not live to see their dreams fulfilled, and many would die believing they had been misled, for progress is long and laborious, beset by many obstacles and delays; yet, in the long perspective, they would be more than justified.

Canadians fortunate enough to live in the better-settled portions of the Dominion enjoyed educational opportunities equivalent to those of other enlightened countries of the time. Nova Scotia had had a system of government-aided schools since 1808, but in 1865 an act was passed instituting a general assessment for school support in all sections of the province. Both primary and secondary schools were brought under the control of the Council of Public Instruction; provision was made for the appointment of school inspectors; and the Superintendent of Education was given power to set uniform courses of study.

Higher education in Nova Scotia was a denominational matter. King's College, founded in 1789, was dominated by the Anglican

Church, but Dalhousie, founded in 1818 by Lord Dalhousie, then governor of the province, was non-sectarian. The Catholics founded St. Mary's in 1840, and St. Francis Xavier, as a college, in 1853, and as a university in 1866. The Baptists, with an academy at Wolfville, opened Acadia College in 1839.

New Brunswick College, now the University of New Brunswick, was founded at Fredericton in 1800; and Mount Allison, at Sackville, founded by the Methodists, was incorporated as a university in 1858.

Dr. Egerton Ryerson had been superintendent of education for Canada West since 1844, and had put the stamp of his forceful personality upon the school system. It was based on what Ryerson conceived to be the best in British, American and German educational systems. Grammar or common schools were responsible for education up to the age of 21. In addition to what would now be called the primary grades, these schools also taught the more advanced work necessary for university entrance.

In 1865, there were 4,303 schools in operation, employing 4,721 teachers and containing 383,652 pupils. Dr. Ryerson reported with regret that 42,141 children were not attending any school.

Separate schools had been provided for by acts of the parliament of United Canada in 1855 and 1863. Under these acts, taxes paid by Roman Catholics were applied toward the support of schools for the education of their children.

Trinity College, opened at Cobourg in 1836 (later transferred to Toronto), was incorporated as a university in 1851; Queen's was founded at Kingston in 1842; King's (University of Toronto) was founded in 1843; Knox College, in 1844; and Ottawa College was founded in 1849 and became a university in 1866. St. Michael's (Toronto) was founded in 1852. Although the need for higher education was well looked after in Canada West, relatively few were able to take advantage of the opportunity. In 1867, less than a hundred students were enrolled at the University of Toronto.

In Quebec, Roman Catholic schools, providing instruction in all grades from primary school to classical college, constituted the public schools of the province. Separate schools for the education of Protestant children (which included all non-Catholics) were similar in status to those in Canada West for Catholics.

In 1865, there were 3,706 primary schools in Canada East, with 4,780 teachers and 172,733 pupils; 210 secondary schools with 1,099 teachers and 28,613 pupils. The 146 separate schools had 4,763 pupils.

Laval University, at Quebec City, received its charter as a university in 1852. McGill's history as a university goes back to 1821, when its charter was received. In 1868, McGill had 254 students.

Despite these educational facilities, large numbers of people, especially in rural areas, were illiterate. Books were scarce and confined to the few.

In a paper read in 1875 before the Literary and Historical Society of Quebec (founded in 1824), its president, James Douglas, lamented the dearth of libraries. 'In Montreal,' he said, 'the commercial capital of the Dominion, whose citizens are ostentatious in the expenditure of wealth for purposes of outward show, there is not a public library worthy of the name.'

Toronto had 'a large university library open for reference only to the public, but no free library of any pretensions; and all our other large cities are as badly or worse off'.

Newspapers, most of which were short-lived, were widely published and circulated, and political pamphlets streamed from the presses. Few Canadians could afford to write books because of the limited market, and of the general belief (surviving almost to the present) that no Canadian book was worth reading. In 1867, the Canadian postal service handled 14,000,000 newspapers; while, in 1868, books to the value of $478,630 were imported into the country, mostly from the United Kingdom.

Frequent attempts had been made to establish monthly magazines, but all had failed. While they lasted, some made an effort to pay contributors; but, generally, the only field open to writers was newspaper work, which, in most cases, called for the ability (and willingness) to sing the praises of one party and vilify the other, irrespective of merit.

Thomas Chandler Haliburton, creator of Sam Slick, who died in 1865, Octave Cremazie, Louis Frechette and François Xavier Garneau are almost the only writers of the period whose names have survived. Yet that age was to produce a group of future writers, born within a few years of each other (Roberts, 1860, Campbell, Lampman, Carman, 1861, Scott, 1862), who were to lay the foundation of Canadian literature.

Although in some sections, lumbering, and in others, fishing, were the chief occupations of people in the new Dominion, the majority got their living from the land. In Ontario, by this time, the frontier of settlement had been pushed back from Lakes Ontario, Erie and Huron almost to the line of the Canadian Shield; arable

SIR JOHN A. MACDONALD

land in the St. Lawrence valley and in the Eastern townships of
Quebec was pretty generally taken up. In New Brunswick, the chief
farming areas were in the St. John river valley and along the Bay of
Fundy. While in Nova Scotia, the Annapolis valley and areas re-
claimed from the Bay of Fundy and along tidal rivers provided the
richest farmlands, but many other regions less favourable had been
put under crop.

Previous to Confederation, the export of squared timber had
been the greatest source of money to the people of the Canadas,
but by 1867 the annual value of agricultural products had increased
beyond that of the forests. This, in large measure, was due to the
greater acreage sown to cereals, chiefly wheat, as well as to the rapid
increase in livestock.

In New Brunswick, agriculture still lagged behind the forest,
but in Nova Scotia the fisheries were in first place. Cod, of course,
was the principal fish, but the inshore fisheries produced large
quantities of herring and mackerel.

Previous to the advent of the railway, each of the provinces had
built trunk roads to open up the country, and for military purposes.
These roads varied in quality, but for every mile of good macadam
there were many miles of plank or corduroy, and even greater
stretches of deeply-rutted earth. Some of the heaviest-travelled roads
were turnpikes, maintained by tolls.

Passengers and mails were carried in stage-coaches; heavy goods
were transported in huge wagons drawn by horses or oxen. As railways reached into the new regions, these more primitive forms of
transport receded with the frontier.

While, in the Canadas and in the Maritimes, railways had existed
since the fifties, it was not till Confederation that they began seriously
to affect people's lives. By now, the Grand Trunk extended to Sarnia,
in the west, to Riviere du Loup, in the east, and to Portland, Maine,
on the Atlantic. The Great Western Railway Company had completed
a line from Hamilton to Windsor, and from Niagara, through
Hamilton, to Toronto. Lake Huron and Toronto were connected by
the Northern Railway, which had its Lake Huron terminus at
Collingwood.

By Confederation, 145 miles of railway had been built in Nova
Scotia, connecting Halifax with Windsor, and with Truro and
Pictou. In New Brunswick, the railway was approaching Woodstock,
and a line had been completed from St. John to Shediac, making
a total of 234 miles for the province.

The modern age of communications had begun in Canada with the completion of telegraph lines connecting Toronto and Quebec City in 1847, and by Confederation time the telegraph had brought all the provinces into touch with one another, spreading to the remotest parts of each. In 1866, the transatlantic cable had been successfully laid from Ireland to Newfoundland.

Railways ultimately drove the palatial passenger boats from the Great Lakes, the St. Lawrence, and the coastal waters of the Maritimes, but at the time of Confederation the steamers still provided the most comfortable means of travel.

The change from wooden to iron ships, as well as the change from wind to steam, affected many people in every part of the new Dominion. The substitution of iron for wood spelt the doom of the thriving shipbuilding industry which had employed large numbers of people in Nova Scotia, New Brunswick, Quebec and along the Great Lakes in Ontario.

Improved transportation in the years previous to Confederation had brought about new industries. By this time, too, steam had begun to replace the use of direct water-power, providing opportunities for many communities in which such power did not exist. Towns, mere villages before the railway, now began to grow and to develop appropriate industries. The number of small foundries increased, and blacksmith shops expanded into factories for the manufacture of buggies and wagons, farm implements and other machinery.

The manufacture of farm implements was one of the first to benefit from the growth of railway transportation. In 1847, Daniel Massey established, near Newcastle, Canada West, a small factory to make farm implements, which by Confederation had expanded into a prosperous business, producing an extensive line of threshers, reapers, mowers, hay rakes and miscellaneous farm implements. And, at Beamsville, in the Niagara peninsula, Alanson Harris, in 1857, had begun manufacturing farm implements, the second progenitor of the future Massey-Harris Company.

Also about the time of Confederation, Robert McLaughlin began to make buggies and wagons at Enniskillen, some 15 miles north of Oshawa, Ontario, founding a firm which, when the automotive age arrived, was to continue as a manufacturer of motor-cars at Oshawa, forerunner of General Motors Company of Canada.

At Montreal, strung along the Lachine Canal, which provided both power and transportation, many factories had been built, including rolling mills, iron works, nail factories, flour mills, a sugar refinery (Redpath's), sawmills and a plant for making candles.

In the woollen industry, once largely confined to the home, machinery had already largely replaced hand labour. Some wool was imported, but most of that used was produced locally. According to the census of 1861, there were 62 carding and fulling mills in Canada West, and 82 woollen mills, while in Canada East there were 88 carding and fulling, and 45 woollen mills.

The boot and shoe industry was even more fully based on domestic raw materials. Tanneries increased with the growth of the livestock industry. In 1861, Canada West had 264 tanneries, and Canada East, 184, chiefly in the Eastern Townships. In 1866, from 3,000 to 4,000 men and women were employed in the manufacture of boots and shoes in Montreal. Many workers were also employed in both provinces in making harness and saddlery.

At Confederation, manufacturing was yet in its infancy in the Maritimes. The manufacture of woollens was still in large measure confined to the farm. Tanneries had been established, and saddlery, harness and boots and shoes were being made in a number of places, both in Nova Scotia and New Brunswick. At the second provincial exhibition, held at Fredericton in 1864, agricultural implements, castings, carriages, furniture, stoves, grates, cloth, hats and boots and shoes were among the exhibits.

In 1861, William Davies, who had previously engaged in the export of pork products, established a modern-type packing-plant in Toronto, which was the beginning of what later became Canada Packers Limited.

Retailing, at the time of Confederation, was in the hands of numerous small merchants, but in St. Mary's, Ontario, an Irish immigrant, Timothy Eaton, was about to transfer to Toronto (1869), where, by his practice of selling for cash, all prices plainly marked, and money refunded if the customer were not satisfied, he was to revolutionize the retail trade and build one of the world's greatest retail organizations.

Robert Simpson, who was to build a rival retail organization across the street from Eaton's, was still in business in Newmarket, Ontario, but within three years would begin doing business on Yonge Street.

Mining, of such future importance to Canada, was then confined to but a few sections, principally in Nova Scotia. In 1861, gold was discovered in Halifax, Lunenburg and Guysborough Counties, and

4

caused a mild boom. In 1863, there were 18,296 men employed as miners in the province, and the production of gold increased from 7,275 ounces in 1862 to 27,583 ounces in 1864.

The coal measures in Cape Breton and in the counties along the eastern seaboard of Nova Scotia had been worked for many years previous to Confederation. In 1863, coal exports to the United States amounted to 263,374 tons, to other parts of British North America, 58,233 tons, and 75,529 tons were consumed at home.

Each of the provinces had established strong banks before Confederation, many of which, as the years passed, were either to close their doors or to be absorbed by more vigorous rivals. The oldest surviving bank is the Bank of Montreal, which received its charter in 1817. The Bank of Nova Scotia, founded in 1831, and the Bank of Toronto, founded in 1855, were flourishing institutions at the time of Confederation. The Canadian Bank of Commerce began business in 1867, but the Gore Bank, with head office at Hamilton, the Halifax Banking Company, the Eastern Townships Bank and the Bank of British Columbia, all subsequently absorbed by it, had been in existence for various lengths of time before that date.

Two of the life insurance companies doing business at the time of Confederation, Canada Life Assurance Company, founded in 1847, and Sun Life Assurance Company, founded in 1865, are now among the largest in Canada. The Mutual Life Assurance Company began business in 1869.

In 1859, petroleum had been discovered at Oil Springs, in Lambton County, Canada West, and by Confederation an extensive oil industry had developed centring at Petrolia. The wells, which were about 200 feet deep, occasionally flowed, but most required pumping. Crude oil was used by the railways for lubrication, and the refined product, called coal-oil, drove out the tallow candle for home illumination in rural communities, and vied with coal-gas in the cities.

Plentiful supplies of cheap grain and increasing population led to the growth of the brewing and distilling industries. Montreal, Toronto, Kingston, Hamilton, London and a great many other towns had flourishing breweries. In 1861, there were 49 distilleries in Canada West, but only 3 were reported in Canada East.

The small number of distilleries in Canada East might suggest that much illegal distilling was going on. This is supported by figures for the number of licensed taverns in Toronto and Montreal, respectively; whereas Toronto, with a much smaller population, was reported to have 218 licensed taverns in 1866, Montreal had only 158, but it was stated that large numbers of unlicensed premises were selling liquor.

As might have been expected in view of the existence of so many liquor outlets, with little or no supervision, the per capita consumption, especially of whisky, was high. In 1867, the per capita consumption of proof spirits was 1·62 gallons, and beer, 1·96 gallons. This may be compared with the consumption of 0·57 gallons of spirits in 1951 and 12·72 gallons of beer.

If, as its defenders contend, the liquor traffic may be credited with the promotion of pleasant social intercourse, it must be debited with responsibility for its share of human misery; and it is this aspect which has caused people in every country to press for the restriction or prohibition of liquor sales.

In 1863, the United Canadian Alliance for the Suppression of the Liquor Traffic was formed at Montreal, and, the following year, through its efforts a local option act was passed by the parliament of Canada. Called after its framer, Christopher Dunkin, the act authorized municipalities, by popular vote, or by the edict of their councils, to prohibit the retail sale of liquor within their limits. At the time of Confederation a considerable number of municipalities, both in Ontario and Quebec, had invoked the provisions of the act.

Commercial sports were yet unknown, but people at Confederation did not lack for recreation. Baseball had not yet got a start in British North America, nor had football, but lacrosse was a favourite summer sport, and so to a lesser extent was cricket. In winter, nearly everyone took part in sports of some sort—tobogganing, snow-shoeing, sleigh-riding, skating or curling. The latter was still confined chiefly to localities where Scots predominated.

Dancing was popular, both the round dances just coming into popularity, and square dances such as have been revived in recent years. Surprise parties were a favourite form of entertainment. Many concerts and lectures were held during the winter months.

Canada had then no labour organizations and no labour legislation had yet appeared upon the statute books. The new factories quite naturally paid as little in wages as they could get away with; hours were long and working conditions were frequently bad. Many factories were poorly lighted, lacking in proper ventilation, and having little or no protection against accidents. Women were employed in the woollen mills and in the boot and shoe factories, and were paid much lower wages than men. Children of 8 and 9 worked long hours for mere pittances.

Lunatic asylums, as they were called, were, more often than not, places of horror, and penal institutions were not much better. Children as young as 8 and 9 were frequently sentenced to the penitentiary for three-year terms and were flogged for trivial breaches of discipline.

It was largely a man's world. Except for teaching, women were not welcome in any of the professions, and women teachers were paid much less than men. In Canada West, for example, the average salary paid a male teacher in country districts was $260 when board was not included, but women, teaching in similar circumstances, received an average of $169. In cities, the average for male teachers was $522 a year, and for women $241.

Despite the fact that schools in Canada West in 1865 contained 179,332 girls, it was not till 1868 that girls could legally attend the grammar schools. As early as 1827, girls in Upper Canada had begun to outrage the susceptibilities of educational leaders by insisting upon having an education. In that year, Dr. Strachan, chairman of the Board of Education, reported that school attendance by girls was 'an inconvenience of a temporary nature which will gradually pass away as the population increases in wealth and numbers'.

In the same year, School Inspector George Paxton Young reported disapprovingly that ten girls were taking Latin, but no woman was yet eligible for entrance to a university anywhere in British North America.

No feature of the social and economic life of Canada has shown such an advance as the change in the position of women since the days of Confederation.

CHAPTER V

WESTWARD MARCH BEGINS

UNION of the eastern provinces was not enough; there still remained the vast empty spaces of the West. From the western limits of Ontario to the Rocky Mountains, and north as far as the arctic watershed, the country belonged in fee simple to and was governed by the Hudson's Bay Company. When, even before Confederation, the government of Canada had considered the possibility of ending this amazing anachronism, the law officers of the Crown had ruled that, although based on nothing more than the fantastic whim of a Stuart king, the Company's title was unassailable. British and Canadian statesmen knew, however, that this title would carry little weight with Americans pursuing their 'manifest destiny'. As early as 1865, Macdonald had written: 'If Canada is to remain a country separate from the United States, it is of great importance to her that they [the United States] should not get behind us by right or by force and intercept the route to the Pacific.'

Thus, some Canadians at least stood ready to assume responsibility for the territory, and the British government was at length prepared to exert the pressure necessary to persuade the Company to give up its claim.

Lying to the north and west of Rupert's Land, as the Hudson's Bay Company's domain was called, was an immense tract generally referred to as the North-Western Territory. This the Hudson's Bay Company had held under lease from the British government from 1821 to 1859. Since then it had remained literally a no-man's-land. This area was assumed to come under Canadian jurisdiction if and when Rupert's Land was acquired.

In October 1868, Georges Cartier and William McDougall went to England on behalf of the Canadian government to conduct negotiations with the Hudson's Bay Company, and eventually succeeded in making an arrangement under which, for £300,000, the Company agreed to surrender its interests in North America, retaining one-twentieth of the land in the area bounded by the United States, on the south; the Rocky Mountains, on the west; the North

Saskatchewan river, on the north; and Lake Winnipeg, Lake of the Woods, and connecting waters, on the east. In addition, the Company retained 45,000 acres adjacent to its trading posts.

This arrangement was duly accepted by the Canadian parliament; the Deed of Surrender was executed by the Company on November 19; and formal transfer was to be made on December 1, 1869. In anticipation of this, parliament passed an act providing for the interim government of the Northwest Territories as soon as title had been acquired. Under authority of this Act, William McDougall was appointed lieutenant-governor on September 28, and immediately set off for the West by way of the United States.

It is necessary now to take a brief look at this new territory into which Canada was about to spread. For two centuries the Hudson's Bay Company had held it almost without change in order that it might continue to provide an unending flow of fur-trade profits. Once, in the early years of the century, that purpose had been challenged by the chivalrous Earl of Selkirk who dreamed of a new home for dispossessed Scottish Highlanders. The story of that attempt adds a glowing page to the history of Canada, the like of which had not been written since Jeanne Mance and Maisonneuve had set an example of unselfish devotion unexcelled in the annals of any country.

While Selkirk's dream of a Scottish haven in the new world was short-lived, the Red River settlement he founded did not die; in fact, its influence continues to this day. The Gaelic tongue has taken on new accents contributed by *Canadien* voyageurs and dark-eyed Cree maidens who became the wives of both Scot and *Canadien*. The resulting blend adhered more closely to the ways of its Indian strain than to those of either Scot or *Canadien* because they were suited to the country.

These people had continued to live on the land as the Selkirk settlers had done, staking out their homesteads in long, narrow strips running back from the river, in the manner of their French forebears along the St. Lawrence. But their husbandry was mainly influenced by the presence of the bison, still 'covering the plains as by a robe'. Why cut hay to feed cattle to supply inferior meat?

The principal objectives of New France had been the prosecution of the fur trade and the christianizing of the natives. Following the Conquest, British traders quickly took over the fur trade, but the missionary effort they were content to leave in the hands of the French. The hardy voyageurs who paddled or lined the heavily-laden canoes up the streams and carried their loads over the numerous portages were nearly all *Canadiens*, but no *Canadien* trader was tolerated.

The supremacy of the Hudson's Bay Company was challenged, but by other British traders. After blood had been spilt, the canny Scots who dominated both sides decided it was more profitable to combine. Following the absorption of the North West Company in 1821, the ancient Company reigned supreme. William McTavish, a one-time Nor'wester, was Governor of Rupert's Land when the Deed of Surrender was signed in 1869.

In spiritual matters, on the other hand, the religion of Old France had no competitor. The *Canadiens*, of course, were Roman Catholics, as were the Indians, and some of the Scots, especially the later generations of them. The ministration of missionaries trained in the seminaries of Quebec was never interrupted and many religious communities existed throughout the country. At their head was Bishop Taché, member of a family that had already contributed a Prime Minister to Canada, whose episcopal seat was at St. Boniface.

Among the Hudson's Bay Company's officers and servants, among the *Canadien* voyageurs, among the Métis, as the people of mixed blood were called, and among the Indians the idea of change met general opposition. To them, the Company had always been the highest authority, next, of course, to the Queen, a legendary figure, and an object of veneration less only in degree than the Deity itself.

The clergy, on their part, chiefly composed of zealots from Quebec, feared that their dream of a French Catholic community on the plains might never be realized if Canada, dominated by an English Protestant majority, should extend its authority westward. Their influence over the people was great, and their antagonism helped to swell the general unrest.

In addition to these, a small number of Canadians, mostly from Ontario, had gained a foothold in the country, and by their energetic behaviour and criticism of existing conditions contributed greatly to the growing tension.

The total population, whites, Métis and Indians, in the Red River settlements was about 11,000.

From first to last, the transfer was badly handled. By ill chance, both temporal and spiritual heads of the community were unavailable. Governor McTavish lay dying of consumption at Fort Garry, while Bishop Taché was away in Rome. Word went round that the

Company had sold its lands to Canada, without consulting the people, or considering their wishes; like cattle, they went with the land. Cut off from the outside world except for the slowest sort of communication, no one knew for certain what had happened; rumour ruled. Yet one thing was plain: the Hudson's Bay Company's governor and council had ceased to function; never before had this happened.

Although no official notice had been given of the change of masters, there were signs that Canada was about to take over. Officious Canadian surveyors, under Colonel Stoughton Dennis, brushing aside the people's remonstrances and refusing all explanations, were surveying land along the Red River which the Métis and others had always considered theirs. Was their land to be given to the pushful Canadians?

People never remain long without government of some sort. Whenever such a situation occurs, someone usually comes forward either to call a meeting to elect some person or persons to take charge, or to nominate himself for the job. Louis Riel, a native of the plains, chiefly of *Canadien* stock, but partly of Indian blood, placed himself at the head of several hundred Métis and other people of the settlement, occupied Fort Garry, which did not resist, seized Company stores and arms, and set up a provisional government.

Riel had been educated in Quebec for the priesthood, but when signs of mental instability appeared, the religious authorities seem to have changed their minds about him. He was a religious fanatic, with definite delusions of grandeur not unknown to history. Joan of Arc had similar hallucinations, but she succeeded in her undertaking. Had Riel succeeded, it is possible he might by now have become the patron saint of Manitoba.

When William McDougall arrived at the border between Dakota Territory and Rupert's Land, he was met by an armed detachment from Riel's headquarters at Fort Garry and ordered not to cross the border on pain of death. The governor withdrew to the nearby village of Pembina, and from there issued proclamations which served no good purpose, and also encouraged some of the Canadians to resist the provisional government. When these efforts failed, he returned to Ottawa and resigned his office.

The Canadians needed little urging from McDougall or anyone else to resist the Riel regime. One of these, Thomas Scott, an Orangeman from Ontario who had come to Manitoba with a survey party, as irrational as Riel in his belief in his own righteousness, absolutely refused to recognize the rebel and his rabble crew. Riel accepted the challenge. Scott was arrested and, after a travesty of a trial, was brutally killed.

Before word of this reached Ottawa, the government had taken steps to correct some of the mistakes already made. Bishop Taché was summoned from Rome to use his influence with the Métis, and three commissioners were sent to Fort Garry to negotiate a settlement. The commissioners were: Colonel Charles de Salaberry, whose father had commanded the Canadian forces at Chateauguay in the War of 1812–14; Vicar-General Thibault, well-known in the Red River settlements; and Donald A. Smith, of the Hudson's Bay Company.

Because of their French origin, Colonel de Salaberry and Vicar-General Thibault could have been expected to carry some weight with the Métis, but Smith, later to be closely associated with the Northwest, was there for the first time. Forty years before he had come to Canada from Scotland as an articled clerk and had gradually worked up from an obscure post in Ungava to a place of power in the Company's counsels. When it became evident that the Company must surrender its charter, many shareholders began disposing of their shares, causing the price to drop. Donald Smith, from his knowledge of the country, believed that the sale to Canada, and the resulting development of the country, would greatly increase the value of the Company's remaining interests, and the value of its shares.

Already on the road to wealth through shrewd investments, and closely associated with the Bank of Montreal, whose president, George Stephen, was his cousin, it was not difficult for Smith to find the money to buy in shares as they appeared on the market. If at this time he had not gained control, he must have done so very soon afterward.

As it turned out, neither the commission nor Bishop Taché succeeded in bringing order out of chaos, and when word of Scott's death—'murder' was the term used in Ontario—reached Canada, all hope of conciliation was over. From one end of Ontario to the other, the country was aflame. Macdonald, more aware of the justification for the Métis revolt than he cared to admit, and stirred by the storm rising in Ontario and its possible consequences, acceded to the demand for the dispatch of soldiers. In May 1870, a force of British regulars and Canadian militia under command of Colonel Garnet Wolseley was on its way. (When at length the expedition reached Fort Garry, Riel and his officers had fled, and all was quiet in the Red River valley.)

Although the date of transfer had been set for December 1, 1869, it was not till May 2, 1870, that the first steps were taken to provide for the establishment and government of the province of Manitoba; and the following day arrangements were made for the payment to the Hudson's Bay Company of the stipulated £300,000. On May 20, A. G. Archibald, M.P. for Colchester, N.S. (who had temporarily held office in the cabinet of 1867), was appointed lieutenant-governor to succeed William McDougall. And finally, on June 23, 1870, an order-in-council of the British government authorized the transfer of Rupert's Land and the North-Western Territory to Canada. By this act, Canada was extended westward as far as the crest of the Rockies, and north to the uncertain boundary of Alaska.

With a vast new territory to organize and settle, one might assume that Canada would have been too busy to indulge in political recrimination, but religious and sectarian passion are hostile to logic. Antipathies, never deeply submerged, rose quickly to the surface; flood-gates, too long held in check, were flung open.

In Ontario, the Orange lodges, ever welcoming an excuse to oppose anything Catholic and French, led the attack. The issue was made to order for them: an Orangeman had been done to death by a French Catholic rebel. The blood of Thomas Scott cried out for vengeance: so far as they were concerned, it must not cry in vain. While the lodges led the attack, their views were echoed by nearly every other non-Catholic in Ontario.

The people of Quebec, except for the small English-speaking minority, were as fiercely determined to justify Riel's acts. They argued that Riel's government, representative as it was of the great majority of the people, was the only existing one, and its actions had the force of law. The execution of Scott, though unfortunate, was but an incident.

Their violence in Riel's defence was heightened by frustration of the hope generally entertained of establishing a *Canadien* province in Rupert's Land to counterbalance the growing preponderance of English-speaking influence in Canada. These fears were increased by the evident intention in Ontario to make certain that any new provinces created in the West should be English and Protestant.

Macdonald needed all his political subtlety to weather the storm. Hitherto, the Orange vote had been solidly behind him; but now the Liberals, by supporting the lodges' demand for Riel's blood, threatened to gain their allegiance. On the other hand, by acceding to the lodges' demand, he was in danger of losing his considerable support in Quebec, without which he could not hope to remain in office.

A good deal of the discussion hinged on whether Riel, as he claimed, had been promised amnesty, which certain incidents supported. In a letter to Bishop Taché, Macdonald had authorized him to offer an amnesty, but that was before word of Scott's death reached Ottawa. Later, while the Ontario government (Liberal) had a price of $5,000 on Riel's head, Macdonald, through Bishop Taché, was paying him to keep out of the way. When Fenians threatened to invade Manitoba, Lieutenant-Governor Archibald successfully appealed to Riel for help in repelling the attack. This, Riel claimed, established him as a supporter of law and order, rather than the reverse, as his enemies claimed. In 1872, he was elected to the House of Commons for the new Manitoba riding of Provencher. In the same election, Cartier lost his seat in Montreal East, and Riel resigned to allow him to contest Provencher. Therefore, to characterize him as a felon and a rebel was, in the circumstances, to accuse the Canadian government of complicity in his alleged crimes. There was much to support his claim.

As in most such cases, with the lapse of time the heat died out of the controversy; and the subject might well be allowed to drop here but for the fact that a young Quebec member, Wilfrid Laurier, made his first speech in English in the House of Commons in a debate on a motion to expel Riel (who, upon Cartier's death, had been re-elected in Provencher), on the ground of his being a fugitive from justice.

After discussing certain legal technicalities and casting doubt upon the legality of the motion, Laurier concluded:

It has been said that Mr. Riel was only a rebel. . . . What act of rebellion did he commit? Did he ever raise any other standard than the national flag? Did he ever proclaim any other authority than the sovereign authority of the Queen? No, never. His whole crime and the crime of his friends was that they wanted to be treated like British subjects and not to be bartered away like common cattle. If that be an act of rebellion, where is the one amongst us who if he happened to have been with them would not have been rebels as they were? Taken all in all, I would regard the events at Red River in 1869-70 as constituting a glorious page in our history, if unfortunately they had not been stained with the blood of Thomas Scott. But such is the state of human nature and of all that is human: good and evil are constantly intermingled; the most glorious cause is not free from impurity and the vilest may have its noblest side.

Despite Laurier's effort, the vote for expulsion carried, only one Ontario member voting against it, but a new voice had been raised in parliament on the side of tolerance. Although eventually religious and sectional prejudice were to strike him down, Laurier was probably to do more than any other person to slake their fires. From time to time they would break out anew; but in after years such occasions would grow fewer and their power to disrupt become less.

CHAPTER VI

NEIGHBOURS AND LINE FENCES

ONE of the chief factors in forming the character and temperament of Canadians is the presence along their southern border of a headstrong people overly confident of their own high destiny and inclined to ignore the feelings, and sometimes even the existence, of others, especially the benighted colonials to the north of them.

This situation was aggravated by the fact that in all official intercourse Canadians must speak through the devious channels of British diplomacy (the Canadian government sent complaints to the Colonial Office in London, which in due course passed them on to the Foreign Office, in Whitehall, which in turn forwarded them to the British Ambassador at Washington, who then handed them to the American Secretary of State).

British diplomatists, among the shrewdest and most experienced in the world when it comes to advancing a British cause, were never able fully to appreciate the importance of questions or interests concerning the colonies. But, on the other hand, it was a decided advantage to have some sop to throw to the Americans in exchange for concessions of greater advantage to themselves.

Even as early as the end of the Revolutionary War, when commissioners were sitting to arrange the terms of the Convention of Peace and Separation which ended the conflict, this tendency is evident. 'Called upon to favour the United States, on the one hand, or the French and Spanish, on the other, the British ministry chose to patronize the rebellious provinces,' write the American historians, Charles and Mary Beard. They also state that 'in the end, the shrewd maneuvers of the American commissioners and the liberality of the British cabinet made the general settlement at Paris in 1783 a triumph for the United States'.

The American commissioners were Benjamin Franklin, John Adams and John Jay, while the British government was represented by one Richard Oswald, described by the biographers of John Adams as: 'a respectable and amiable private gentleman, nominated at the suggestion of Dr. Franklin, with whom he was to treat, because he thought he would get along easily with him; but by no means a match for a combination of three such men as Franklin, Jay and John Adams'.

Great Britain was reconciled to the loss of the colonies, still having Canada, large and undefined, farther north. But Oswald had a poor opinion of those regions and was not above expressing his opinion to Franklin, telling him as well that before leaving England he had let members of the cabinet know 'that in his opinion Canada should be given up to the United States as it would prevent occasions of future differences, and as the government of such a country was worth nothing, and of no importance, and that he was not without hopes it would be agreed to'. What was of more importance to the British government at the moment was the restoration of seized Tory property and the collection of debts due British merchants by American citizens.

Such being the case, it is fortunate for Canada that only that portion of British North America south of Lakes Erie, Huron, Michigan and Superior, extending southward to the Ohio, and westward to the Mississippi, aggregating about 415,000 square miles, and eventually comprising nine states, and marginal areas elsewhere, should have been handed over to the United States by the 'amiable private gentleman' to whom the fate of the future Canadian nation was entrusted.

This region was well known to the American negotiators, and they took good care to see that the new boundary was more or less definitely defined. They were also aware of the value of Canada's fisheries, access to which they insisted upon. But when it came to defining the boundary between Acadia and Massachusetts the wording of the treaty was not so definite.

The logical boundary on the east was, of course, the Penobscot river, once called the St. Croix, which, according to the charter of the colony of Massachusetts, separated that colony from Nova Scotia. Long before the revolution, Acadians had settled on the Penobscot; but the American commissioners evidently wished to acquire territory to the east and north of that boundary.

Article II of the treaty provided that the boundary should follow the middle of the St. Croix river from its mouth in the Bay of Fundy to its source, and from there directly north to the highlands dividing the rivers flowing into the St. Lawrence from those flowing into the Atlantic. From this point, it would follow a line across the said highlands to the northwest head of the Connecticut river, continuing down the middle of that river to the 45th parallel of north latitude.

The year after the treaty was signed, the province of New Brunswick was established, and Loyalists settled along the Schoodic river, believed to be the St. Croix of the treaty. Even at this early date, some United States citizens were claiming that the Magaguadavic, farther east, was the true St. Croix.

Because of this, and other disagreements, a new treaty was negotiated in 1794, the fifth article of which provided for a new commission to decide the point. This commission consisted of three members, one appointed by each of the parties, and the third chosen by the first two. The findings of this commission were to be final.

It began work in 1796, continuing until the fall of 1798, the United States commissioner contending for the Magaguadavic, the British commissioner holding for the Schoodic. The third commissioner, an American, decided the issue in favour of the British claim. But the Schoodic has two branches, roughly 50 miles apart in their upper reaches, the western, called the Schoodic, and a north one, called the Chiputnaticook. The commission decided that the west branch was the main one.

Having done this, however, the commission now proceeded to do something beyond its instructions. It decided that the boundary should follow the Chiputnaticook, at the source of which a boundary monument was erected. But no highlands corresponding to the description given in the treaty could be found by projecting a line northward from that point. So matters were back where they started.

The next move in this comedy of errors was made in 1797, when the contracting parties, realizing that the commission had exceeded its authority, proceeded to ratify its act. Here, for some unknown reason, the British government, having a perfectly good case, seems to have deliberately tossed it aside.

The boundary still remained to be settled, and when the Treaty of Ghent was made in 1814, two commissioners were appointed to finish the job, but met with the same difficulty that had stopped their predecessors, since they were bound to accept the Chiputnaticook as the boundary.

Yet, if the commission of 1794, after having determined that the *west* branch of the Schoodic was the true St. Croix, had stopped at that point, the highlands referred to in the treaty could easily have been found a short distance north of the source of that branch, and

south of the St. John valley. And, as Sir Sandford Fleming, familiar
with the geography of that region, has pointed out, this would have
saved for Canada an area of 11,000 square miles, and would have
made much easier Fleming's task of building the Intercolonial
Railway.

Naturally, in determining a boundary, negotiators are usually
guided by maps, and what more natural than that the line agreed
upon should be traced on a map, which is precisely what happened
in this case. The line was drawn on several maps, one of which, with
the line marked in red, was, during the course of the negotiations,
supplied by Franklin to Count de Vergennes, the French Foreign
Minister, accompanied by a letter in which Franklin stated that he
had 'marked with a strong red line . . . the limits of the United States
as settled in the preliminaries between the British and American
plenipotentiaries'.

This map and letter were afterwards found in the archives of the
Foreign Office in Paris by Jared Sparks, the American historian,
who forwarded them to the United States government, admitting
that they not only supported the British claim, but more than was
claimed for. 'It is evident', he said, 'that the line from the St. Croix
to the Canadian highlands is intended to exclude all the waters
running into the St. John.'

Farther west, between Vermont and New York and Canada, the
boundary was to be the 45th parallel, which, one would think, could
scarcely have led to complications. But in surveying the line a mistake
was made, giving a slice of Canadian territory to the United States
which, in due course, provided another opportunity for horse-trading
at the expense of Canada.

During the French regime, and particularly after the conquest,
fishermen from the New England colonies had taken fish in Canadian
and Acadian waters, and had been in the habit of landing on nearby
shores to dry their fish. The American commissioners were anxious
to have these privileges continued and they were confirmed by the
treaty, only to be wiped out by the war of 1812.

The Americans refused to admit that the war had had this effect,
and while the British government supported the Colonies' contention in principle, nothing was done to prevent Americans from
continuing to take fish in Canadian and Acadian waters. A few ships
were seized, but when the American ambassador protested, the
British government, in a convention signed in 1818, sought to soothe
the Americans by extending rights previously held by them on the

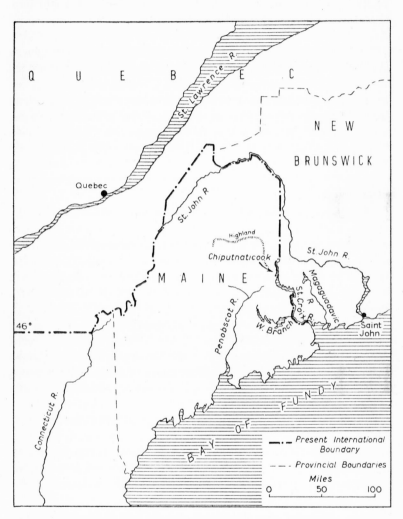

MAINE–NEW BRUNSWICK BOUNDARY

Newfoundland and Labrador shores, although excluding them from the inshore fisheries.

In 1820, the State of Maine was carved out of Massachusetts, and shortly after the boundary question became a lively issue. The State o' Mainers, unable to expand in any direction but northward, interpreted the treaty of 1783 to their own advantage, claiming a boundary that almost severed Nova Scotia and New Brunswick from the rest of Canada. In this they were actively supported by the full force of United States diplomacy, and for sixty years the matter was a cause of international dissension, more than once leading almost to bloodshed. Several attempts at settlement were made. The dispute was once referred to the King of the Netherlands, of all people, who, with respect to the New Brunswick–Maine boundary, conceded everything the Americans claimed, and more, but Canada was saved, for the moment, by the refusal of the Americans to accept the award because of dissatisfaction over its provisions concerning the line farther west.

At length, in 1842, the United States government under President John Tyler and the British government under Sir Robert Peel decided to end the controversy by making a new treaty. Peel appointed Lord Ashburton, head of the international banking house of Baring, as special ambassador for the purpose, and the United States was represented by Daniel Webster, Secretary of State.

Ashburton had no diplomatic experience, but had lived at various times in the United States; his firm had extensive financial interests there; and he was married to the daughter of a Pennsylvania senator. He had also been in Canada, but knew practically nothing about the country, least of all its geography. Pitted against this tyro was a self-made man of great force and ability, one of the shrewdest politicians that the United States has ever produced.

The result was as might have been expected, and is evidenced by the wedge of territory which sunders New Brunswick from south-eastern Quebec. Admittedly a man of greater ability than the unfortunate Oswald, Ashburton was nevertheless also an amiable amateur, outclassed and outmanœuvred from the start. It is inconceivable that had a man like Joseph Howe been chosen as the British representative, such a settlement could ever have been agreed upon. Ashburton did not even take advantage of all the evidence in support of his own case. He had a map marked similarly to that which Franklin had forwarded to Count de Vergennes in 1782, but failed to establish it as evidence. It was alleged that Webster also had a copy of the Franklin map in his possession as well as a copy of the letter from Franklin to de Vergennes.

Ashburton did not know at the time of Webster's map, nor of the letter, but when their existence was disclosed in a debate in Congress, he confided to Charles Greville, the diarist, that:

it was very fortunate that this map and letter did not turn up in the course of his negotiation, for if they had, there would have been no treaty at all, and eventually a scramble, a scuffle, and probably a war. Nothing, he said, would have ever induced the Americans to accept our line, and admit our claim; and with this evidence in our favour, *it would have been impossible for us to concede what we did, or anything like it.* He never would have done so, and the matter would have remained unsettled; and after all, he said, . . . *the whole territory we were wrangling about was worth nothing*, so that it is just as well the discovery was not made by us. At the same time, our successive governments are much to blame in not having ransacked the archives at Paris, for they could certainly have done for a public object what Jared Sparks did for a private one, and a little trouble would have put them in possession of whatever that repository contained.

Between Quebec and Vermont–New York, where the treaty set the 45th parallel as the boundary, and no doubt could be cast on the intentions of the negotiators, Lord Ashburton agreed to accept the mistaken line as the boundary, in order that the United States might retain Fort Chamblee at Rouse's Point, which was found to be north of the true parallel.

In spite of the obvious injustice of the treaty that resulted from these negotiations, and every other similar treaty from 1783 to 1903, most Canadian historians pass over the circumstances as of little consequence. Thus George M. Wrong dismisses the subject: 'Since objectors in each country charged that its interests had been sacrificed to the other, we may conclude that a fair compromise was reached.' It is true there were objectors in both countries. That there should be none in Canada would be strange; and, in spite of its one-sidedness, there were some American objectors, but it is significant that the treaty passed the United States Senate by a vote of thirty-nine to nine. Most of the objections came from disappointed State-o'-Mainers and Webster's political opponents. In a comprehensive speech in the Senate a few years later Webster, in defending the treaty, demonstrated conclusively that the United States had gained the advantage at every important point.

Meanwhile, despite the convention of 1818, the fisheries question continued to be a point of dissension between the United States and Canada, the latter, hampered, of course, by having to deal with the

United States through reluctant British channels. United States fishermen simply refused to be bound by any agreement, and the Canadian authorities were powerless, in the circumstances, to do anything to put an end to the unlawful traffic.

At length, in 1854, Canadians were fortunate in finding a British diplomatist who not only sympathized with their cause, but was capable of doing something about it. This exceptional person was Lord Elgin, then governor-general, who proceeded to Washington, and 'on a sea of champagne', negotiated a treaty under which, in consideration of the opening of Canada's inshore fisheries to the Americans, a reciprocal arrangement was made for the free exchange of the principal natural products of both countries, including those of the sea. This agreement continued in force until 1866, when it was abrogated by the United States, even though in the twelve years it was in force a great increase in trade had resulted.

The abrogation of the Reciprocity treaty of 1854 brought further turmoil among the fishermen. Accustomed to fish in Canadian waters, American fishermen refused to pay any attention to Canadian protests or injunctions. Finally, under pressure from the British government, the Canadian government agreed to permit Americans to continue fishing upon payment of a nominal licence fee. Although the number of ships increased each year, fewer ships bothered to take out a licence; and, after 1868, when the fee was increased, the number sharply declined.

Then, in 1870, the Canadian government by order-in-council abolished the licensing system and prohibited fishing by foreigners. This led to a serious situation. Canada's inshore fisheries were invaded by Americans, fighting occurred between Canadian and American crews, nets were destroyed, and American vessels were seized and condemned.

In addition to losses sustained by Canadian fishermen from these illegal operations, Canadian soil was invaded by Irish Fenians who were allowed to raise money openly in the United States, recruit armies, and, without hindrance on the part of United States authorities, to invade Canada, destroying life and property and requiring the expense of many millions of dollars in repelling them. Canada's protests to the British government failed to bring about any effective representations on its behalf.

The principal reason for the British government's lack of vigour in pressing Canada's claims was that the United Kingdom itself was in a delicate situation with respect to the United States. During the

American Civil War, the *Alabama*, built in a British shipyard, had, before it was captured, caused much destruction of northern commerce, resulting in a feeling of hostility toward Great Britain, and also toward Canada. At times, the United Kingdom and the United States had come perilously near war, which, had it occurred, would have been on Canadian soil.

Besides these sources of trouble, a dispute had arisen concerning the ownership of San Juan Island, in the strait that separates the southern end of Vancouver Island from the American mainland. If the boundary followed one channel, the island would belong to the United States, but if it followed a more southerly one, the island would be Canada's.

Thus there was ample ground for concern in Canada, and the government continued to urge the British government to make some effort to settle the various grievances. Canadian urging at length resulted in the appointment by the Gladstone government of a Joint High Commission, and Lord Kimberley, the Colonial Secretary, asked Sir John Macdonald to act as one of the five British commissioners.

This put Macdonald on the spot. In the first place, a precedent was created by asking a colonial to act at all, even though he would be guided by instructions, not from his own, but from the British government. His first thought was not to accept; but, on further consideration, he decided that

if Canada allowed the matter to go by default, and left its interests to be adjudicated upon and settled by a commission composed exclusively of Americans having an adverse interest, and Englishmen having little or no interest in Canada, the government here would be very much censured if the result were a sacrifice of the rights of the Dominion.

The chief British commissioner was Lord de Grey, a member of the cabinet. The principal other commissioner, aside from Macdonald, was Sir Stafford Northcote, a member of the opposition in the British parliament, and, at the time, governor of the Hudson's Bay Company. The British ambassador, Sir Edward Thornton, was also a commissioner. Heading the American panel was Hamilton Fish, Secretary of State in the Grant administration. Of the four others, selected on a regional basis, three were judges; but it must be remembered in this connection that the position of judge in the United States is often more political than judicial.

The commission began its deliberations early in March 1871, and took up first the question of access by Americans to Canadian inshore fisheries as well as fishing in the Great Lakes and other adjoining waters. It was obvious that Macdonald's British colleagues hoped to use this as a bargaining point in getting a settlement from the United States in connection with the *Alabama* claims, of greater interest to the United Kingdom.

Macdonald, on his part, hoped to exchange the fishing rights for a renewal of the provisions of the Reciprocity treaty of 1854, but he soon learned that the United States would not agree to this. The administration did not wish to antagonize strong protectionist interests in the Senate. The best that seemed possible would be the entry into the United States market of a few specified commodities and, as an added inducement, a cash payment.

Macdonald was averse to giving up the fishing rights in perpetuity, as the British government had suggested, but if he failed to make a suitable trade arrangement, he was prepared, as a last resort, to accept a cash consideration. Writing to Tupper, he said that

It would be out of the question for Canada to surrender, for all time to come, her fishery rights for any consideration, however great. That we had no right to injure posterity by depriving Canada, either as a dependency or as a nation, of her fisheries, and in my opinion any surrender must be for a term of years renewable by either party, but liable to be terminated by either party.

He kept in close touch with his colleagues at Ottawa, writing either to Tupper or Cartier frequent long, interesting letters giving a racy account of the negotiations and his impressions of the negotiators. Occasionally, it was of assistance to him to be able to defer an answer to de Grey until he had consulted the council at Ottawa, and often the answers he received were suggested by him in code messages. Nothing shows the quality of Macdonald's mind better than his letters, not only in this instance, but throughout his career. He had a fluent pen and wrote a flowing hand, but back of all can be discerned a keen and perceptive mind.

What Macdonald did not know was that his letters to his cabinet colleagues at Ottawa were being secretly relayed to Sir Edward Thornton by the governor-general, Lord Lisgar. It is interesting to speculate upon what might have happened had Macdonald discovered this treachery.

Although Macdonald was in a difficult position, and continually found himself ranged not only against the American commissioners but his British colleagues as well, he was able on occasion to play one against the other. He was not so successful in dividing the British commissioners, although for a time he had hopes of gaining the support of his fellow-Conservative, Northcote, but found that British solidarity was proof against political partisanship. He did once, however, succeed in causing a division between the Colonial and Foreign Offices on a point at issue.

Lord de Grey had been putting pressure on him to agree to a cash consideration for the fisheries in perpetuity in lieu of the reciprocal trade agreement for which he had been holding out. Sir John instructed the Canadian cabinet to send a cable to Lord Kimberley, the Colonial Secretary, protesting against any attempt to sell the fisheries without the consent of Canada, and received in reply the assurance that the British government never had any intention of selling the fisheries without Canada's consent.

It was a most fortunate thought to send a telegram to Lord Kimberley [Macdonald wrote to Tupper a week or so later], as on my expression of disinclination to enter upon the question of sale or lease of the fisheries, communication was had with Lord Granville, the Foreign Secretary, who authorized the commission to discuss the question of sale, at the same time expressing a preference for sale in perpetuity. Upon this I produced Lord Kimberley's answer, which was a floorer. Lord de Grey is now doubtless communicating with Lord Granville as to the apparent discrepancy between his statement and that of Lord Kimberley.

The situation was one that appealed to Macdonald's sense of humour, and he must have had many a quiet chuckle over the discomfiture of his noble colleague. But he was not to be allowed to enjoy the sensation very long, for as a result of the situation caused by his ruse, Lord Granville instructed Lord de Grey to proceed with the negotiations concerning the fisheries, despite Macdonald's objections, but to insert in the treaty a clause requiring ratification by the Canadian parliament, which he believed would be forthcoming when the time came.

This instruction, though satisfactory in some respects [Macdonald wrote], places me in an extremely embarrassing position. If a majority of my colleagues should at any time conclude to accept terms which I do not approve of, I must, of course, either protest or withdraw, or remain on the commission and trust to the non-ratification of the treaty by Canada. If I take the first course, it will disclose to the Americans the existence of a difference of opinion—a conflict, in fact, between England and Canada. This the Americans are anxious to establish, in order to get up a sort of quarrel between the two, and to strengthen that party in England which desires to get rid of the colonies as a burden. If I continue to act on the commission I shall be attacked for making an unworthy sacrifice of Canada's rights, and may be compelled to vote in parliament against a treaty which I had a share in making. . . .

After much jockeying back and forth, the matter narrowed down to American fishermen being allowed the free use of Canada's inshore fisheries for ten years, after which the arrangement might be terminated by two years' notice given by either side, in exchange for the free entry into the United States of Canadian coal, salt, fish and lumber.

At intervals during the fisheries negotiations, questions at issue concerning the navigation of jointly-owned or adjacent waterways were discussed. The Americans argued that in consideration of the free navigation by Canadian ships of Lakes Michigan and Champlain, and the use of the Sault Ste. Marie and St. Clair Flats canals, American ships should have the right to free navigation in the St. Lawrence and the use of Canadian canals.

Macdonald argued that

the navigation of the St. Lawrence, in its natural state, should be considered an equivalent for Lake Michigan. That we had the same right to use the channels through the St. Clair Flats as the Americans, and if they chose to improve any one of them by artificial means, they could not deprive us of the right to use them, though they might have a fair claim to a contribution to the cost of construction. That the only thing that remained was the Sault Ste. Marie canal of one mile, against our Welland and the St. Lawrence canals of seventy miles.

As an additional consideration, Canadians were granted the right to navigate the Stikine, Yukon and Porcupine rivers, in British Columbia and the Yukon, each of which rises in Canadian territory, but flows through portions of Alaska in order to reach the sea.

The best that could be done in connection with the *Alabama* claims was an agreement to submit the question to an arbitration tribunal at Geneva, while the San Juan Island controversy was to be submitted to the arbitrament of the German Emperor (who subsequently decided in favour of the United States). Macdonald, who could see little gain to Canada from the loss of its fisheries, hoped to get something by way of indemnity for the damage caused by the Fenians, but Sir Edward Thornton had somehow neglected to have the subject included in the agenda, and consequently Macdonald could not get the matter considered at all. He finally succeeded in securing a rather grudging promise from de Grey that the British government, rather than irritate the Americans further, might in some way compensate Canada, and with this, Macdonald was forced to be content.

Then, having once more put on record his opposition to the conclusions arrived at, and under instructions from the British government, Sir John signed the treaty with the other nine commissioners on May 8, 1871, but that was not the end of the matter so far as he was concerned. He still must secure ratification of the fisheries provisions by the Canadian parliament, and he was not sure in his own mind whether to support or oppose ratification.

Macdonald's return to Canada was far from that of a conquering hero. His supporters were bewildered, but his political enemies, led by George Brown, were loud in their condemnation. This was one time when he welcomed criticism. If he should find it necessary to condemn the treaty, he would at least have Canadian opinion unitedly behind him. Furthermore, he still hoped to arrange some sort of reparation payment with Great Britain for the Fenian losses, which might justify ratification. In the end, that is what happened. The British government, after months of consideration, offered to guarantee a loan of £2,500,000, and then, although criticized in some quarters for submitting on such a paltry consideration, Macdonald began the task of deploying his own forces in support of the treaty.

'I have screwed up my colleagues to the sticking-point,' he wrote a friend, 'and after many weary months of labour and anxiety we have finally agreed to go to parliament for an act to carry the fishery articles into force.' Having once determined on his course, Macdonald cast all doubt and indecision aside, and in a four-hour speech which is among his best parliamentary efforts defended his actions at Washington and advocated acceptance of the results of his labours. The bill carried by a vote of 121 to 55.

Macdonald's early biographers and other historians have painted him as a great imperialist, and so, in a sense, he was. But, like most of those who followed him in his high office, he found that there was often a clash between what was in the best interests of Canada and what was wanted by British statesmen, and in every case he remained true to the trust reposed in him by the Canadian people.

CHAPTER VII

FROM SEA TO SEA

THE province of Manitoba had been set up, a small square patch in the midst of the Northwest Territories, like a postage stamp on the map of North America. But, as Macdonald had written in 1865, if Canada were to remain a country separate from the United States, it was of great importance that the United States should not get behind it by right or by force and intercept the route to the Pacific. There still remained a 600-mile gap between the Rockies and the Pacific through which the American tide might flow northward to coalesce with the newly-acquired territory of Alaska.

If this should ever happen (and looking back, the wonder is that it did not), all hope must be abandoned of Canada's ever becoming a really great country. With a front on both oceans, there might be some chance of adequately developing the vast interior, but if restricted only to an outlet on the far-away Atlantic, the prospect would have been absolutely hopeless. Fortunately for Canada, men of courage were at the head of affairs and this contingency did not have to be faced.

British Columbia, then called New Caledonia, was part of the Hudson's Bay Company's domain, under lease from the British government, but after the discovery of gold on the lower Fraser river in 1858, it was created a Crown colony. Vancouver Island, owned by the Company since 1849, became a separate colony, but in 1866 it was joined to British Columbia. Victoria, near the southern end of Vancouver Island, became the capital of the new colony.

Victoria was a small trading post, and others had been established at a number of points on the mainland, but otherwise there was no settlement. Then, with the discovery of gold in Cariboo, far inland, in 1860, many thousands of goldseekers and adventurers rushed into the district. Within a year or two, 5,000 people had congregated in the towns that had mushroomed on the banks of the principal placer creeks.

James Douglas, who had been governor of British Columbia under Hudson's Bay rule, continued as governor of the colony, and it fell to his lot to build a highway from the head of navigation on the Fraser river to Barkerville, the principal point in the Cariboo gold-fields, a distance of over 400 miles. This highway, considering the time at which it was built, and the facilities at the disposal of the builders, was relatively as great an undertaking as the Panama Canal half a century later. Even before Confederation, it had been completed. Toll gates speedily recouped the colonial treasury for the million dollars it had cost, and gold dust flowing from the diggings produced boom conditions throughout the colony.

Although probably a majority of the people at the time were Americans, and some talk of annexation was heard, there was a general desire to become part of Canada. But no one favoured this unless Canada would promise to build a railway connecting the eastern provinces with the Pacific. Such a project, however, must wait until Rupert's Land and the North-Western Territory had been acquired by Canada, for upon this the British government insisted.

Governor Seymour, successor to Douglas, was against union. Macdonald, through the governor-general, had already arranged with the British government to have him supplanted when he died suddenly. Macdonald's choice was Governor Musgrave of Newfoundland, who, although unable to induce that colony to join, was favourable to Canada. Consequently, within a week of Seymour's death, Musgrave received the appointment. In his instructions to the new governor, Lord Granville, the Colonial Secretary, wrote: 'I shall probably have occasion to address you on the question, now in agitation, of the incorporation of British Columbia with the Dominion of Canada.'

Consequently, as soon as Rupert's Land and the North-Western Territory had been acquired, negotiations were begun and speedily concluded. The principal clause of the agreement was:

The government of the Dominion of Canada undertake to secure the commencement simultaneously, within two years of the date of union, of the construction of a railway from the Pacific towards the Rocky Mountains, and from such point as may be selected, east of the Rocky Mountains, towards the Pacific, to connect the seaboard of British Columbia with the railway system of Canada; and, further to secure the completion of such railway within ten years of the date of union.

Contrary to the procedure followed in the Red River valley, the people of British Columbia were given a voice in deciding their own future. The agreement was approved at a general election held in the autumn of 1870; on the 20th of January, following, it was ratified by the legislature; and on July 20, 1871, it was also ratified by the Canadian parliament. Thus was Canada extended from sea to sea.

Canada was extended from sea to sea inasmuch as people who looked out on both the Atlantic and the Pacific were entitled to call themselves Canadians and elect representatives to sit in parliament at Ottawa. As an actual fact, however, long stretches of wilderness still separated the people of both coasts from those living in the central provinces. In both cases the federal government had promised to build a railway. The Intercolonial, under the direction of the ablest railway engineer in Canada, Sandford Fleming, was already under construction, slowly though steadily narrowing the gap between the Maritime provinces and Quebec. Built as a government undertaking, it attracted little attention from the shrewd manipulators of men and money soon to begin exercising their talents on the Canadian scene.

Although in ratifying the agreement with British Columbia, parliament had stipulated that the Pacific railway should be built by a private company, aided by subsidies of cash and land, the project actually began as a government enterprise. In 1871, Sandford Fleming, still engaged in building the Intercolonial, was also entrusted with the surveys for the Pacific railway. Parliament provided a subsidy of $30,000,000 in cash and 50,000,000 acres of land, chiefly on the prairies.

The agreement was no sooner ratified than two groups of financiers were competing for the contract to build the railway. Both had powerful supporters in parliament and within the government. One was headed by Sir Hugh Allan, shipping magnate of Montreal, already receiving subsidies from the government in connection with steamship lines, who was associated with American financiers. The other was led by Senator D. L. Macpherson, of Toronto, who had already amassed a fortune through railway transactions. Behind each were varying interests in their respective cities, and soon the contest developed into a rivalry between Toronto and Montreal.

For political and other reasons, Macdonald tried to amalgamate the two groups, insisting upon the elimination of Allan's American associates, but neither Allan nor Macpherson would take second place to the other. Allan went through the motions of cutting loose from the embarrassing Americans, but, as later disclosed, they were still very much in the picture.

By now, the government's term of office was drawing to a close. Since the high point of 1867, the political skies had clouded somewhat for Macdonald. In the key province of Ontario, the Sandfield

Macdonald government, the first under the provisions of the British North America Act, which Macdonald had hoped might remain a support for his own administration, had been defeated and a Liberal government now ruled at Toronto under the premiership of Edward Blake.

In Quebec, however, no cause for alarm existed in the provincial field. The Conservative government of J. P. O. Chauveau, set up in 1867, continued in office, the ablest men in the legislature, on both sides, being also members of the federal House, a practice not yet abolished.

But important changes had occurred in the ministerial ranks at Ottawa. Although Galt's pique over the title had been mollified by the G.C.M.G., he never was quite reconciled, and when Macdonald refused to come to the aid of the Commercial Bank, which consequently failed, Galt, heavily interested in the bank, resigned as Minister of Finance and eventually went into opposition, although he did not join the Liberals. His place was taken by John Rose, also an English-speaking Quebec member, who in turn resigned to accept an important financial position in England. Thus, in the end, Macdonald was forced to be content with Sir Francis Hincks, lately returned to Canada after a long sojourn in the West Indies as a British proconsul. Unknown now to any but those of an earlier generation, he was also out of touch with Canadian affairs.

McDougall, of course, after his Manitoba fiasco, had gone back to the opposition, and since representative Liberals could not be induced to enter Macdonald's cabinet, the coalition idea had practically gone by the board, except that the political party over which Macdonald presided was still referred to as the 'Liberal-Conservative' party.

The elections were held in the autumn of 1872. Those were the days of open voting, when elections were spread over a month or more. Abuses of all sorts were common, and after each election many members were charged with corruption in attempts to unseat them, which in a good many cases were successful. Sometimes 'saw-offs' were arranged, when protest proceedings were withdrawn by mutual consent.

Macdonald set a fast pace in the campaign, particularly in Ontario, and undoubtedly saved the situation there. The Orangemen were still agitated about Riel, and suspicious about the government's sincerity in attempting to arrest him. Macdonald, in turn, blamed the Ontario government for scaring Riel away with its offer of a huge reward. Fortunately for Macdonald, his trafficking with Riel was still a secret.

The government won, but by a decreased majority, due largely to losses in Ontario. In Nova Scotia, thanks to the energy of Tupper, the silencing of Howe, the settlement of the fisheries question, and the good progress being made with the Intercolonial, a substantial gain was made. In Quebec, the government lost two or three seats, one of which hurt. Cartier was defeated in Montreal East. British Columbia, with six seats, sent a solid block of Conservatives to Ottawa; and of Manitoba's four, three were supporters of the government; the fourth was Louis Riel, who shortly resigned in favour of Cartier. Among the Conservatives was that Donald Smith who had been one of the three commissioners who failed to come to terms with Riel in 1870; he had been elected in Selkirk.

So, with the political decks cleared for another five years, and good prospects for an immediate start on the Pacific railway, Macdonald seemed free to undertake some of the tasks of organization and consolidation badly needing his attention. But the fates decreed otherwise. Without warning, the bright skies were overcast by a cloud that seemed likely to blot out his political career.

Early in the first session (April 2, 1873), L. S. Huntington, Liberal member for Shefford, in the Eastern Townships of Quebec, charged that Sir Hugh Allan had contributed large sums of American gold toward the election expenses of Macdonald, Cartier, and other members of the government in consideration of his being granted the Pacific railway contract. He moved that a committee of the House be appointed to investigate the matter. Since Huntington produced no proof, and since charges of corruption were frequent in political skirmishing, the affair created little stir. No reply was made on the government side, and the motion was voted down by the ministerial majority.

But the matter was not to be brushed off so easily. With some on the government benches Huntington's thrust had reached its mark. The next day, in order to allay growing uneasiness, the Prime Minister, while declaring the charges as without foundation, himself moved for a committee. It was duly appointed and continued its investigation throughout the session, although obstructed by various delaying devices. Since the committee could not continue after the House had prorogued, parliament was adjourned on May 23 till August, when it was agreed that, after receiving the committee's report, the House would be prorogued.

On July 4, however, the Montreal *Herald* published letters and telegrams from Allan to his American associates directly implicating members of the government. The following day, the Montreal *Gazette* contained a statement made by Allan under oath in which he denied the truth of the Huntington charges; but this was followed a short while later by a letter in the *Herald* from G. W. McMullen, of Chicago, confirming the charges and directly involving the Prime Minister and Sir Georges Cartier.

Cartier had written to Allan on July 8, 1872:

The friends of the government will expect to be assisted with funds in the pending elections, and any amount which you and your company shall advance for the purpose shall be recouped to you. A memorandum of immediate requirements is below.

(*Signed*) E. CARTIER

Memo:

Sir J. A. Macdonald	$45,000
Sir G. Cartier	$85,000
Sir H. Langevin	$32,600

On August 24, Cartier had written to J. J. C. Abbott, Sir Hugh's solicitor, asking for another $25,000 for himself and an additional $10,000 for Macdonald. Finally, there was a telegram from Macdonald himself to Allan:

I must have another ten thousand, it will be the last time of calling. Do not fail me.

In a letter to McMullen, a copy of which was published, Allan stated that up to November 15 he had contributed a total of $443,000 to the government's election fund.

After prorogation on August 13, a Royal Commission consisting of three judges was appointed to continue the investigation; parliament was summoned for October 23 to receive its report. And on that day, Alexander Mackenzie, the Liberal leader, moved as an amendment to the Address that in view of the facts already disclosed the government had merited the 'severe censure' of the House. This was a motion of want of confidence. Debate on the amendment then followed, lasting till the 23rd of November.

On that date, in an impassioned speech of four hours' duration, Macdonald attempted his defence. It failed to convince any but his own most devoted followers. He admitted having received money from Allan, which, of course, was not in doubt, but he claimed that acceptance of that money did not commit the government in any way so far as the Pacific railway negotiations were concerned. With such extensive interests as Allan represented, it was important to him or anyone else so situated that a government favourable to such enterprises should be sustained, and naturally, as a business man, Allan had spent his money accordingly. In closing, he made a last desperate plea which, in the reports available, appears artificial and unconvincing. As a literary effort, with its strained reiteration, it was far below Macdonald's own standard, and could have been improved upon by many of his listeners. But with the old actor speaking the lines, in a supreme effort to avert disaster, the scene, with every seat in the Chamber filled and the galleries overflowing, must have been greatly moving.

Prince Edward Island had joined Confederation on July 1, 1873, and its six representatives (the fruit of a hard bargain) sat in the House for the first time. Elected as supporters of the government, their allegiance wavered as the debate continued, showing the way of the wind. But it was the harsh, staccato accents of Donald A. Smith which turned the tide. The Speaker had called for the question before Smith rose in his place. At first, the ministerial forces were hopeful of a favourable verdict as he carefully winnowed straw already threshed and re-threshed. He was confident, he said, that the Prime Minister had not accepted money in consideration of a promise to award the contract to Sir Hugh Allan. Then, in the conscious rectitude of one with the power and wealth of the Hudson's Bay Company behind him, sitting himself for a pocket-borough, he indulged in a few homilies concerning political morality. Ministerial hopes were now at their lowest and could go no lower when he wound up with the assertion that to receive money from an expectant contractor was a very grave impropriety, and for that reason he could not support the government.

The House adjourned before a vote was taken, and the next day Sir John placed his ministry's resignation in the hands of Lord Dufferin, the governor-general.

The recital once again of this familiar incident may seem unnecessary, but it serves to introduce a subject too often ignored in discussions of Canadian affairs. Elections cost money, sometimes a very great deal of money, but no provision is made for securing the money. Theoretically, those who believe in a party's policies may be expected to contribute whatever they choose to its campaign funds. But any party naïve enough to proceed on such an assumption would have a very short life. Organized groups of workers whose dues can be levied upon are an exception to the general rule; and in periods of political excitement considerable amounts are sometimes raised by new groups trying their hand in the political field. These can usually depend upon election-workers who do not require to be paid.

But the principal parties, year in and year out, depend upon individuals or firms with a large stake in the country who can be counted on to contribute in order either to maintain things as they are or in the hope of bringing about a change. Everyone knows that these contributions are levied, and paid, but very little is ever said about it; in a sense, the matter is taboo.

As is perhaps natural, those to whom the duty of collecting campaign funds is delegated are often looked down upon by some of those who benefit most from their efforts. And since most of this business is conducted under the table, without receipts being given or asked, the opportunities for petty graft—sometimes not so petty—are considerable.

The type of concerns from which contributions can be obtained varies from time to time. Railway promoters were the first important sources. Before Confederation, when the Grand Trunk Railway was the chief contributor, the working of the plan was very simple and almost out in the open. The railway was continually receiving subsidies of one sort or another from the government, and often a portion found its way back for campaign purposes. This was in addition to direct fees or stipends paid members of parliament, including cabinet members, in the employ of the railway.

The building of the Canadian Pacific Railway was a much greater enterprise than any yet undertaken in Canada, and it was only natural that its promoters should have been expected to contribute to political campaign funds. Taking all things into consideration, even the sum contributed by Sir Hugh Allan was not unreasonably large. After all, as a political realist of a later day was wont to explain: Elections are not won with prayers!

Macdonald knew that too; he had been through many a close-fought campaign where the results were often in direct proportion to the money available. His principal mistake this time was in allowing himself to be caught. This is not easily condoned in politics; but that it is not considered an unforgivable sin is shown by the fact that, after a short setback, he was to lead his party to victory four times in a row. Did he do it without campaign funds? He did not, but he never made the same mistake again. In addition to the railways, he was soon to add, as a source of campaign funds, the manufacturers of Canada.

6

CHAPTER VIII

LIGHT AND SHADOW

UPON Macdonald's resignation, the governor-general called on Alexander Mackenzie to form a government, which he shortly did. In the elections which followed (1874), the Mackenzie administration was confirmed by an overwhelming majority. In the House, all the seats to the right of the Speaker were occupied by Liberals, and some of the seats opposite. The followers of Macdonald were reduced to 73, out of a total membership of 206.

Canada's greatest periods of advancement have been when men of daring and imagination have been at the helm. Now intervened a period when those at the head of affairs, though honest, sincere and well-meaning, were temperamentally incapable of devising large-scale plans and prosecuting them to a successful conclusion. Alexander Mackenzie, the Prime Minister, able in his way, was slow, cautious, penurious, and so concerned with the details of the Department of Public Works, which he insisted on holding in addition to the premiership, that he rarely had time or energy for the larger issues of statesmanship. His chief lieutenant, Edward Blake, the despair of his contemporaries and an enigma to everyone since, had the type of mind that exhaustively converts the simple into the complex. He could marshal more arguments against a proposal than he could ever discern in favour of any. Richard Cartwright, the Minister of Finance, a brilliant parliamentary orator and debater, an ex-Tory who had come to hate Macdonald with a fervour of which only he was capable, was so imbued with the philosophy of *laissez faire* that he found nothing incongruous in the idea that less than 4,000,000 people could ever take possession of half a continent and colonize and develop it by merely sitting back and letting nature take its course.

The Liberal leaders, and their followers as well, were convinced that Macdonald's precipitate action in expanding the boundaries of Canada to take in first the Hudson's Bay and North-Western Territory and then British Columbia, and particularly his Pacific railway scheme, was certain to involve the country in ruin. Although they believed that the possibilities of these western lands were greatly exaggerated, since the word of Canada, unwisely as they believed, had been pledged, they were prepared to proceed with the railway, but only by taking a step at a time, utilizing the waterways and building stretches of railway between. Instead of building a line from Ontario to Manitoba, they preferred to build a line southward to connect with lines in the United States.

But the underlying difficulty during the Mackenzie administration was one for which the government was not responsible: financial conditions in the United States. Coincident with the advent of the Mackenzie government, the United States had sunk into one of its periodical depressions. The boom of railway and land speculation which had followed the end of the Civil War had collapsed with the usual crash of large financial houses and the bankruptcy of railway companies. Canada's chief customer, then as now, was the United States, and consequently markets for Canadian fish, lumber and other products were drastically curtailed. The national revenue, derived chiefly from duties on imports, dwindled when prices fell and Canadians were forced to reduce their imports because they had not the money to pay for them.

Macdonald's expansiveness had greatly increased the country's fixed charges, and no provision had been made for a corresponding rise in revenue. Having now to meet these charges—which they had strenuously opposed when forced through parliament—was particularly galling to Mackenzie and his colleagues. Even by the most rigorous economy and retrenchment, Cartwright could not make ends meet; and each year he was forced to face parliament with the admission of deficits for which the government was in no way responsible. The author of their difficulties sat opposite, chuckling at their discomfiture.

The government had much to its credit in the way of useful legislation. Voting by ballot was substituted for the pernicious system of open voting, and election protests were transferred to the courts instead of being left to parliamentary committees, as in the past. The Supreme Court of Canada was set up; and the famous Northwest Mounted Police began their reign of law and order on the western plains. The Scott Act, providing for the prohibition of the sale of liquor in any county in which a majority of the voters so decided, not only threw the support of powerful liquor interests to the Conservatives, but created an issue that has bedeviled successive governments, both federal and provincial, ever since.

In 1876, the Intercolonial Railway was completed to Riviere du Loup, thus providing railway connection between Halifax and Saint John and Quebec. The Pacific railway was also building, but so slowly that more than once British Columbia threatened to secede. Built under the careful scrutiny of Mackenzie, whose department included railways, it provided no easy profits for contractors and, in other respects, did little to lift the pall of depression hanging over the country.

Much as Mackenzie and Cartwright disliked raising the tariff, they were obliged to do so because revenues fell with the fall in prices, and they were considering slight additional increases when protests from the Maritimes deterred them from doing so. Nevertheless, in other parts of the country, particularly in the industrial regions of Ontario and Quebec, an agitation developed for increases in the tariff, not so much as a means of raising revenue but for the purpose of protecting Canadian manufacturers against low-priced goods being imported from elsewhere. Even some of those who for years had hoped for reciprocity with the United States, now began to demand a 'reciprocity in tariffs'.

Macdonald was quick to grasp the significance of this development. He sought a policy upon which he could not only attack the record of the administration, heaping blame on them for the stagnation in which the country was sunk, but which also seemed to offer hope of better times to come. He and his colleagues at length formulated such a policy, which he launched in the form of a motion in the House during the session of 1878, as follows:

That this House is of the opinion that the welfare of Canada requires the adoption of a National Policy, which, by a judicious readjustment of the tariff, will benefit and foster the agricultural, the mining, the manufacturing and other interests of the Dominion; that such a policy will retain in Canada thousands of our fellow-countrymen now obliged to expatriate themselves in search of the employment denied them at home, will restore prosperity to our straggling industries, now so badly depressed, will prevent Canada from being made a sacrifice market, will encourage and develop an active interprovincial trade, and moving (as it ought to) in the direction of a reciprocity of tariffs with our neighbours, so far as the varied interests of Canada may demand, will greatly tend to procure for this country, eventually, a reciprocity of trade.

It proved to be a historic pronouncement. The Liberal majority, of course, voted it down. To those like Mackenzie and Cartwright, steeped in the tenets of Cobdenism, it was anathema. But among those who cared little for theoretical economics, it had strong appeal.

It promised something for everybody, and was at the same time a gesture of defiance at the United States. Only the most stupid failed to see that someone would have to pay, but each hoped that the money would come out of someone else's pocket. Macdonald had found as nearly an ideal program as the heart of politician could hope for, not only in the forthcoming elections, but in elections extending over the next forty-odd years.

In September 1878 the voters went to the polls. In vain did the Liberals point with pride to their legislative achievements, which were considerable; in vain did they explain the cause of their deficits and attempt to show how much the taxpayer had been saved through their careful budgeting. The continuing depression and three bad harvests in a row were obstacles too great to be overcome. And, perhaps the greatest factor of all, we have it on the authority of the Liberal Minister of Finance himself that Mackenzie 'went into action with a remarkably empty war chest, in point of fact, with nothing but a few casual subscriptions, not too freely given, from a few of the wealthier members of the party'. No wonder the Liberals were slaughtered!

The Liberal majority of 60 in 1874 was converted into a minority of 68. Macdonald had emerged once more into the bright sunlight of public favour. The ignominy of the Pacific Scandal was forgotten. Not only did the electorate smile on him, but the financial clouds began drifting away. Careful at first, the Conservatives embarked on no new enterprises, content for the time to follow Mackenzie's policy of building the Pacific railway as a government enterprise. Even their new policy of protection was applied in moderation, but it encouraged the dispirited manufacturers, causing them to increase production, thereby helping to reduce unemployment, creating additional consumer demand. The country began to rise from its lethargy.

In the meantime, events had been shaping which were to effect a radical change in Canadian affairs. Donald A. Smith, George Stephen, and R. B. Angus, of the Bank of Montreal, J. J. Hill, later to become a famous American railway magnate, and some others, had secured control of the St. Paul, Minneapolis and Manitoba Railroad, which held extensive land grants in the American west. The line had been looted by successive groups of speculators and this enabled the Canadian group to buy out the Dutch bondholders on very favourable terms. Smith and his friends gained control just as the depression was lifting, and when immigrants again began pouring into the northwest they each reaped a fortune.

Now Smith held out hopes to them of similar quick profits in Canada if they could get the government to reverse its policy concerning the building of the Pacific railway. An ostensible Liberal since his vote had tilted the scales against Macdonald in 1873, he had been unsuccessful in his efforts to get the Mackenzie government even to think of turning the project over to another private company.

With the return of the Conservatives, however, his hopes revived, but he was still *non persona grata* with Macdonald, who did not easily forget. In fact, as late as the final day of the 1878 session, after an altercation with a number of Conservative members, including Sir Charles Tupper, the report of which fills several pages of *Hansard*, consisting mostly of interrupted remarks, taunts and insults, Macdonald got in the last word as the Gentleman of the Black Rod interrupted the proceedings. Shouted Macdonald over the hubbub: 'That fellow Smith is the biggest liar I ever met!' It was therefore necessary for the negotiations to be conducted without Smith's connection being known, but Smith was accustomed to working from behind the scenes.

Stephen and Angus were well known and they held out promises of financial support in England and in continental Europe. The details of the arrangement were quickly agreed to, and in October 1880 an agreement was concluded between the government and a syndicate consisting of George Stephen, R. B. Angus, James J. Hill, Duncan McIntyre, Morton Rose & Company, and Kohn, Reinach & Company. In consideration of the construction and operation of a railway from Lake Nipissing, through Canadian territory, to the Pacific, the syndicate was to receive, in addition to the 700 miles of railway then under construction by the government, $25,000,000 in cash, and 25,000,000 acres of land, chiefly selected in the fertile belt within 24 miles of the railway. Furthermore, they were promised freedom from import duties on construction materials, freedom from taxation on their land for twenty years after the patents were issued, freedom from taxation on stock and other property forever, and from regulation of rates until 10 per cent was earned on the capital. Furthermore, for twenty years the government was to charter 'no line of railway south of the Canadian Pacific, except such lines as shall run southwest or westward of southwest, or to be within fifteen miles of latitude 49°'.

Before the end of the year, the agreement had been ratified by parliament. Although the opposition strenuously objected, the government's large majority ensured its passage; and throughout the country there was general support for what seemed a more hopeful and energetic approach to the problem. A rise in speculative interest all along the proposed line followed ratification, and the last vestiges of the depression were dissipated.

The victorious Tories would listen to no criticism of their deal; but they might have saved the country much later difficulty if some of the provisions of the agreement had been left out, such as those providing for exemption from taxation and rate regulation, and the monopoly clause concerning lines within 15 miles of the border. They might, too, have saved the country, and incidentally the Canadian Pacific Railway itself, a great deal of expense and inconvenience if they had insisted that the line should follow the course marked out by Engineer-in-Chief Sandford Fleming, through the Yellowhead Pass, which would have brought about the development of a more northerly zone across the prairies, with much better grades through the mountains, and might have prevented much later railway-duplication.

Despite the difficulty of the route finally selected, the company, under the energetic management of William C. Van Horne, completed the line in half the time allowed by the contract, a remarkable feat of engineering and organization. The railway quickly became a financial success and has been an object-lesson in efficient railway management. It is often put forth as an example of a privately-built railway, but that is not quite accurate; without the large subventions it received in cash, land and railway lines actually constructed, it could not have been built, because traffic available for many years would not have provided sufficient revenue to pay a return on the money invested. As it was, the company was forced to go back to the government more than once for loans and other financial assistance in order to carry its plans to a successful conclusion.

The settlement that followed the building of the railway across the plains brought another problem to a head. Recognizing the prior rights of the Indians, the government had made arrangements to recompense them by the payment of treaty money, and in other ways, however inadequate, but there were a great many Métis who were not classed as Indians and consequently were not eligible for compensation. Many of these had already been living on homesteads of their own, staked as in the Red River valley and along the St. Lawrence in long, narrow strips running back from the rivers. Now, as in Red River, surveyors were plotting the land into checkerboard squares, on the plan of thirty-six sections, each a square mile, to the township, irrespective of the boundaries of the Métis' homesteads. And, as in the Red River valley, there was trouble.

The Métis sent deputation after deputation to Ottawa, but with little result. Even with the experience of 1870 to guide it, the government was strangely indifferent to the danger of the situation. The Prime Minister himself was Minister of the Interior from 1878 to 1883. He had never set foot in the west, and was not particularly interested in its problems. Furthermore, his habit of procrastination was most unfortunate in this connection. When Macdonald finally relinquished the department, he turned it over to Sir David Macpherson, a wealthy man who had retired from business to indulge a fancy for politics without any desire to assume its responsibilities. In the circumstances, it is not to be wondered that the Métis at last despaired of a peaceful solution to their problems.

It was then that they turned to Louis Riel, who for years had been living in Montana. In the summer of 1884, four representatives of the Métis, chief of whom was Gabriel Dumont, travelled from Saskatchewan to Montana and induced Riel to return with them and head their campaign for what they considered justice. Even then, had decisive action come out of Ottawa, violence might have been averted. Not till the spring of 1885 was any overt act committed. Then a provisional government was set up at Batoche, on the South Saskatchewan river, with Riel at its head and Gabriel Dumont as military chief. The government post at Duck Lake was occupied and stores seized, and the inevitable happened. A fight occurred between a party of armed Métis and a detachment of Northwest Mounted Police under Major Crozier in which twelve constables were killed. The time for peaceable settlement had passed. The government immediately began recruiting an army. Three thousand men were quickly raised in eastern Canada and 2,000 in the west. General Middleton was appointed to command the forces.

Five hundred Métis, headed by Gabriel Dumont, with Riel in attendance, were gathered at Batoche. Poundmaker, an Indian chief, rallied his braves to the Métis cause at Battleford, on the North Saskatchewan; and Big Bear, with his braves, joined the uprising farther up the river, between Battleford and Edmonton. In all, about 1,000 Indians and Métis were on the warpath, although many additional thousands might have been drawn into the quarrel, which is what terrified people in isolated prairie homesteads.

A stretch of about 250 miles of the Canadian Pacific Railway between Ontario and Manitoba, chiefly along the north shore of

Lake Superior, was still uncompleted. In some places, the tracks had been laid, but not ballasted; in others, the right-of-way had been cleared, but no tracks had been laid. In some places only a tote-road existed. General Manager Van Horne, of the C.P.R., undertook to get the troops through. They were transported across some of the gaps in sleighs, which were then loaded on flat cars and hauled by rail to the next gap, where horses were substituted for steam. In some places rails were laid across the ice, and trains run over them. Six days after leaving Ottawa, the troops were in Winnipeg: in 1870 the trip had taken two months.

Middleton's forces encountered the rebels first at Fish Creek, in April, without decisive result; but on May 12, a force under Dumont was overwhelmed by greatly superior numbers. Further sporadic attacks occurred along the Saskatchewan, but after the fall of Batoche the rebellion was over. Dumont escaped to the United States, but Riel was captured.

Riel, tried at Regina before a jury of six men, all English-speaking, was found guilty with a recommendation for mercy. The recommendation was ignored and he was sentenced to death. After Riel's lawyers had made a number of unsuccessful attempts to have the sentence set aside, he was hanged at the Police barracks in Regina on November 16, 1885. Eight Indians were also executed in connection with murders during the uprising, and eighteen Métis received gaol terms of from one to seven years.

Once more the fires of passion and prejudice burned throughout the land. English-speaking Canadians, almost solidly, supported the verdict and its outcome, but those with French blood in their veins, almost without exception, while not condoning rebellion and murder, put the blame for what had happened upon the mismanagement of the government. Others contended that Riel was insane and, as such, should not have been put to death. Back and forth, in parliament, in the press, and everywhere that the two religious and linguistic groups came in contact—and in many places where they did not—the wordy battle raged. For a time it seemed that the most pessimistic prognostications concerning the possibility of preserving unity in Canada were about to be justified. But, fortunately, passion by its very nature sooner or later burns out. The fires die down until some other stimulus revives them. The next occasion was not far off, but, till then, an armed truce, if not peace, prevailed.

CHAPTER IX

END OF AN ERA

A S the twentieth anniversary of Confederation approached, those
who surveyed the Canadian scene must have had great faith in
the future of their country to contemplate the prospect with any
degree of satisfaction. Corruption, widespread and flagrant, set the
tone of a political morality too complaisant to blush for its own shame.
Ontario and Quebec were at each other's throats in a manner not
equalled by any outbreak during the union of 1841. In addition to
sectarian squabbles, litigation was almost constant between the
Macdonald administration and Mowat's Ontario government over
the question of 'provincial rights'. Mowat won most of these contests,
thereby increasing the power of the legislature at the expense of the
federal authority.

In the Maritimes, the legislature of Nova Scotia had adopted
(1886) a resolution to secede from Canada, either to become a separate colony, or else part of a purely maritime union. In Ontario,
various proposals for ending the country's stagnation were advanced,
from 'commercial union' with the United States to outright annexation. The chief reason for disappointment was the slowness of the
country's growth. Between 1851 and 1861, what then comprised
Canada—Upper and Lower Canada—had grown by over 600,000;
in the following decade, the increase had been nearly 700,000; but
it was feared that, unless some great change occurred in the meantime, the next census figures would show the population had increased by even a smaller amount. Boston was attracting the best
Maritime brains at an alarming rate; the young people of Quebec
were flocking to the factories and mill towns of New England at a
still faster rate; and Ontario was losing people, not, as had been
expected, to the vacant lands of the Canadian west, but to the plains
of Dakota and other western United States territories. Border towns
and cities all along the line were filled with Canadians, and it was
said that there was scarcely a Canadian family which did not have
one or more relatives beyond the border.

Perhaps the most widely-discussed remedy for some of these ills was the move toward imperial federation. This appealed to many whose emotional ties with the British homeland were strong. The British North American colonies had formed a federation, why not a federation of British countries? At first sight, the idea was attractive. But when an attempt was made to work out the details, an irreconcilable clash between imperial and national interests was seen to exist.

At the same time, there was also an upsurge of national feeling and aspiration. The suggestion of a group of British nations, independent in everything but allegiance to a common Crown, which had been envisaged by Macdonald during Confederation days, found some influential adherents who even suggested that Victoria might be regarded as Queen of Canada, as her great-great-grand-daughter is now regarded.

In this frame of mind the people went to the polls in February 1887. Edward Blake, Liberal leader since the defeat of the Mackenzie government in 1878, with the able support of Laurier in Quebec and Cartwright in Ontario, had maintained a vigorous attack upon the administration, which, now becoming moribund, provided ample grounds for criticism. The Liberals were hopeful of victory. In the preceding year, elections had been held in each of the principal sections of Canada. With the exception of British Columbia and Manitoba, which remained Conservative, the rest of the provinces had returned Liberal governments. But a new political factor had arisen which helped to nullify the general trend. The fortunes of the Canadian Pacific Railway and the Conservative party were too closely associated for the railway to allow the party to fail. Its influence and resources were openly thrown into the scale on the side of the government. More money was spent in this election than in any in the history of the country. The Conservatives won, and the 'Old Man' was safe for another term. Probably the most important result of the elections was the resignation of Blake as Liberal leader and the choice of Wilfrid Laurier as his successor.

For a number of years the people of Manitoba had been striving for lower freight rates by trying to provide competition to the C.P.R. between Manitoba points and the United States. But each time a railway charter was granted by the Manitoba government the federal government had disallowed it as contrary to the monopoly given the C.P.R. in the 1880 agreement. Before the question was finally settled in 1888, armed conflict had been narrowly averted, and this had caused the federal government to induce the C.P.R. to relinquish its rights.

In compensation for this the government guaranteed the interest on C.P.R. bonds issued on the security of the company's lands.

That one need only scratch the surface of Canadian life to reach underlying sectarian prejudice was once more demonstrated in the Jesuits' Estates controversy. For reasons that have nothing to do with Canadian history, the Jesuits were expelled from one European country after another, including Great Britain, and the Pope had decreed their suppression. After the Conquest, their lands and other property in Canada were confiscated to the Crown, in 1841, transferred to the Province of Canada, the proceeds to be used for education; and at Confederation they passed into the keeping of Quebec.

In the meantime, the papal ban had been lifted; the Jesuits returned to Quebec, and had re-established themselves, mainly as teachers. They then sought the restoration of their former property, or at least some compensation for its confiscation. To this there was opposition, but purely as between one set of Catholics and another.

Then the impetuous Honoré Mercier came to the front; and when he had established himself at the head of the government (Liberal), undertook a settlement of the issue. In 1888, he introduced a bill under which the Jesuits were to receive $400,000 and the Protestant schools $80,000 for a complete renunciation of their claims. The bill passed the legislature without a dissenting vote.

But in Ontario, dissent was forthcoming. The most fervent defenders of Protestantism in Canada are usually Irishmen, and at that time the most fervent of them was D'Alton McCarthy, an Ontario Conservative M.P., whose activities were often an embarrassment to Macdonald, dependent as he was on Quebec votes which had never deserted him. An address, moved in the House of Commons by one of McCarthy's followers, demanding disallowance of the Quebec legislation, precipitated a debate which ranged far and wide. The issue was taken up by sympathetic newspapers and societies outside the walls of parliament. When the vote was taken, however, only thirteen supported the motion, and the leaders of both parties breathed more easily, for although Macdonald's chief concern was for the unity of his party, Laurier had from the first made the unity of Canadians the chief plank in his political platform.

Out of this agitation grew the Equal Rights Association, formed in 1889 by McCarthy and his associates. Shortly afterward it found another issue. The act of 1875, setting up the framework for a government of the Northwest Territories, permitted the use of either French or English in debates of the council or assembly and in the courts, requiring the printing of all legislative papers and records in both languages. French immigration, however, had been negligible; and thus the legal necessity for the use of two languages was in many ways a nuisance and an unnecessary expense.

McCarthy and his friends, although not greatly concerned with the convenience of the handful of settlers on the prairies, welcomed an issue which permitted an attack upon the official use of the French language anywhere but in Quebec, and a motion was introduced in the House to that general effect. This was another question cutting across the parties, and further conflict was avoided by the adoption of an amendment permitting the legislature to determine what language it cared to use with respect to its own proceedings and records. While this displeased both the McCarthyites and those *Canadiens* who feel that their nationality is slighted if their language is not always placed on terms of absolute equality with English, the amendment carried by a vote of 117 to 63.

Although the term of parliament did not expire until 1892, and a pledge had been given that an election would not be held until after the redistribution of seats following the census of 1891, a combination of circumstances persuaded the Macdonald administration to bring the election on earlier. Signs were multiplying of lessening support throughout the country; discontent was seething in the civil service; dissension continued between the Catholic and Protestant wings of the party; and persistent charges of corruption were being made, threatening at any time to involve the government in wide-open scandal.

In fact, the exposure had already begun. Israel Tarte, owner of an influential Montreal newspaper, and himself a power in the Conservative party, in pursuing a personal feud with Sir Hector Langevin, Macdonald's Minister of Public Works, had published documents proving that Thomas McGreevy, Conservative member for Quebec West, and collector of campaign funds for the party, had made large sums for himself, the party fund, and others by securing contracts from the Department of Public Works at highly inflated prices.

The final argument for an early election, however, and the most cogent, lay in the necessities of the Canadian Pacific Railway, then engaged in floating a bond issue in London in connection with its financing of connecting lines in the United States.

Skelton [1] gives an obviously inside account of what happened.

[1] *Life and Letters of Sir Wilfrid Laurier*, vol. 1, p. 411.

In discussing the possible date for the election, Macdonald told John Henry Pope, his Minister of Railways, of the assurance given to George Stephen and William Van Horne, of the C.P.R., that an election would not be called for at least a year.

'That makes this just the time to bring on the election,' Pope declared.

'How's that?' the Prime Minister enquired.

'The C.P.R. crowd simply can't let you lose, with all they have at stake; they will have to shell out as never before.'

Parliament was dissolved on February 3, 1891, and the date of the elections set for March 5. The campaign was brief but bitter. The opposition, scenting success, fought all along the line. The Conservatives, their ranks closed in the face of the common danger, fought with their backs to the wall. Macdonald, despite his age and the inclement season, was everywhere. Appeals were made for just another victory for the 'old man'. The slogan became: 'The old man, the old flag, and the old policy.'

Although in a minority of one in Ontario and Quebec, the outlying parts of Canada saved the day for the Conservatives. Seemingly, the 'old man' had not appealed in vain; but it was the C.P.R. that weighted the scales in favour of the Conservatives. Quoting Skelton again: 'In every constituency but one—that of Marquette, where Robert Watson won a six-vote victory, wholly through oversight, Van Horne declared—through which the main line of the Canadian Pacific ran, a Conservative was elected.'

But the 'old man' had won his last fight. The labour of a winter campaign had been too much for his waning strength. He was stricken by a paralytic stroke on May 29, 1891, and died a week later. Condolences and eulogies poured in from far and near, and as he lay dead, friend and foe knew that, despite his failings and his handicaps, he had been a great man. Most public men so shield their shortcomings that only later can their true worth be assessed. In many cases, men who bulk large to their contemporaries dwindle in the critical light of history. Macdonald did not hide his deficiencies; indeed, at times, he even seemed proud of them. Perhaps that is why, with the passing of time, his stature has grown; the worst that could be said of him had already been said many times over.

The pulse of a nation paused for a moment, and then life went on.

Sometimes the measure of a great man is the size of the gap he leaves when he departs. In the case of the Conservatives, the gap was large indeed, and seemingly hard to fill. The general expectation was that Sir Charles Tupper, in London as High Commissioner, would be chosen, but he was pushed aside. The prize went to J. J. C. Abbott, onetime solicitor for Sir Hugh Allan, now also solicitor for the C.P.R. In the nature of things, the choice was appropriate, for undoubtedly the strongest influence in the Conservative party was the Canadian Pacific Railway.

The Liberals had supported Tarte's charges against Langevin, and Tarte had switched his allegiance. Although charges against his department were confirmed, Langevin himself had been exonerated by the investigating committee. Now the Liberals were to squirm in their own turn when it was disclosed that the contractor for the Baie des Chaleurs Railway had received large sums from the Quebec government, out of which $100,000 had been paid a newspaper proprietor for use in paying debts of the provincial Liberal party. A Royal Commission cast some doubt upon whether Premier Honoré Mercier had had any knowledge of the affair, but he was dismissed from office by the lieutenant-governor, precipitating another federal-provincial conflict which is no longer of interest.

Prime Minister Abbott resigned on November 25, 1892, and was succeeded by Sir John Thompson, the former Minister of Justice, who was immediately faced with another of the issues peculiar to Canada—the Manitoba School question.

The constitution of the province of Manitoba provided for the setting up of separate schools. In its first session, the legislature had established a school system modeled on that of Quebec. Although the bulk of the people were Protestant and English-speaking, no great objection had been found to the system. Then D'Alton McCarthy appeared on the scene and in an address at Portage la Prairie urged his hearers to 'make this a British country in fact and in name'. Either he succeeded in convincing Joseph Martin, Attorney-General of the Greenway (Liberal) government, that a change was necessary, or Martin merely took advantage of the opportunity to advance his own views, but an announcement was made that changes, both in respect to language and schools, were contemplated.

Following this, Martin prepared a bill to abolish denominational schools, which was passed by the Manitoba legislature in March 1890. The Catholics decided to fight; they appealed to the federal government to disallow the act, and brought an action in the courts to have the law declared unconstitutional.

The appeal for disallowance came at an inopportune moment—in the midst of the 1891 election campaign. The cabinet decided to await the verdict of the courts: if the law were declared unconstitutional, they would not need to act; and if the courts found otherwise, the question whether to intervene or not could then be settled.

The courts held conflicting views. The Manitoba Court of Queen's Bench upheld the validity of the law; the Supreme Court of Canada unanimously held it to be invalid; and then, in July 1892, the Judicial Committee of the Privy Council reversed the decision of the Supreme Court of Canada.

This threw the matter back into the lap of the federal government. It was a thorny question and the government would make enemies whatever it did, but there still remained a chance of avoiding a decision; there was some slight possibility that the government had no legal right to intervene at all. So the matter made its dreary way through the courts again.

In December 1894, Sir John Thompson died while on a visit to Windsor Castle, and the choice of his successor was another compromise. Since the late Prime Minister was a Catholic, a convert from Methodism, it was probably felt that the balance might be restored by the selection of Mackenzie Bowell, one-time head of the Orange Order in Canada. He was no sooner installed in office than the Privy Council handed down its decision in the Manitoba School question to the effect that the government *did* have jurisdiction.

And this government, led by a former head of the Orange Order, proposed to introduce a measure in support of the Catholic minority, and in coercion of the Manitoba government. But, two days after parliament met in special session, seven members of the cabinet resigned in a body, and returned to the fold only on the assurance that Premier Bowell should resign at the end of the session in favour of Sir Charles Tupper, who had suddenly returned from his sojourn in London.

When the Remedial Bill was introduced, Laurier, speaking for the Liberals, declared his party's opposition, not because it did not believe the minority had rights, but because it was averse to the federal power being used to force a law on Manitoba which the majority obviously did not want. He pointed out that the Manitoba government had more than once offered to make some provision for the minority, but that this offer of compromise had never been accepted. The Liberals favoured conciliation rather than coercion.

Laurier had now to face the organized opposition of the Catholic hierarchy, and was threatened with everything including hell fire. For once he had the McCarthyites on his side, while some Liberals

supported the government. At the end of a speech in which he outlined the arguments against the measure, he moved the six months'
hoist, which in parliamentary procedure provides the most effective
end to a motion.

The debate occupied two weeks, and when the vote was taken
the government's majority was cut to 24. Encouraged by the defec-
tions from the government ranks, the opposition began to filibuster
in the committee stage. This doomed the measure because the life
of parliament was running out, and other business must be attended
to before it expired. On April 15, Sir Charles Tupper, leading the
House, gave up the attempt; and on April 23, the final session of the
seventh parliament came to a close.

In a day of bitter elections, the campaign of 1896 was one of the
bitterest. The Conservatives, in office without a break for seventeen
years, and still having the powerful support of the Canadian Pacific
Railway and the Catholic hierarchy, fought with stubborn bitterness.
The Liberals, on the other hand, scenting long-deferred victory,
pressed hard their advantage.

The elections were held on a day in June, and when the votes
were counted an era was ended and another opened. Canada had a
new Prime Minister, Wilfrid Laurier. Despite the injunctions of the
Church, read from the pulpits a week before polling day, forty-nine
of the sixty-five Quebec constituencies had returned Liberal members. As might have been expected, the voters of Quebec, not greatly
concerned with what type of schools Manitoba might have, nor
deterred by the directives of their Church, voted to make one of their
own Prime Minister of Canada. Blood is thicker than dogma!

The four provinces of 1867 were now seven; and through births,
addition of territory and immigration, the 2,283,000 Canadians of
that day had, by 1891, increased to 4,833,235, a disappointing total,
it is true, when the hundreds of thousands of exiles beyond the
border were considered.

Canada had been enlarged in another way. The Geological Survey
of Canada, founded in 1842, had, after Confederation, assumed the
stupendous task of exploring the vast new regions gained by the
acquisition of the Northwest.

In 1887, George M. Dawson and Richard G. McConnell had
made a reconnaissance survey of a large part of northern British
Columbia and Yukon Territory; and Dawson's report had fore-
shadowed the discovery of gold in the Yukon ten years later. In 1893,
Joseph B. Tyrrell and his brother James had made an exploratory

journey across the 'barren lands' from Lake Athabaska to Chesterfield Inlet, on Hudson Bay.[1] Albert P. Low had spent most of the nineties in Labrador and Ungava, and had explored and described the iron ranges which, with deposits already uncovered in Algoma and others to be discovered near the head of Lake Superior, would one day establish Canada as a leading iron ore producer.

Although its full significance was understood by few, the first steps had been taken to provide Canada with that breadth without which it was but a long string of isolated communities which must in time break apart.

[1] James W. Tyrrell's *Across the Sub-Arctics of Canada*, published by William Briggs, Toronto, in 1897, is now a classic of Canadian exploration.

Laurier

CHAPTER X

TURN OF THE TIDE

THERE had been *Canadien* premiers before. La Fontaine, Taché, Cartier, and others, had headed ministries. But these were hyphenated ministries; in each case the nominal premier was bracketed with an English-speaking minister having equal power and authority. Furthermore, Canada then consisted only of Upper and Lower Canada, more or less accustomed to an uneasy association. The Canada of 1896, on the other hand, extended from coast to coast and contained many who looked upon French Canada as a strange and unknown country.

Various factors had contributed to the long rule of Macdonald, chief of which was the virtually unfailing support of Quebec. Quebec Conservatives were divided into two hostile and often warring factions, the Castors, representing the ultramontane, or clerical, wing of the party, and the Bleus, no less Catholic in their allegiance, but not so much under the thumb of the hierarchy. Macdonald succeeded in keeping the two factions, in federal politics at least, from each others' throats; Cartier, a Bleu, and Langevin, a Castor, sat in the same cabinet.

With the death of Cartier, the Castor interest seemed likely to preponderate; and it was to meet this threat that Chapleau, who succeeded to the Bleu leadership, formed an alliance with the Montreal journalist, J. Israel Tarte. One result was the exposure by Tarte of graft and corruption in Langevin's Department of Public Works, which eventually caused Tarte to be thrown out of the Conservative party into the ranks of the Liberals. It was Tarte who, in 1896, had managed the Liberal campaign in Quebec, and by his delivery of Bleu votes played a large part in the victory which gave Laurier 49 seats to 16 for the Conservatives. Needless to say, most of the Bleus were still Conservative in their political views; and this Laurier had in mind when forming his cabinet.

The key office of Public Works, rich in patronage, therefore went to Tarte, presumably familiar with its affairs from the campaign he had waged against its late incumbent. Angry protests arose from many Liberals who through the years had borne the heat of battle in Quebec, but they and others were now to learn that the courtly, gracious Laurier had another side to his nature; that he could be inflexible when his mind was made up.

This was evident again when he came to the all-important office of Minister of Finance. Sir Richard Cartwright, who had held the thankless post during the Mackenzie regime, and had continued as the Liberal financial critic, naturally expected the call. Cartwright, a brilliant debater with a sardonic sense of humour, was, however, an ardent Cobdenite to whom free trade was a moral matter. For two decades, in parliament and on the hustings, he had bitterly denounced the Macdonald policy of protection, heaping scorn upon its parasitical beneficiaries. Laurier, a 'moderate protectionist', not willing to alienate the support of manufacturers, and realizing that the appointment of Cartwright would be an affront to them, persuaded W. S. Fielding, for ten years Premier of Nova Scotia, more amenable in his views, to accept the post. Cartwright, like a good soldier, accepted the verdict (and the more pedestrian Department of Trade and Commerce); but it was remarked that the zest for battle had died within him.

The Department of Agriculture went to Sydney Fisher, a Quebec 'gentleman' farmer. Because he had a university education, then considered by 'dirt' farmers a handicap, and by reason of inherited wealth was free to indulge a passion both for farming and public service, the farm fraternity was at first inclined to look upon him with mild tolerance, but, as Skelton observed, he proved to be 'immensely better fitted . . . than the lawyers and doctors and brewers and near-farmers who had preceded him'.

With these important posts gone to representatives of other provinces, it was necessary to do something to mollify Ontario, and there Laurier was able to kill a flock of birds with a single stone. By appointing, as Minister of Justice, Sir Oliver Mowat, Premier of Ontario for twenty-five years, Laurier not only ensured the allegiance of Mowat's large following among Ontario Protestants, since George Brown's day inclined to fear French-Catholic domination, but brought to an end the interminable series of legal squabbles with Ontario of which Mowat had been largely the instigator.

As a foil to the pious and meticulous Mowat, Laurier appointed to the office of Postmaster-General, hitherto a minor one, the politically ruthless farmer-lawyer Mulock. As the Irish-Catholic member of the administration, Laurier chose, for Secretary of State, another Ontario member, the veteran Richard W. Scott, who as a member of the pre-Confederation parliament had framed the act which gave Ontario its separate schools, and who, in 1878, had also framed the temperance legislation known to history as the 'Scott Act'.

Another recruit from the provincial field was Andrew G. Blair, Premier of New Brunswick, a shrewd hard-hitting politician who had reached the top in the rough-and-tumble politics of that province through a process of survival of the fittest. Quite appropriately, he became Minister of Railways.

The office previously held—and neglected—by Sir John A. Macdonald himself, that of Minister of the Interior, was temporarily left unfilled; but when the unfinished business in connection with the Manitoba School question had been attended to, Clifford Sifton, Attorney-General of Manitoba, was brought in as the sole representative of the vast region extending from the Ontario border to the Pacific Ocean. One of the most efficient administrators ever to hold office at Ottawa, his career of many contradictions presents a challenge which no unbiased historian has yet seen fit (or been able) to accept.

In accordance with Laurier's contention that the Manitoba School question could be settled by compromise rather than by coercion, an early attempt was made to come to an agreement with the Greenway government, representatives of whom were invited to discuss the matter with a subcommittee of the cabinet. As a result of these deliberations, the Manitoba government agreed to amend its legislation to provide for religious teaching. If requested by the parents of ten children in a rural school, or twenty-five in an urban school, religious instruction could be given after regular school hours. Provision was to be made for the employment of teachers of the same religion as the minority where the average attendance at an urban school reached forty, or twenty-five in rural schools. It was further provided that 'when ten pupils in any school speak the French language, or any language other than English, as their native language, the teaching of such pupils shall be conducted in French, or such other language, and English upon the bilingual system'. The latter clause was meant to include other groups such, for example, as the Mennonites (revoked in 1916).

The controversy was not ended, however. Ecclesiastical diehards refused to accept it, but were eventually silenced when, after investigation by an apostolic delegate, the Pope issued an encyclical which, after making provision for face-saving on the part of the clerics, suggested that 'the rules of moderation, of meekness and brotherly charity' should not be lost sight of. This ended the famous Manitoba School question.

Liberal writers and politicians tend to credit the Laurier administration with the change that soon spread over the land. There is much to justify this contention. Fired by Laurier's own faith, decades ahead of its time, in the possibilities of Canada, the Liberals, by their demonstration of that faith, revived hopes shattered by long years of stagnation. The Laurier government had appeared on the scene at a fortunate moment. The previous administration, over-long in office, corrupt and moribund, with five different leaders in as many years, was unable to cope with the situation. The speculative boom which followed the era of railway-building in the eighties had inevitably collapsed, bringing financial ruin to people all over the country. A period of declining commodity prices had accentuated the economic distress, reaching its lowest level with the panic of 1893, when hundreds of banks in the United States closed their doors.

The Laurier government had come to power as prices began to rise. The force of the depression was spent. The country was now ready for another forward movement; and the Liberals did not fail to take advantage of this opportunity. Mr. Fielding, in his first budget—April 1897—without altering the protectionist nature of the tariff, introduced comprehensive changes and made important additions to the free list, which did not include iron and steel, as promised previous to the elections, but duties were lowered on certain iron and steel products.

A new departure, and one which was to play a large part in Canadian affairs in the future, was the introduction of the British preferential tariff. The budget of 1897 provided for a maximum and a minimum tariff, the latter to apply to British goods; but existing British treaties with various countries automatically had extended the preference to the latter as well. The law was therefore amended in 1898 to provide for a specific reduction of one-fourth of the regular customs duties on imports from the United Kingdom and certain low-tariff British countries; and the government of the United Kingdom took steps to end the troublesome treaties.

The most pressing task that faced the new government was the settlement of the West. In the past, this had been left to railway and other companies with land to sell, and very little effort was made to place people on Crown lands. In 1874, the Mackenzie administration had been responsible for settling about 1,400 families of German Mennonites in southern Manitoba, near Emerson. Opposed to war and other manifestations of force, these people had left their homeland to avoid conscription and had first settled in southern Russia. When, eventually, they were threatened with being impressed into the Czar's armies, they enquired about Canada, and on being assured that here they would be free from military service, once more gave up their homes.

Two years later, a similar number of Icelandic families came, under arrangement with the federal government, to settle in lands set aside for them on the shore of Lake Winnipeg, at a place they named Gimli, meaning 'Promised Land'. They were faced with many hardships in their first years, and some moved away to more desirable locations in what was then Dakota Territory; but those who remained did well in time, and their descendants, now spread widely over the prairies, have made a definite contribution to the Canadian mosaic.

Clifford Sifton, the energetic young minister from the West, realized the need for people on the plains, and set about getting them. As a preliminary, he stopped the practice of handing out lavish land grants to railways, and, on the other hand, made homestead regulations much easier. Following this, he inaugurated an intensive campaign for settlers. Soon the spectacle of long immigrant trains shuttling across the country was a typical sight, and Winnipeg, the first distribution-point for these new Canadians, became a polyglot metropolis of diverse accents and nationalities.

A special settlement scheme involved a colony of Doukhobors, who, like the Mennonites, had left Russia because of a distaste for fighting. In 1899, through the intervention of Count Leo Tolstoy, about 7,000 of them were settled on lands near Yorkton, now in Saskatchewan. Because of their social customs, some have come in conflict with their neighbours and with the laws of the province, but the great majority have justified the faith of those who brought them to Canada.

While absorbed with these purely domestic affairs, Canadians were being drawn into the orbit of wider events. Joseph Chamberlain, representative (in his own words) of 'that proud, persistent, self-asserting and resolute stock that no change of climate or condition can alter, and which is infallibly destined to be the predominating force in the future history and civilization of the world . . .' had chosen the post of Colonial Minister in the Salisbury government formed in 1895, and meanwhile had been promoting his ideas of imperialism in which Canada, in his estimation, held an important place.

The credo of this cult, enunciated, strangely enough, by one who was not himself of 'that proud, persistent, self-asserting and resolute stock', had been pronounced by Benjamin Disraeli many years ago:

Self-government, in my opinion, when it was conceded, ought to have been conceded as part of a great policy of imperial consolidation. It ought to have been accompanied by an imperial tariff; by securities for the people of England for the enjoyment of the unappropriated lands which belonged to the sovereign as their trustee; and by a military code which should have precisely defined the means, and the responsibilities, by which the colonies should be defended, and by which, if necessary, this country should call for aid from the colonies themselves. It ought, further, to have been accompanied by the institution of some representative council in the metropolis, which would have brought the colonies into constant and continuous relations with the home government.

Although Canada had taken some steps along the road to political independence, and was to take others in the near future, it had not yet thrown off many of the shackles of colonialism, chief of which was the tendency, especially of many Canadians of so-called Anglo-Saxon parentage, to consider Canadian citizenship as somehow inferior to that pertaining in Great Britain; they seemed to take a sort of pleasure in subordinating themselves and their country to the continued domination of English imperialists.

This, in some ways, stemmed from anti-American prejudice. The British element in Canada was descended largely from those who had left the United States after the Revolution, and their prejudices were not lessened by the lapse of time since that exodus. Their loyalty to what to them was the 'mother country' was increased by the lack of similar feelings on the part of people whose ancestors were French. It seemed never to occur to them that feelings such as theirs could scarcely be expected of people who knew no other country but Canada and who had in their veins no Anglo-Saxon blood.

When Laurier sailed for England in June 1897 to attend the Diamond Jubilee of Queen Victoria, he was subjected to the full force of imperialist influence. His distinguished appearance and courtly bearing marked him out from all the other colonial statesmen present. As the representative of the leading Dominion, he would have been accorded the honour of first place in any event, but with typical,

SIR WILFRID LAURIER

though unconscious, condescension, the London *Daily Mail* declared that 'for the first time on record, a politician of our New World has been recognized as the equal of the great men of the Old Country'. Due to the officiousness of Donald A. Smith, himself a knight and angling for a peerage, Laurier found himself in a position in which it was impossible to avoid accepting a title.

It is perhaps not surprising, in the circumstances, that, on occasion, he was influenced by the prevailing trend (a New York newspaper credited Sir Donald Smith's champagne!).

Although he was to realize later the futility of any such scheme, he spoke of the necessity for some federative plan which should bring the representatives from Great Britain and the Dominions overseas in a grand council or legislative assembly.

Before the National Liberal Club, he declared that, 'It would be the proudest moment of my life if I could see a Canadian of French descent affirming the principles of freedom in the parliament of Great Britain.'

But when he sat in council, free from the influence of 'the applause of tumultuous crowds, the hospitality of famous men and gracious women', he parried every attempt of Chamberlain to entangle Canada in his grandiose schemes. Nor did Chamberlain succeed much better with most of the fourteen other premiers, consequently no plan of imperial federation emanated from the meetings. It was not the end of Chamberlain's campaign, which, in another quarter of the globe, was shortly to entangle the Dominions in British imperial affairs in spite of themselves.

Lord Aberdeen, a Liberal, had been governor-general for five years, and in May 1898, the Earl of Minto, more to Chamberlain's liking, was appointed. He had been military secretary from 1883 to 1885 to Lord Lansdowne while the latter had been governor-general of Canada, and had acted as General Middleton's chief-of-staff in the Riel Rebellion, but his experience had been confined to soldiering.

Relations were strained between Boer and Briton in far-off South Africa, but no one then thought that the quarrel would lead to war, and it is not likely that Chamberlain could have foreseen the use to which Minto would soon be put. It is not necessary at this late date to review the details of that unfortunate episode in British history whose sordidness is relieved only by the statesmanlike manner in which the Boers were later granted self-government.

Sir Wilfrid Laurier sympathized with the Boers in their desire to retain their independence, but, knowing only one side of the story, he criticized them for denying the franchise to the Outlanders. This, however, did not, in his mind, justify making war on them, especially by Canada. In July 1899, he moved a resolution expressing sympathy for the Outlanders' cause, which was seconded by George E. Foster, of the Conservatives. The resolution also expressed the hope that this mark of sympathy 'might cause wiser and more humane counsels to prevail in the Transvaal and possibly avert the awful arbitrament of war'.

The resolution was not quite what Mr. Chamberlain and his envoy wanted. Lord Minto expressed his regret that an offer of material assistance had not been made, and continued his efforts to commit the government to a more definite course of action. Mr. Chamberlain cabled the governor-general expressing 'high appreciation of signal exhibition of patriotic spirit of people of Canada shown by offers to serve in South Africa', adding information concerning the organization of any forces raised into 'units suitable for military requirements'.

There had been individual offers of war service, but no offer had been made by the government, and it is not clear whether Chamberlain's cable was due to someone's error or whether it was an attempt to force the government's hand.

As the certainty of war increased, feeling ran high in Canada. Among English-speaking Canadians the desire was almost general that Canada should participate, while in French Canada little enthusiasm for war existed. Without knowing much about the circumstances, many *Canadiens* had a feeling of kinship for the Boers, pushed about by outsiders. This caused a split in the cabinet.

Laurier was torn between two forces. While at all times he was jealous of Canada's growing freedom of action, he was not motivated by anti-British feeling. He was intensely proud of the British connection, but the England that engaged his heart and mind was that of Milton, Burke and Gladstone.

On the other hand, most Canadian imperialists thought of England in terms of Cromwell, Marlborough and Wellington, of Wolfe and Clive. To them, Rhodes, Milner and Chamberlain were continuing a glorious tradition.

Laurier saw that the two viewpoints could not be reconciled; and he saw that if one side must give way it must be that represented by himself and others less concerned than he with maintaining the British connection. When aroused by any threat, fancied or real, to their spiritual homeland, Canadian imperialists would plunge the country into civil war rather than let it appear that Canada was deficient in what they conceived to be its duty.

After a two-day cabinet discussion, it was decided that the government should equip and transport volunteers up to 1,000 men, and, on October 30, only eighteen days after the first shot was fired in South Africa, a force of 1,150 men under Lieut.-Col. Otter was on its way. A week later, a second contingent was offered, consisting of four squadrons of mounted troops and three batteries of artillery. Sir Donald Smith, who meantime had succeeded in achieving the peerage as Lord Strathcona, equipped at his own expense a detachment of 600 mounted rifles, known as the Strathcona Horse. Eventually, some 7,300 Canadians went to South Africa, one-third of whom were in official contingents; the others, besides the Strathcona Horse, had been recruited through the Department of Militia, but at the expense of the British government. The total cost to the Canadian treasury of this imperial gesture was about $2,800,000.

In the session of parliament which met in February 1900, and in the general elections which followed, the question of the government's action was hotly debated. The Conservative opposition criticized the government for doing too little and that little too late. One Tory taunted Sir Wilfrid on having been 'first in the Jubilee parades, and last in the test of action'.

The attack from the other side was led by Henri Bourassa, grandson of Louis Joseph Papineau, who sat as Liberal member for Labelle, onetime friend and admirer of Laurier, and a brilliant and forceful speaker. He stated the case soon to become familiar as the Quebec nationalist position with respect to participation by Canada in Britain's wars.

Bourassa used arguments which in other circumstances might have been used by Laurier himself, and in answering them Laurier was far from effective, but he gave expression to the thought which lay behind his every public action when he said:

I put this question to my honourable friend. What would be the condition of this country today if we had refused to obey the voice of public opinion? It is only too true that if we had refused our imperative duty, the most dangerous agitation would have arisen, an agitation which, according to all human probability, would have ended in a cleavage in the population of this country upon racial lines. A greater calamity could never take place in Canada. My honourable friend knows as well as any man in this House that if there is anything to which I have given my political life, it is to try to promote unity, harmony and amity between the diverse elements in this country.

Bourassa's vote of censure was overwhelmingly defeated, only 9 members, all from Quebec, 5 Liberals and 4 Conservatives, supported him.

In the election campaign that followed the close of the session, the debate continued on a larger scale, and, if possible, especially in Ontario and Quebec, with greater acrimony. Some idea of the depths to which prejudice can descend may be obtained from the threat of the Toronto *News* 'that British Canadians would find means, through the ballot-box or otherwise of emancipating themselves from the dominance of an inferior people that peculiar circumstances have placed in authority in the Dominion'.

But the ballot-box was not yet to come to the aid of the extremists. The government lost 14 seats in Ontario, but, despite the fury of Bourassa's attack, gained 9 in Quebec. The Maritimes and the West both returned a majority of government supporters, while Sir Charles Tupper, the leader of the opposition, and his chief lieutenant, George E. Foster, who ran in Saint John, lost their seats.

The end of the century found Canada carried along on a rising tide of prosperity, looking eagerly forward to the new century which Laurier was to claim for Canada.

CHAPTER XI

THRESHOLD OF A CENTURY

CANADIANS had reason to be glad that the old century was over. It had been one of strife and struggle, even though during its course it had witnessed the creation of a Dominion stretching from sea to sea. With prosperity, with a new government, and with a feeling of satisfaction at storms weathered together, the people of the seven provinces could look forward with hope to the future.

Canadians were still fighting and dying in South Africa, but the war was far-off; few in Canada were greatly disturbed by it, and everyone felt that the end would not be much longer deferred. They recited Kipling's *The Absent-Minded Beggar*, and sang songs the soldiers sang, but the most popular tune of the year was *Under the Old Apple Tree*.

The year 1901 had scarcely begun when Queen Victoria died, an event almost incredible to a generation grown used to thinking of her as a symbol of changeless time. Singing *God Save the King* seemed an act of disloyalty; speaking of the King's government, and referring to lawyers as *King's* Counsel, was awkward and unnatural. But the old customs and memories soon mossed over, and the new was quickly accepted.

For Canadians, that year 1901 was to hold more memories than usual of royalty. In September and October, the Duke and Duchess of Cornwall and York, later King George V and Queen Mary, paid the Dominion a visit, crossing the country from coast to coast.

The Canadian Pacific Railway provided a special train of nine coaches which surpassed all previous efforts anywhere. It was 750 feet long and weighed 595 tons. Finished outside in natural mahogany, the interior was 'a revelation of the possibilities of luxury and comfort of modern railway travel'. Telephones 'of a new pattern' were installed in every coach, and, as a novelty, were so arranged that all the instruments could be 'in use at the same moment without any one of them interfering with the other'.

One coach, named 'Canada', was finished in white mahogany and upholstered in terra-cotta and olive green plush. It contained six staterooms, fitted with every convenience. At one end was a bath, and at the other, a large lavatory and shower, 'the latest novelty, even in royal trains'.

By 1901, the population had reached 5,371,315, which was more than had been generally estimated. Ontario was still in the lead with 2,182,947; Quebec had 1,648,898; Nova Scotia, 459,574; New Brunswick, 331,120; Manitoba, 255,211; Northwest Territories and Yukon, 186,159; British Columbia, 178,657; Prince Edward Island, 103,259; with 25,490 in regions yet unorganized.

Culturally, Canada had advanced considerably over the Confederation period. Cities were now better equipped with libraries, even though partly due to the generosity of an American steel manufacturer. Music, art and literature, while still struggling against heavy odds, had at last gained a foothold. During the visit of the Duke and Duchess to Toronto, they had been regaled by a chorus of 2,000 picked voices accompanied by a 'large and efficient orchestra' under the baton of F. H. Torrington, director of the Toronto College of Music. The numbers rendered were 'high class', and included Handel's *Hallelujah Chorus* and a 'special patriotic song written for the occasion by Mr. Torrington'.

The year 1901 was a prolific one in the literary field. Among the books published were Agnes C. Laut's *Lords of the North*, Gilbert Parker's *The Right of Way*, Sir William Dawson's *Fifty Years of Work in Canada*, Charles G. D. Roberts' *The Heart of the Ancient Wood*, and *Johnnie Courteau* by W. H. Drummond.

Canadians were finding time to indulge in sports, and to witness them. Golf had already won a large number of devotees in every part of the Dominion. The Canadian Golf Association had been organized in 1895, and the following year was permitted to add the title 'Royal'.

Where facilities existed, both rowing and yachting were popular. At Philadelphia, in 1901, the Winnipeg Rowing Club had won the intermediate race for eight-oared shells, and the Argonauts of Toronto had won the senior championship. In sculling, Lou Scholes, of the Don Rowing Club, Toronto, carried off the intermediate championship of America. Aemilius Jarvis, sailing the *Invincible*, was successful in bringing the Canada Cup back to Canada.

The principal spectators' game was lacrosse, and large crowds turned out to watch the rival teams race up and down the playing-fields. The Montreal Shamrocks won the Minto Cup and the championship of the world in 1901. The Toronto Tecumseths, the

Ottawa Capitals, the New Westminster Salmon-Bellies and the Cornwalls were some of the other well-known teams. Every community down to the smallest had its lacrosse teams and leagues. It was the heyday of what was then called Canada's national sport. Baseball also attracted large crowds, and much more cricket was played than at any time since.

In point of population, Canada was one of the smaller and unimportant countries of the world. But Canadians had already gone a long way, in their own estimation, since Confederation; and had developed a confidence in their future which, upon dispassionate analysis, their circumstances did not quite justify.

It is true that, away off in the Yukon, Dr. J. B. Tyrrell, the geologist and explorer, in an interview published in the Dawson *Daily News* on January 1, 1901, predicted that 'as the great feature of the last century has been the entry of the United States on the stage of the world's history', so 'in the next century, Canada may be expected to assume a somewhat similar position to that occupied by the United States in the last'. And he went on to prophesy that Canada's virgin agricultural land would all be tilled, the forests would be cut so as to conserve them, the lakes would furnish enough fish to feed millions,

and it is not improbable that the mineral wealth will equal or even exceed that of the United States itself . . . As yet there are between one and three million square miles of country in Canada practically unprospected and the mineral wealth that lies hidden in this vast area will be an important factor in the progress of this northern continent.

Tyrrell, however, was one of the very few men in Canada who could speak from first-hand information. He had spent a large part of each year for two decades travelling over the North and West, examining the rocks and other natural features of a large portion of the area of which he spoke. He knew what he was talking about, and few predictions made at that time concerning Canada's future have come so close to the truth.

Sir Wilfrid Laurier had also claimed the twentieth century for Canada, and time is likely to justify him as a true prophet, yet his was a sublime act of faith. Certainly, not much evidence was yet available. The two most populous provinces were without coal, and the value of hydro-electric energy was not yet fully demonstrated. Although the great nickel-copper deposits at Sudbury were being worked, not for two years yet would the silver mines of Cobalt be discovered; and a dozen years must elapse before the gold of Porcupine and Kirkland Lake would provide further clues to the treasures locked

8

within the rocks of the Canadian Shield, hitherto, and for many years to come, considered a wasteland and a liability.

And even if the extent of the minerals within the rocks had been realized, their value could scarcely have been appreciated, for the motor-car, the airplane, and all the mechanical equipment and appliances since developed which require metals in their construction, and have so greatly revolutionized the way of life in most modern countries, were yet unthought of.

Canada's mineral exports in 1901 amounted to only $40,367,683, of which $24,445,156 consisted of gold. The next largest item was coal, valued at $5,397,060. Copper amounted to $2,655,467; lead, to $2,512,061; and silver, $2,420,750; while nickel, later to become one of Canada's chief mineral exports, was valued at $958,365. Little here to suggest that Canada would some day become one of the chief mineral-producing countries in the world!

Canada was still largely an agricultural land; and although the drift to the cities had begun, rural population would for some time to come outnumber the urban. Sawmills provided the bulk of forest products, but the pulp and paper industry was already growing fast. Sydney, N.S., was in the throes of a boom resulting from the recent organization of the Dominion Iron and Steel Company; at Hamilton, forerunners of the Steel Company of Canada, and the Algoma Steel Company at Sault Ste. Marie, were also helping to lay the foundations of Canada's steel industry.

Motor-cars on the streets and highways were no longer objects of curiosity. But not many people besides the adventurous were prepared to depend on them to get with certainty from one place to another. Roads built for wagons and buggies, and likewise the materials out of which this newest instrument of locomotion was constructed, were not yet equal to the unusual strains imposed upon them. Either could generally be counted on to add to the hazards and uncertainties of motoring. Many of the more staid members of the community held that the horseless carriage was but a passing fad.

While electric railways had already driven horse-cars from city streets, the turn of the century may be said to have marked the beginning of the electrical era which, before many decades, was to transform the Canadian economy. At the end of 1900, however, the total installed electrical energy was estimated at only 170,327 horse-power, more than half of which was in Quebec. Ontario was close behind, with Nova Scotia, New Brunswick and British Columbia showing promising beginnings; but Manitoba had only 1,000, and the Northwest Territories only 280 horsepower.

Perhaps the most exciting event at the turn of the century was the Klondike gold rush, which began in a small way in 1896, and swelled to a wild stampede in 1898. In that year, it is estimated that Dawson City had 30,000 people. By 1901, the population of the whole Territory had shrunk to 27,000. Such is the fickle nature of placer-mining booms!

Gold production followed a similar curve. In 1898, gold to a total of $10,000,000 was taken from the creeks, reaching its peak in 1900, with $24,275,000, dropping then in 1901 to $17,000,000, and declining steadily thereafter.

The sight, even the thought, of gold often robs people of their wits. Stories of millions to be washed out of the gravels of Klondike creeks excited the cupidity of many who could not tell the difference between a ground-sluice and a sluicebox. It was staggering to think of what this inaccessible corner of the globe might yet produce; and if it could attract 30,000 people in so short a time, what would the picture be in five, ten years?

While thousands battled their way over the Chilkoot and other mountain passes, or toiled up turbulent streams, various schemes were afoot to provide easier access to Eldorado. Naturally, a railway was the first thought; but the Klondike was so situated as to be almost unreachable by railway, except at enormous cost. The best that could be suggested was a system consisting of part railway and part waterway, which Canadians wished to be wholly within Canadian territory. The boundary between Alaska, Yukon Territory and British Columbia was still in dispute, and the nearest ports were claimed by the United States.

The southern terminus of the nearest all-Canadian route was at Telegraph Creek, head of navigation on the Stikine river. Although the river reached the sea through territory claimed by the United States, navigation was free to Canadians. From Telegraph Creek, a line could be built to Lake Teslin, 150 miles northward, and from there an uninterrupted water route to the goldfields was possible. Goods must still be transferred, however, to and from river and ocean steamers at Wrangel, in United States territory; but it was hoped that eventually the line could be extended to a more southerly port, in Canadian territory. In view of the development now in progess there, it is interesting to note that Kitimat was one of the ports suggested.

The Telegraph Creek-Teslin Lake plan was adopted by the federal government, and a contract was signed by Clifford Sifton, as Minister of the Interior, with Mackenzie and Mann—not yet so famous as they later became—to build a 30-inch railway from Telegraph Creek to Teslin Lake, and also to provide appropriate shipping for goods and passengers from that point to the goldfields.

In return, the contractors were to receive 25,000 acres of land for each mile of railway constructed. This land could be selected any-where, with certain exceptions, in Yukon Territory, but must be taken in blocks not less than 24 miles by 6, which should be divided into eight parts, four of which should be the property of the con-tractors, or their assigns, alternate tracts of the same size to be retained by the government. The contractors were allowed three years from September 1898 in which to select one-half of the lands earned by them, and six years to select the remainder. Mackenzie and Mann were to have a five-year monopoly of railway transportation within the Territory.

The contract was vigorously assailed in parliament by the Conservatives, the debate on the second reading extending over fifteen days. Quoting from government reports, which assumed the existence of 125,000 square miles of gold-bearing ground, Conservative speakers, taking as a basis the $1,000,000 per square mile actually recovered from some creeks, attempted to prove that the government proposed to confer fabulous wealth upon a pair of favoured contractors, and hinted at something even more nefarious.

The government had an obedient majority, and the bill easily passed the House, but the Senate, still largely Conservative, threw it out. As events proved, this was fortunate for both government and contractors, for, as a transportation route, it was unworkable; and since it was predicated upon a fanciful exaggeration of the value and extent of the Klondike goldfields, the contractors, had they carried out their bargain, would have become bankrupt.

In the same year, the White Pass and Yukon Railway, a privately-financed enterprise, began construction of a line from Skagway to Whitehorse, 111 miles, thus by-passing the only serious obstacle to navigation on the Yukon River, and by June 30, 1900, it was in operation. Although the W.P. & Y. originates in United States terri-tory, passes into British Columbia, and ends in Yukon Territory, it has been signally free from jurisdictional disputes.

Meanwhile, through the fertile invention of Robert W. Service, a

Dawson bank-clerk, the world's store of folklore had been enriched and its gallery of heroes enlarged by the creation of Dangerous Dan McGrew, Sam McGee, The Lady That's Known as Lou, and other similar characters.

CHAPTER XII

THREE-CORNERED DIPLOMACY

IN these early days of the new century, many of the problems that had beset Canadian statesmen during the previous century remained unsolved. Prominent among them were relations with the United States. And linked with these was the difficulty of achieving any satisfactory results under the system of three-cornered diplomacy which still prevailed. The day when Canada itself should deal directly with the United States had not yet come, but the Laurier administration was now about to take a first step in that direction.

The fisheries situation was still unsatisfactory to Canadians; the Bering Sea fur-seal fisheries controversy, temporarily shelved in 1893, awaited permanent settlement; and the discovery of gold in the Yukon had made the determination of the Alaska boundary an urgent matter. In addition to these and other questions, there were the ever-present trade problems. Until the adoption of the National Policy by the Conservatives in 1878, the aim of both parties had been to re-establish reciprocity with the United States; and with the Liberals that continued to be a main objective. By one of the ironies of fate, however, the Liberals had come into office as the low-tariff Cleveland administration had given place to the Republicans under McKinley, who produced the highest tariff in the country's history.

Nevertheless, the Canadian government was determined to prevent Anglo-American relations from becoming worse, and to improve them if possible. At one of the early meetings of his cabinet, Laurier had stated that the establishment of close and friendly relations with the United States must be a cardinal feature of Canadian policy, and that the government should not allow itself to be swayed by prejudice. He insisted that, with this end in view, the government should play a greater part than in the past in negotiations with Washington.

Through John Charlton, a Liberal M.P., with business interests in the United States, the government sounded out responsible officers of the Washington administration. This led to further conferences between Canadian and American officials in which Laurier himself joined. Eventually, Sir Louis Davies, Canadian Minister of Marine and Fisheries, with the British Minister to Washington, Sir Julian Pauncefote, met officers of the State Department and drew up terms of reference for a joint commission to which it had been decided that the various questions should be referred.

The commission consisted of Lord Herschell, the British Lord Chancellor, Sir Wilfrid Laurier, Sir Richard Cartwright, Sir Louis Davies, Mr. Charlton and Sir James Winter, of Newfoundland, representing the British government; and Senator Fairbanks, Senator Gray, Nelson Dingley, chairman of the Ways and Means Committee of the House of Representatives, and three officers of the State Department, representing the United States. Whereas, in 1871, Sir John Macdonald had been the only Canadian on a panel of five, this time four Canadians and one Newfoundlander were on a panel of six. But in 1871, the principal question at issue, from the United Kingdom's standpoint, was that of the *Alabama* claims.

The commission met first in Quebec—August 23 to October 10—and resumed in Washington on November 9, continuing till February 20, 1899, when it adjourned. A number of relatively non-contentious matters were adjusted, but of the four main issues, viz., reciprocity of trade, the fisheries, the Bering Sea sealing question, and the Alaska Boundary, the results varied. In view of the American administration's high-tariff tendencies, the Canadians were satisfied with the concessions they had secured—free entry for minerals, quarry products and some agricultural products. No progress was made with the fisheries dispute; better results were achieved with respect to the Bering Sea question; but no progress at all was made with respect to the Alaska boundary.

Northwestern British Columbia is cut off from the sea by a long strip of territory extending southward from the main part of Alaska; and although many deep inlets probe far inland, this strip is wide enough to contain them wholly within United States territory. How this comes about constitutes another tragic episode in British-Canadian-American relations insofar as Canada is concerned.

Out of the expeditions of Vitus Bering, who died in 1741 on one of the Shumagin Islands, but who never reached the mainland, grew the Russian claims to territory in North America. The coast as far north as Cook Inlet was explored by Captain James Cook in 1778, who took formal possession of the adjacent territory in the name of the British sovereign. In 1793-94 Captain George Vancouver completed a careful survey of the coast from what is now the state of Washington to Alaska. Sailing his ships as far into the bays and inlets as he could with safety, he continued from there with boat parties, mapping the coast, its indentations, and the islands offshore. The names he gave the various geographical features may still be seen on the map, commemorating his shipmates, his friends and relatives, eminent persons in English public life and place-names from his beloved Norfolk County. No clearer claim to ownership could have been established.

In 1799, Emperor Paul I, of Russia, granted a monopoly for twenty years to the Russian American Company of the trade, hunting and fishing on all the coastal territory claimed by Russia in northwest America. The southernmost Russian establishment was at Sitka, on Baranof Island; but in 1811 the company established a post called Fort Ross, far to the south in approximately latitude 38°, but no effort was ever made to occupy any of the intervening territory, and no claim to ownership was made by the Russian government.

The grant to the Russian American Company was renewed in 1821, by Alexander I, who at the same time issued a ukase prohibiting foreign ships from approaching the coast of northwest America nearer than 100 Italian miles. Although no government challenged the territorial pretensions involved in this ukase, the British government saw in it an attempt to interfere with the right of its subjects to roam the seas in pursuit of trade wherever they wished to go. British diplomatic machinery was soon in motion, and the United States also went into action.

The United States and Russia agreed (April 1824) that

hereafter there shall not be formed by the citizens of the United States any establishment upon the northwest coast of America, nor in any of the islands adjacent, to the north of fifty-four forty minutes of north latitude; and that, in the same manner, there shall be none formed by Russian subjects, or under the authority of Russia, south of the said parallel.

Since the Russian government had made no claim to territory so far south, and no American had by exploration or otherwise established a claim to territory so far north, it is difficult to understand why latitude 54° 40′ should have been chosen as the dividing-line.

Negotiations between the United Kingdom and Russia extended at intervals from 1821 to February 1825. The Russians began by making extravagant claims, finally insisting on a strip, or *lisiere*, along the coast as far south as latitude 54° 40′. This, they claimed, was essential to preserve their establishment from the encroachments of the Hudson's Bay Company.

The British case was conducted by Sir Charles Bagot, then Ambassador at St. Petersburg, and his successor, Mr. (later Sir)

Stratford Canning. Count Nesselrode, the Russian Foreign Minister, and M. de Poletica, onetime Russian Ambassador at Washington, were the Russian negotiators. Sir Charles stoutly contended for a settlement that would preserve as much British territory as possible; but after his departure, on instructions from Foreign Secretary George Canning, Stratford Canning agreed to most of the Russian demands. None of the negotiators had the remotest idea of the territory involved, and apparently the British negotiators failed to take advantage of the undoubted claims established by Cook and Vancouver.

As defined in the treaty, the boundary line was to extend eastward from the southernmost point of Prince of Wales Island (surveyed and named by Vancouver, and on which no Russian probably had ever set foot) to Portland 'Channel' (Vancouver's Portland *Canal*), and northward along that inlet to latitude 56°; and 'from the last-mentioned point, the line of demarcation shall follow the *summit of the mountains situated parallel to the coast* as far as the point of intersection of the 141st degree of west longitude. . .'

It was further provided

that wherever the summit of the mountains which extend in a direction parallel to the coast . . . shall prove to be at a distance of more than ten marine leagues from the ocean, the limit between the British possessions and *the line of coast* which is to belong to Russia, as above mentioned, shall be formed by a line parallel to the windings of the coast, and shall never exceed the distance of ten marine leagues therefrom.

In 1867, the Russians, apparently considering the territory of little value, sold Alaska to the United States, but it was not till 1871, after British Columbia became part of Canada, that the Pacific coastal area came under Canadian jurisdiction. For some years, however, British Columbia was much more concerned with securing a railway than with defining its northwestern boundary.

For British Columbia to make representations to the United States was a slow, roundabout process. The matter must first be taken up with the appropriate federal official, and from Ottawa it would traverse the usual triangular diplomatic channel by way of the Colonial and Foreign Offices in London. The Canadian government, urged by British Columbia, repeatedly requested action, but Congress steadily neglected to comply.

The discovery of gold in Cassiar District in the sixties caused trouble because the easiest route to and from the diggings was by way of the Stikine river, which reaches the ocean through United States territory (the *lisiere*). Trouble flared once more after gold was struck

in the Klondike in 1896, when, again, it was necessary to travel by
way of Skagway, at the head of Vancouver's Lynn Canal, which,
although 90 miles long, was claimed by the United States as entirely
within its territory.

Now, the wording of the Russo-British treaty became of prime
importance. Did the boundary cut across the inlets, or did it follow
the shoreline round their heads? In a region of jumbled mountain
masses, which ones were 'the mountains situated parallel to the
coast'? What was meant by coast? Did it mean the *general direction*
of the coast or follow its sinuosities? What was meant by *ocean*? Did
the ocean penetrate into the inlets? What was meant by Portland
Channel, and where did the line run with respect to four islands at the
entrance to Portland Canal?

After much discussion back and forth, the United States offered
to leave its interpretation to a board of 'six impartial jurists of repute',
three to be appointed by each country; and, despite Canadian objections, the United Kingdom agreed. The commissioners were to act
as judges, to decide upon the evidence presented to them what, in
their opinion, was the intention of the framers of the treaty so far as
it was possible to do so. They were not to set aside the wording of the
treaty and to substitute something else. They were not given power
to compromise; and the convention under which they were appointed
stipulated that each should 'subscribe an oath that he will impartially
consider the arguments and evidence presented to the tribunal and
will decide thereupon according to his true judgment'.

If the commissioners had indeed been impartial jurists, they would
still have had a difficult task, but President Theodore Roosevelt,
determined to win, appointed commissioners who were far from
impartial, and except one, were not jurists. They were Elihu Root,
Secretary for War, Senator Henry Cabot Lodge, of Massachusetts,
and Senator George Turner, of Washington. Secretary Root was a
member of the government whose case he was asked to try; Senator
Lodge was well-known as an uncompromising advocate of the undiminished American claim; while Senator Turner represented the
one state which more than any other claims a direct interest in Alaskan
affairs.

The Canadian government and people were indignant at the
appointments. Sir Wilfrid Laurier strongly urged the British government not to proceed, but the latter, as usual, was anxious to maintain
amicable relations with the United States and, of course, was less
concerned than the Canadian government with the importance of

territory in far-off British Columbia. Lord Lansdowne, the British Foreign Secretary, did facetiously suggest that perhaps the British government might retaliate by appointing three County Court judges!

The Canadian government, unwillingly accepting the situation, finally nominated Lord Alverstone, Lord Chief Justice of England, Sir Louis Jette, Lieutenant-Governor of Quebec, a former judge of the Supreme Court in that province, and Mr. (later Sir) Allen Aylesworth, an outstanding member of the Ontario bar, in 1906 to become Minister of Justice for Canada. Clifford Sifton was appointed British 'agent'.

That President Theodore Roosevelt was determined on winning is shown by a number of circumstances, and he made sure that the commissioners appointed by him were fully aware of his attitude. Previous to the sitting of the tribunal, which met in London, September 3 to October 20, 1903, he dispatched troops to Alaska. There is also evidence that the British government, if not Lord Alverstone, was made aware of what might happen if the tribunal did not succeed in finding a verdict favourable to the United States.

Henry White, secretary of the United States Embassy in London, paid a visit, while the tribunal was in session, to Prime Minister Balfour at his home, and made quite clear to him the President's determination to secure a favourable verdict. He reported on his mission in a letter to John Hay, Mr. Roosevelt's Secretary of State :

. . . I left no doubt upon his mind as to the importance of a settlement nor as to the result of a failure to agree.

.   .   .   .

I explained to him very fully the position of Alverstone, and intimated that I thought it would be very desirable that he should be told that the government, without in any way wishing to influence him, was very anxious for a decision.

.   .   .   .

Whenever things seemed to be approaching a deadlock—as they did once or twice, during the past week—I only attributed it to Lord Alverstone's very natural and proper desire to do the best and make all the fight possible for the Canadians on the question of the width of the *lisiere*, and I never for a moment doubted that the undercurrents of diplomacy, the force and quiet working of which you and I can appreciate, would bring about a decision in the end.

When the decision was handed down, it became evident that 'the undercurrents of diplomacy' had not failed to operate with 'the force and quiet working' anticipated by Secretary White.

With respect to whether the line should cut across the inlets or

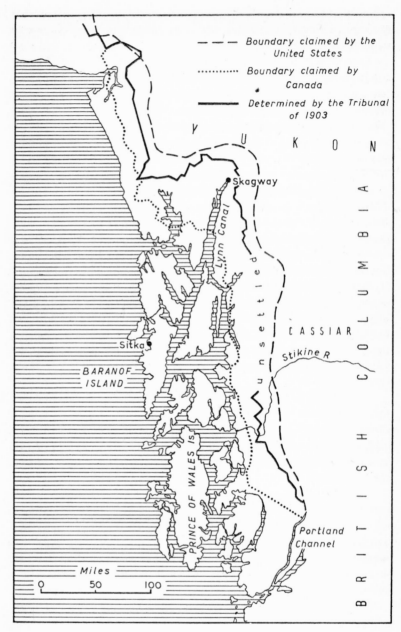

Boundary claimed by the United States

Boundary claimed by Canada

Determined by the Tribunal of 1903

Y U K O N

Skagway

Lynn Canal

unsettled

CASSIAR

Stikine R

BRITISH COLUMBIA

Sitka

BARANOF ISLAND

PRINCE OF WALES Is.

Portland Channel

Miles

0   50   100

ALASKA BOUNDARY

follow round them into the hinterland, Lord Alverstone supported the United States contention, Sir Louis Jette and Mr. Aylesworth dissenting.

Concerning the mountains parallel to the coast, the United States commissioners, with Lord Alverstone's concurrence, arbitrarily selected certain mountain peaks further inland than those the Canadians claimed were meant by the treaty-makers, and nearer the coast than the 35-mile line contended for in the American brief.

On the question of the outlet of Portland 'Channel', the decision was also a compromise: of the four islands in dispute, the majority award gave two to Canada and two to the United States.

Sir Louis Jette and Mr. Aylesworth refused to sign the report. This was not an exhibition of poor sportsmanship. While naturally sympathetic to the Canadian case, they insisted that they had been prepared to act as judges and to arrive, as nearly as possible, at a decision based upon what they believed had been in the minds of the framers of the treaty.

Lord Alverstone, on the other hand, with respect to the question as to whether the line cut across the inlets or followed the shore round their heads, had exercised his right as a judge and found for one of the two points presented to him. When, however, it came to the other major points, he had not acted as a judge, but had joined with the United States representatives to render a verdict supporting neither case.

The majority award not only ignored the arguments of both sides, but also ignored the wording of the treaty. There might have been some doubt concerning which of the two contentions was more clearly in line with the spirit of the treaty, but it was clear that the award with respect to these questions was tantamount to re-writing the treaty itself.

Furthermore, Lord Alverstone had at first concurred with his colleagues as to the ownership of the islands and later, presumably after pressure had been put upon him, changed his opinion. In doing so, he had merely altered a few words in his previously-written memorandum, reversing its conclusions, but leaving as before the arguments leading up to those conclusions. Consequently, the document, while in the main supporting the British case, unaccountably ended in favour of the position which its main arguments did not support.

Not only that, but the Canadian commissioners were not told of his change of mind till the vote was taken, when to their surprise he cast the deciding vote against the position he had taken in the memorandum he had himself written, a copy of which was in his colleagues' possession.

In his dissenting opinion, Mr. Aylesworth declared the action of the majority in dividing the islands 'is "according to my true judgment" nothing less than a grotesque travesty of justice'. And in a statement to the London *Times*, the two Canadians stated: 'We have been compelled to witness the sacrifice of the interests of Canada, powerless to prevent it.'

John S. Ewart, one of the most eminent constitutional lawyers Canada has produced, in a closely-reasoned review of the case, published in parallel columns Lord Alverstone's memorandum, as originally written, and as amended, and on the evidence provided by that document characterized the Lord Chief Justice's conduct as 'treachery'.

If this was an isolated case, Canadians might look on it as the fortunes of war, and let it pass, but with Ashburton's wedge in the east, and this further mutilation on the west staring them in the face whenever they look at a map, those who know the facts find it hard to be complacent.

CHAPTER XIII

PEOPLING THE PLAINS

THE Canadian Pacific Railway had reached the Pacific coast in 1886, but till the Laurier administration took office, ten years later, very few settlers had found homes in the vast region the railway had opened up. Those who had succumbed to the lure of a pioneering life were having a decidedly hard time. Freight rates, and consequently the necessities of life, were high, while markets were few, and for the same reasons prices realized were low. The Laurier administration, largely through the efforts of Clifford Sifton, was to change much of this.

Sifton believed that immigrants could be secured in the British Isles, the United States and continental Europe, and he planned to attract them. Successful settlers, among others, were selected as agents of the department to solicit immigrants in the communities from which they themselves had come; and advantage was taken of every conceivable means to advertise Canada and its opportunities.

Results were immediate. By 1899, the tide of immigrants had risen to 44,500, swelling to 67,379 in 1902, to 189,000 in 1906, reaching a high of 402,432 in 1913 and 384,878 in 1914. From then on, because of the war, the stream dwindled to a mere trickle.

Homestead entries, numbering 7,800 in 1900, were 22,000 by 1902, and by 1906 had reached 41,000, continuing at a high level until the war sharply reduced the number of immigrants.

In 1901, the area occupied by the present prairie provinces contained a total of 419,492 people, which by 1911 had increased to 1,322,709, a gain of 200 per cent. While Manitoba had grown from 255,211 in 1901, to 455,614 in 1911, Saskatchewan had increased from 91,279 to 492,432 and Alberta from 73,002 to 374,663.

The growth of the cities shows in a graphic way the numbers who flocked to the prairies during the decade. By 1911, Winnipeg's 42,340 of 1901 had jumped to 136,023; but Saskatoon, only a village of 113 in 1901, had grown to a small city of 12,000. Regina, with 2,249, had increased to 30,213; Edmonton, from 2,626 to 24,900; and Calgary, from 4,392 to 43,704.

With the increase in people, greater railway facilities were needed. In 1897, the federal government had granted the Canadian Pacific Railway a cash subsidy of $10,000 a mile, or a total of $3,405,000, to assist in building a line from Lethbridge, Alberta, through Crow's Nest Pass, to Nelson, B.C. In return for this, the company agreed to reduce freight rates to and from western Canada on certain specified commodities, including grain for export. These Crow's Nest Pass rates were to set the pattern for western freight rates for many years.

The Canadian Pacific built branch lines on the prairies as fast as settlement warranted. By 1900, it had built about 500 miles of branches to the north of its main line, and, including the Crow's Nest Pass line, about 1,000 miles to the south. It was not the C.P.R., but the Canadian Northern, however, which was chiefly responsible for the network of lines that soon spread across the plains.

The story of the Canadian Northern Railway, and of the two men who spun it out of nothing, is one of the most fantastic in the history of Canada, or anywhere else, for that matter. William Mackenzie and Donald Mann grew up in rural Ontario, and without much education or other qualification but their native wit, learned to build railways when the C.P.R. was building. They also learned to appreciate, and never to underestimate, the Canadian West and its possibilities.

They were an ideal pair. Mackenzie, a financial wizard, could present a business proposition in its most entrancing form, juggling millions until his hearers were swept off their feet. Mann, the master-builder, was a genius in handling men and materials. It was he whose crews moved more dirt and rock, and strung more rails, than had ever been done before. Mann supplied the substance for Mackenzie's dream of a railway empire which, if their plans had not miscarried, would have meant power and riches for both.

The promoters planned to build this empire out of the proceeds of land subsidies, bond issues guaranteed by municipal, provincial or federal governments, as well as cash subsidies from whatever source they could be obtained. Boldly proposing that the public should pay for the railways, they planned to retain complete control. As they saw it, the idea was beautifully simple: they kept in their own hands the entire common stock, in which the only voting rights were vested.

The scheme might easily have succeeded had they been content to confine their efforts to the prairies, where construction costs were relatively low, and where traffic, in most cases, was available from the moment the last spike was driven. In fact, some of their lines on the prairies were put into operation even before the final spike was driven. It was not till the audacious promoters sought to realize their dream of a transcontinental line that they were stricken down. The Canadian Pacific's unpopularity in the West was Mackenzie and Mann's opportunity. William Van Horne's ruthlessness, an asset in thrusting a railway through the wilderness, ceased to be one after the railway was built and public goodwill was needed. In its relations with the people of the country, the Canadian Pacific, at that time, displayed a deplorable lack of tact, as when Van Horne threatened to 'make the grass grow in the streets of Winnipeg'.

When the Manitoba government tried to bring down freight rates by securing railway competition, the Canadian Pacific invoked the monopoly clause in its contract and challenged both government and people until the federal government finally stepped in and saved the situation by inducing the C.P.R., for a consideration, to waive the rights it should never have been granted.

Mackenzie and Mann began their career as railway magnates in 1896, when they bought the charter of the Lake Manitoba Railway and Canal Company providing for a line from Gladstone to Winnipegosis, 123 miles. From then on, by acquiring existing charters, by leasing lines built by others, and by securing new charters and building their own lines, the Canadian Northern network spread rapidly across the prairies.

In 1901, the Manitoba government transferred to them its 999-year lease of the 345 miles of the Northern Pacific in Manitoba, and later guaranteed the interest on bonds for a line from Winnipeg to Port Arthur. In return for this, the Canadian Northern reduced its rate on grain between Winnipeg and the lakehead from the 14 cents a hundredweight of the Crow's Nest Pass agreement to 12, and later to 10 cents, forcing the Canadian Pacific to follow suit.

Mackenzie and Mann, drunk with success, not content with building a profitable system on the prairies, must have a transcontinental, and as early as 1903 had begun to acquire bits of line in various parts of the East which were of little use to them if not linked together. At the time there was justification for a second transcontinental, but not for a third, for which plans were already in the making.

In 1903, the Laurier government concluded a deal with the Grand Trunk Railway which made a third transcontinental inevitable. In that year, the government was at the height of its power; Canada was

9

riding the crest of a prosperity wave; settlers were streaming into the country; new towns were springing up; and Laurier hoped to realize his dream of a Canada having breadth as well as length by building a northern transcontinental that would open up a new zone of settlement across the country.

Whether because of previous commitments to the Conservatives, or because of inability or unwillingness to meet the required terms, Mackenzie and Mann made a fatal error in not arriving at a definite understanding with the Laurier government before proceeding with their own transcontinental plans. The government did attempt to arrange an amalgamation between the Grand Trunk and the Canadian Northern, but the Grand Trunk, under the dynamic leadership of Charles M. Hays, also had the bit in its teeth. When the attempt failed, the government continued with its plans in co-operation with the Grand Trunk, plans which, in the end, were to result in the bankruptcy of both the Grand Trunk and the Canadian Northern.

The arrangement with the Grand Trunk provided for the building of what was called the National Transcontinental, a line beginning at Moncton, N.B., crossing the St. Lawrence at Quebec, and following an almost direct course across the Canadian Shield of northern Quebec and northern Ontario to Winnipeg.

From Winnipeg westward, by way of Saskatoon and Edmonton, through Yellowhead Pass, to a new port on the north Pacific (now Prince Rupert), the Grand Trunk undertook to build a line to be known as the Grand Trunk Pacific.

By the time the National Transcontinental and the Grand Trunk Pacific had been completed, the collapse of the boom, the outbreak of World War I, and greatly increased construction costs had made it impossible for either to earn its fixed charges. The government was forced to take both over, thus providing the basis for the future Canadian National Railways System.

Laurier's idea of a northern transcontinental was sound; without depth Canada could never hope to survive. But, prescient as he was, he could not foresee the war and the depression that were to defer his dream for two generations.

No provision had been made for the control of railway rates until 1897, when the Crow's Nest Pass agreement provided a basis. In 1903, the Board of Railway Commissioners (now Board of Transport Commissioners) was formed with supervision over all rates. Thenceforth, no common carrier within its jurisdiction could vary its rates without permission of the Board.

While freight rates were now controlled, the people of the prairies, especially grain-growers, had other causes for complaint. As the railways spread across the plains, that structure which was to become so typical of the prairie scene—the grain elevator—made its appearance at intervals along the right of way.

Farmers could load grain directly into cars at the nearest siding or station, on consignment to a dealer in Winnipeg, or they could sell outright to the elevator. But later, as an inducement to elevator companies to build along its line, the Canadian Pacific began forcing farmers to sell exclusively through elevators in places where an elevator was located, by refusing, or neglecting, to spot cars for them.

This threw the growers into the hands of the elevator companies, who, in many cases, set their own prices, declared their own weights, and arbitrarily decreed such 'dockage' as they chose. Dockage covered such items as dirt, weed seeds, broken kernels, etc. In such matters, the grower was at the mercy of the elevator.

Since what the grower received was the price set in the world market, less elevator charges and transportation, the charges often tended to absorb an undue share of what was left after transportation costs. And many complained that at the time when, because of money owed the banks, they must sell their grain, prices were usually at their lowest; but so soon as the grain had passed into the hands of the elevator companies, prices often advanced.

The grain growers forced attention to their grievances and, in 1899, a Royal Commission was appointed to investigate every aspect of grain-handling. Its report became the basis of the Manitoba Grain Act of 1900, which the grain growers looked upon as their Magna Charta. But, like King John, the railway and elevator companies had a way of forgetting the Great Charter.

Stung to action by these conditions, a group of some sixty grain growers gathered at Indian Head (then in the Northwest Territories) on December 18, 1901, and formed the 'Territorial Grain Growers' Association' with William R. Motherwell, of Abernethy, as president, and John Millar, of Indian Head, as secretary. It was a non-political organization whose object was, by co-operative action, to improve the lot of the grain growers by every possible means.

Since C.P.R. agents still neglected to assign cars for growers desiring to ship direct, as provided by law, the association decided to bring an action against the C.P.R. agent at Sintaluta, and information was sworn before Magistrate H. O. Partridge. The agent was found guilty and fined fifty dollars and costs. The case went to the Supreme Court of Canada, which sustained the magistrate's decision. Thereafter the C.P.R. respected the decision and instructed its agents to supply cars on the basis of first come, first served.

The grain growers also had cause to complain about grading methods. They secured tests of the bread-making qualities of grain that had been graded No. 1, hard, and of grain grading No. 3, which showed that whereas the difference in price was considerable, the quality of the bread was scarcely distinguishable. The difference was chiefly one of bran-colour. The growers also pressed for the right of a shipper dissatisfied with the grade given his grain to apply for re-examination, and these changes were eventually secured.

Gains such as these encouraged the farmers to join the organization, which, with increasing membership, was able more and more to influence legislation. But some farm leaders saw new opportunities opening before them with increasing membership. Among these was A. E. Partridge, of Sintaluta, whose faith in the value of co-operative effort amounted almost to a religion.

Partridge talked of a farmers' co-operative association for the marketing of grain, but, like most of the grain growers of that time, he knew little about the mysteries of the grain market. He decided to find out; in January 1905, with $100 contributed by neighbouring farmers, he arrived in Winnipeg, prepared to stay while the money lasted in an attempt to learn how the grain exchange operated.

As a result of this, and further organizing, the Grain Growers Grain Company was formed the following year at Winnipeg, with shares valued at $25 each, no shareholder to have more than four shares. Each shareholder had but one vote, no matter how many shares he might hold. Partridge was the first president, with John Kennedy, of Swan River, Man., as vice-president.

The organizing committee worked hard, but cash was scarce, and, as one historian of the movement puts it, 'although ten per cent on each share was all the cash that was asked, apparently some farmers were so hard up that if yarn were selling at five cents a mile, they couldn't buy enough of it to make a pair of mitts for a doodlebug!'

Eventually enough members had been signed on to justify a start in business, and a small office was rented in Winnipeg and opened for business in September 1906. The first thing needed was a seat on the Winnipeg Grain Exchange, which at that time sold for $2,500. But, after paying the expenses of organization, the company had only about $1,000 left in its treasury. Back to Sintaluta went Partridge and persuaded a number of his neighbours to join him in pledging their credit at the bank to raise the additional $1,500.

Despite the organized opposition of the established commission houses, the new company thrived. A rule of the Exchange was that traders must charge a commission of 1 cent on each bushel of grain handled. Serving its own members and friends, the Grain Growers Grain Company could do well on such a commission, and members were notified that they would receive a share of the profits in accordance with established principles of co-operative societies.

This led to trouble. Such a distribution of profits was interpreted by the Exchange as 'splitting' commissions with the customer, which its rules expressly forbade. The company was then forced to change its method of dealing, thereafter paying dividends on its shares only. But no sooner had this threat been repelled than another attack was begun. The Exchange now suspended the commission rule, allowing brokers to handle grain for nothing if they chose to do so; and since many were linked with elevator companies, buying and selling on their own account, they could afford to do without the commission, but it represented the Grain Growers Grain Company's sole source of revenue.

Now was the testing time. The company issued a circular explaining to its customers how matters stood, with the result that it handled more grain than ever. The farmers were not slow to realize what was behind the move, and although they might, for the moment, have had their grain handled at a lower rate, they were long-headed enough to stand by their own organization.

At the end of the first year (July 1907), Partridge resigned to devote greater attention to association affairs, and T. A. (Alex) Crerar, a young farmer and elevator-operator at Russell, Man., was appointed to succeed him as president, the first step in an interesting career.

Early in the company's history, the decision was reached to publish a weekly paper so that those interested in the farmers' movement might be kept informed of developments, and to carry on general educational work among farmers. *The Grain Growers' Guide* was the result, a publication which shortly came to exert wide influence on the prairies. Its first editor was Roderick McKenzie, secretary of the Manitoba Grain Growers Association, who was soon followed by George F. Chipman, a trained newspaperman, who made the *Guide* one of the most important farm weeklies in Canada.

Meanwhile, some of the farmers had become convinced that elevators should be publicly owned. At the annual conventions of the associations in the three prairie provinces in 1908 the idea was endorsed. After strong representations had been made to the Roblin government in Manitoba, an announcement was made (December 6, 1909) that the principle of publicly-owned elevators had been accepted by the government.

The grain growers disagreed with the government, however, over how the elevators should be operated. The growers wanted them to be operated by an independent commission, but the government did not wish to surrender control, and the government had its way. When after three years a crisis occurred because the system had steadily lost money, an arrangement was made for a group of farmers to assume control on a co-operative basis, under the management of the Grain Growers Grain Company.

In Saskatchewan, the question was referred to a Royal Commission, whose report, issued on October 31, 1910, recommended the co-operative ownership and operation of elevators. This was followed, in the spring of 1911, by an act to incorporate the Saskatchewan Co-operative Elevator Company Limited. The act provided that if farmers in a given locality should subscribe the amount necessary to build an elevator, paying 15 per cent in cash, the government would advance the remaining 85 per cent to be secured by a mortgage, repayable over a period of twenty years.

Within a few months, 46 units had been organized in Saskatchewan, representing a capital of $405,050 ; 6 elevators were bought and contracts were let for 40 others. During the following two years, the number of elevators owned by the company had increased to 192.

Then, in the spring of 1913, the Alberta Co-operative Elevator Company Limited was organized, the government of Alberta advancing 85 per cent of the money necessary to buy or build the elevators. The company contracted for 52 elevators, but had not sufficient capital with which to carry on business. When the government refused further aid, the Grain Growers Grain Company came to the rescue.

By 1916, the farmers of the three prairie provinces owned over 500 country elevators, in addition to terminal elevators at the head of the lakes with a capacity of 3,000,000 bushels. In that year, the elevators handled over 90,000,000 bushels of grain, and the shareholders in the three concerns totalled over 45,000. In 1917, the Alberta Co-operative Elevator Company and the Grain Growers

Grain Company were amalgamated to form the United Grain Growers Limited.

These activities of prairie farmers were confined chiefly to the marketing of their products, but at the same time farmers' associations existed in each province to promote activities such as educating the farmers in co-operative action and bringing pressure to bear on governments in connection with desired legislation. In 1903, the Manitoba Grain Growers Association, eventually known as the United Farmers of Manitoba, had been formed; in Saskatchewan the farmers had been organized at different times under various names; while, in Alberta, by the consolidation of two previous organizations in 1909, the United Farmers of Alberta came into existence.

In 1909, also, the Canadian Council of Agriculture was formed to co-ordinate the activities of farmers' associations in the various provinces, in other parts of Canada as well as on the prairies. It was largely responsible for the 'Siege of Ottawa' in 1910, and drew up 'The Farmers' Platform', representing the demands made upon the government at that time.

During this period, important political changes had occurred in the Northwest Territories. When this region passed from the Hudson's Bay Company to the Dominion of Canada, the latter embarked upon a unique form of imperialism. Still a colony, it nevertheless governed an area much greater than itself in a manner quite as absolute as any that Downing Street had ever imposed upon a subject territory.[1] The first legislation concerning the Northwest Territories was passed by parliament in 1875, during the administration of Alexander Mackenzie. It provided for the control of local affairs by a lieutenant-governor and an elected assembly, leaving control of lands and other natural resources in the hands of the federal government under the authority of the Minister of the Interior.

Among other things, the act provided for a school system similar to that in Quebec. Provision was made for a majority of the rate-payers in any district to establish a school such as they saw fit, the minority, Catholic or Protestant, being empowered to set up a separate school. This provision was modified by subsequent ordinances of the assembly (of doubtful validity, but allowed to go unchallenged), with the result that by 1901 the schools had lost nearly all of their denominational character. The law, as amended, provided

[1] See Martin, Chester: *Confederation and the West*, Canadian Historical Association, Annual Report, 1927.

that the first school in any district should be a public school, but the minority could organize a separate school and levy taxes upon its adherents for its support. Both public and minority schools were put under the control of a commissioner of education and must adhere to authorized studies, with religious instruction confined to the last half-hour of the school day.

As the population increased, the people of the prairies became more and more insistent upon their right to control their own affairs. F. W. G. Haultain, for many years Premier of the Territories, took the lead in a new fight for responsible government, which, by the turn of the century, was completely successful except for the attainment of provincial status. This, in the election campaign of 1904, Sir Wilfrid Laurier promised to implement, and in 1905 bills were introduced providing for the establishment of the provinces of Alberta and Saskatchewan.

This legislation was of particular interest to Clifford Sifton, as Minister of the Interior; but, following his strenuous efforts in the recent elections, he had been forced to take a rest, leaving for the southern states after he believed the terms of the proposed bills had been agreed upon. The bills were introduced before he learned that the provisions governing schools did not, as he expected, embody the existing regulations, but had re-established the provisions of the act of 1875. He immediately returned to Ottawa and resigned from the cabinet.

Undoubtedly, Laurier was remiss in introducing the bills without having fully cleared with Sifton, who was known to hold strong views concerning religious teaching in the schools. It is inconceivable that Laurier could have been unaware of the implications of the school clauses, and it is probable that, having been forced by circumstances to oppose his fellow-Catholics on the Manitoba School question, he welcomed a chance to appear for once on their side. The offending clauses were drafted chiefly by Charles Fitzpatrick, the Minister of Justice, which was a further affront to Sifton, who did not forget that in 1902, when he had requested the post of Minister of Justice, to which he believed he was entitled, Fitzpatrick had been preferred over him.

Sifton was not the only member of the cabinet displeased with the autonomy bills. Fielding also threatened to resign, and Laurier hastened to effect a compromise, eventually accepting a section drafted by Sifton himself, but he could not mend the rift with Sifton. J. W. Dafoe, Sifton's biographer, blames Sifton's deafness for the break. Had Sifton been able to take part in discussions current in Ottawa before he left for the south, he would doubtless have seen the way matters were tending and would have had a showdown before the bills were introduced. Dafoe believed that if this had happened the subsequent history of the Liberal party might have been vastly different.

Haultain was the logical person to head one of the new governments, preferably that of Saskatchewan, but he was a Conservative, and to have chosen him would probably have precipitated another party crisis. Consequently, to Walter Scott, who had previously represented the Regina constituency in the House of Commons, was given the honour of being the first Premier of Saskatchewan, and Dr. A. C. Rutherford became the Premier of Alberta.

CHAPTER XIV

CANADA GOES ITS WAY

WITH Canada's growing trade and interests abroad, the round-about methods of dealing with other countries which had obtained in the past were gradually discarded in negotiating agreements in connection with trade, immigration and similar subjects. Cabinet ministers and other departmental officers were usually given special authority to negotiate such agreements in the King's name on behalf of Canada. With respect to a formal treaty with France, Mr. Fielding and Mr. Brodeur, Minister of Marine and Fisheries, were appointed plenipotentiaries to act with the British Ambassador to France, whose principal function was to sign the document, a formality not yet thought proper for Dominions' ministers. In the case of less formal agreements, termed conventions, Canadian ministers were empowered both to negotiate and sign. It was during this period that a consular service was established and trade commissioners were sent to some of the principal countries.

All this made necessary additional machinery at Ottawa, and in 1909 a Department of External Affairs was created with Charles Murphy, already Secretary of State, as minister and Joseph Pope as deputy minister. Action was taken in 1909 to end the long-standing fisheries dispute when Mr. James Bryce, the British Ambassador at Washington, and Mr. Elihu Root, the United States Secretary of State, signed a treaty under which that question was submitted to The Hague Tribunal. In June of that year, the case came before the Tribunal, which consisted of Dr. Lammasch of Austria, Dr. Lohman of Holland, Dr. Drago of Argentina, Justice Gray of the United States Circuit Court of Appeals, and Sir Charles Fitzpatrick of the Supreme Court of Canada. An imposing array of legal talent was in attendance, representing Canada, Great Britain, Newfoundland and the United States. This time Theodore Roosevelt was safely out of the White House, hunting big game in Africa or up the Amazon, and the Big Stick was not in evidence. The result was a decision, unanimous except for a dissent on one point by Dr. Drago, which, on every important point, sustained Canada's contention.

In 1909, also, Messrs. Bryce and Root negotiated a treaty which, in some respects, provided for the appointment of a body unique in international affairs. For many years there had been friction along the Canadian-American border arising out of conflicts concerning the use of boundary waters. In Montana, Alberta and Saskatchewan, armed conflict had been narrowly averted over disputes as to the division of the waters of the St. Mary and Milk rivers. The St. Mary rises in Montana, crosses into Alberta, and its waters eventually find their way to Hudson Bay. Milk river likewise rises in Montana, flows into Alberta and Saskatchewan, but then re-crosses the boundary and flows into the Missouri. It was possible for farmers along the upper reaches of the St. Mary to divert water to the detriment of Alberta ranchers; and it was also possible for Alberta and Saskatchewan ranchers and farmers to divert water from Milk river to the detriment of those south of the line. The Detroit river and other boundary waters were being polluted, and neither country had the authority to correct the evil. These are typical of the many occasions for friction that existed in connection with boundary waters.

Under the treaty signed in 1909, the International Joint Commission was set up, consisting of three members on each side, one of whom is designated as chairman. At meetings held in the United States the American chairman presides, and at meetings held in Canada the Canadian chairman presides. Each section has a secretary, and the two work in co-operation. Into the custody of this tribunal both countries have entrusted a portion of their sovereignty. In this way the commission has in some respects greater authority than either of the legislatures which it represents, for whereas neither the Canadian parliament nor the United States Congress has any control over the waters belonging to the other, this body has jurisdiction over waters belonging to both.

In the intervening years, the Commission has quietly and unobtrusively dealt with a great variety of questions; and in practically all of them its decisions have been unanimous. As a result, there has been a complete absence of the sort of disputes common before its creation. Its methods are quite democratic. When a question comes before it for decision, public hearings are held throughout the area concerned, and anyone who has an interest or an opinion may be heard. The commissioners then sift the evidence before them and in a spirit of fairmindedness arrive at a decision. There are no fireworks and little unnecessary publicity. So quietly do they work that many Canadians and most Americans are not even aware of their existence. Yet they have saved the people of both countries a great deal of money, and have prevented untold friction, which, if neglected, might easily have resulted in serious conflict.

The question of Asiatic immigration was complicated by the fact that whereas Canada, spurred by British Columbia, desired to restrict Oriental immigration, the exclusion of Japanese was difficult since Japan was an ally of the United Kingdom, while with respect to Hindus, who were British subjects, exclusion was even more difficult. The Chinese, however, were protected by neither British citizenship nor an alliance and all Chinese, except officials, merchants and students, had been subject since 1885 to a head-tax. Originally the tax had been $50 per person, but in 1901 it was raised to $100, and in 1904, to $400. This maintained the influx of Chinese at a fairly low level.

Canada got around the problem of Japanese immigration by an arrangement made through the Japanese consul-general that the Japanese government itself should control the number of immigrants. This did not remain satisfactory, however, for in 1906, 3,000, and in the following year, 7,000 Japanese entered the country. Riots occurred in Vancouver, which caused the federal government to rush Rodolphe Lemieux, then Postmaster-General, to Tokio to arrange a definite understanding with the Japanese government, as a result of which Japanese immigration fell to but a few hundred a year.

The delicate situation of one British country forbidding the entrance of the citizens of another was handed for settlement to the newest cabinet recruit, William Lyon Mackenzie King, the first head of a separate Labour ministry. A way out was found by inserting a clause in the Immigration Act barring immigrants who did not come direct from their country of origin, and since no steamships plied between India and Canada, it was believed that Indians would be automatically excluded. A group of Hindus chartered a ship, however, and sailed direct to Vancouver but were prevented from landing by armed citizens who defied both the immigrants and the authorities.

With the approach of the coming struggle in Europe, pressure from those, both at home and abroad, who would enmesh Canada in some sort of federation, or Empire defence scheme, became more insistent. It was the day of the British Empire League and the Round

Table Group, all attempting by one means or another to accomplish their desires.

The British government favoured cash contributions to a single navy; but when this did not seem to appeal to Canadians or Australians, it was prepared to consider the alternative of Dominion units, under Dominion control, except during times of war. This, however, did not satisfy Canadian imperialists, who denounced and ridiculed the idea of a 'tin-pot' navy.

At first, the two political parties seemed to be in accord. In the session of 1909, George E. Foster, the veteran Conservative member, speaking to a resolution proposed by himself in favour of action by Canada to protect her coastline and seaports, opposed an annual contribution to the British navy and advocated a Canadian navy, with perhaps an emergency gift of a dreadnought. Sir Wilfrid Laurier then moved a resolution proposing a Canadian naval service; and Robert L. Borden, who, in 1901, had succeeded Sir Charles Tupper as Conservative leader, supported the idea of a 'Canadian naval force of our own'. Both Mr. Foster's and Sir Wilfrid's resolutions were adopted without division.

In January 1910, Sir Wilfrid Laurier introduced his Naval Service legislation. It provided for the creation of a naval establishment comprising a permanent corps, a reserve, and a volunteer force, all on a voluntary basis. Provision was made for the establishment of a naval college, and a naval board to advise the Department of Marine. This naval force would be completely under the control of the Canadian government, but in times of emergency any or all of it might be placed at the disposal of the British authorities. It was proposed, as a start, to build five cruisers and six destroyers for service on both coasts. The cost of the ships, if built in England, would be $11,000,000, increased by about one-third if built in Canada. The annual cost was estimated at about $3,000,000.

In his speech in support of this program, Sir Wilfrid, in referring to opposition from imperialists, denied that 'in them alone is to be found the true incense of loyalty', and in dealing with those whose opposition came from the other extreme, asked,

did these men forget that Canada was a country with two sea-coasts and exposed cities, a country with a large ocean trade? . . . . If England is at war, we are at war and liable to attack [he continued]. I do not say that we shall always be attacked, neither do I say that we would take part in all the wars of England. That is a matter that must be guided by circumstances upon which the Canadian parliament will have to pronounce, and will have to decide in its own best judgment.

The Liberal party, with few exceptions, supported the government's policy. There were few imperialists among them. Such opposition as there was, and it was not very vocal, took the stand that so great a departure from past practice was not required in the circumstances; they preferred not to prod a hornets' nest when there seemed to be no good reason; they were inclined to hand over a dreadnought or two and let the United Kingdom worry about defence, as in the past.

The Conservatives were sharply divided. Mr. Borden and Mr. Foster had already put themselves on record as favouring the creation of a Canadian navy. This Mr. Borden re-affirmed in his speech on the Naval Bill, but he insisted that an emergency existed which called for the immediate contribution by Canada of two dreadnoughts. On the other hand, one of his chief lieutenants from Quebec, F. D. Monk, roundly denounced the bill in terms that were to become familiar in the months to come. Other Conservatives opposed the legislation as likely to lead to the break-up of the British Empire; as a declaration of independence on the part of Canada; and as an exhibition of disloyalty.

Except for an occasional patriot of the imperialist school, there was—outside Quebec—little opposition throughout Canada; but in Quebec, Henri Bourassa and his chief aide, Armand Lavergne, made the issue their own. Around them gathered the nucleus of a new political party, the Nationalists. *Le Devoir*, a daily, was established in Montreal with Bourassa as director. Having from the start a strong religious slant, it fanned the smouldering embers of ultramontanism, once more providing leadership for the Castors, young and old, who had hitherto been leaderless. Bourassa dropped naturally into the position.

On the other hand, stripped of their passion and prejudice, Bourassa and his followers were often more consistent, in the circumstances, than Laurier. Laurier insisted that Canada must have the right to decide whether or not to participate in British wars because Canadians should not be compelled to fight in support of policies they had no voice in deciding. Yet he opposed all attempts to inveigle Canada into advisory councils of one sort or another on the ground that the giving of advice would inevitably lead to a sharing of responsibility. The anomalous term, Commonwealth, had not yet come into general use, and the British Empire was still a reality. Laurier had no desire to withdraw from the Empire, but the status he envisaged for Canada had not yet come to be recognized. Hence it was but natural that to those who placed the Empire before everything else, Laurier's policy seemed to threaten the Empire's very existence. They believed—as was soon to become evident—that Canada could not remain neutral while the Empire was at war in any part of the globe and for any purpose; and that any such attempt, if successful, must lead to independence.

It was not the first nor the last time that Laurier, in his desire to follow a path which would appeal to the growing feeling of independence stirring in Canada, and still allow the Dominion to continue in association with the group of emerging British nations, would seem strangely inconsistent to many, and find himself the target of a cross-fire from extremists in both camps. A letter he wrote to an Ontario friend in 1909 (quoted by Skelton) gives a good picture of the problem as he saw it:

... if we were disconnected with Britain, we would have less occasion of conflict with Europe than we have at the present time; but if British connection has some disadvantages, in my judgment it has advantages which far more than outbalance the objections. No one at this moment thinks or would wish for a severance from Britain; I certainly do not. We are happy, free, content, and prosperous as we are, and so long as the nation has those blessings, no one will ever think of changing the political conditions. We are all the same a nation, though under the suzerainty of Great Britain, and we have to assume the duties and responsibilities of a nation. Part of these duties is the keeping of some armed force, both on land and at sea.

.   .   .   .

I would ask you further to consider this point: our existence as a nation is the most anomalous that has yet existed. We are British subjects, but we are an autonomous nation; we are divided into provinces, we are divided into races, and out of these confused elements the man at the head of affairs has to sail the ship onwards, and to do this safely, it is not always the ideal policy from the point of view of pure idealism which ought to prevail, but the policy which can appeal on the whole to all sections of the community. This has been my inspiration ever since I assumed the leadership of the party and up to the present time this policy has if it has done nothing else, given to the people these blessings which I have just mentioned: peace, harmony and prosperity.

If you were in the position in which I am, you would have to think night and day of these different problems... It has been my lot to face such problems again and again, throughout my political career, and on every occasion I have had to disappoint scores of my friends on some point or other. In the Manitoba School question I imposed upon my friends from Quebec what was to them at that time a difficult problem to face. On the Autonomy Bills of Saskatchewan and Alberta I imposed upon my friends from Ontario what was to them undoubtedly a similar problem to face. I do not expect that the task will be as heavy in the present instance as it was in the two last; still it will be of such a character as to give me many troubled hours. It is some consolation to think, however, that it will probably be the last one.

Little did he know!

The debate on the Naval Bill continued through the session, and on a motion for second reading, on February 3, Mr. Borden, in an attempt to please both wings of his following, proposed an amendment which, among other things, urged the contribution of 'such an amount as may be sufficient to purchase or construct two battleships or armoured cruisers of the latest dreadnought type'. The amendment was defeated on March 9 by a vote of 129 to 74, after a subamendment by Monk calling for the submission of the question to a referendum had been defeated by a majority of 157. The bill was passed on April 20 by a majority of 41.

That ended the matter in parliament, but not in the press, nor on the platforms of Quebec. And now occurred one of those strange strokes of fate which turn the tide of events. Sir Wilfrid appointed to the Senate the member for Drummond-Arthabaska, thus making necessary a by-election in that constituency. Evidently the Liberal strategists saw no danger in such a move. Had not Laurier himself formerly held the seat, even though once defeated there? and was not his summer home still there? The Nationalists, however, were deterred by no such considerations. Sensing their opportunity, they descended upon the constituency in droves, nominating a farmer, Arthur Gilbert, against the Liberal candidate, J. E. Perrault. In order to clear the way for the Nationalist, no official Conservative candidate was nominated. The eyes of all Canada were soon on Drummond-Arthabaska, as the battle raged up and down the countryside. November 3, 1910, was polling-day. The Nationalist candidate was elected by a majority of 207. The Liberals were aghast. Were the foundations of Laurier's hold on Quebec at last beginning to crumble? To the farseeing, the result in Drummond-Arthabaska was a portent of things to come.

At the Imperial Conference of 1907 it had been agreed that periodic conferences should be held, the next one in 1911. Sir Wilfrid again attended. This conference marked the last stand of the advocates of parliamentary federation for the Empire, whose spokesman, Sir Joseph Ward, of New Zealand, proposed the creation of an imperial parliament to have jurisdiction chiefly over foreign policy and defence.

Whether some proposal less sweeping might have found favour

will never be known; but none of the representatives of the principal Dominions would have anything to do with Sir Joseph's scheme. Laurier, for Canada; Fisher, for Australia; Botha (attending his first Conference), for South Africa; Morris, for Newfoundland, all opposed the proposal, which was given its quietus when Asquith, speaking for the United Kingdom, declared that:

We cannot, with the traditions and history of the British Empire behind us, either from the point of view of the United Kingdom, or from the point of view of our self-governing Dominions, assent for a moment to proposals which are so fatal to the very fundamental conditions on which our Empire has been built and carried on . . . .

Imperial Federation was not yet dead, but it had received its death-thrust. To many it had great appeal. Had not the union of the United States, the Canadian provinces, and the South African and Australian states been a great success? Why should not a federation of the various parts of the British Empire be equally successful? The proponents of the idea envisaged a central army and navy to which all should contribute, and many predicated an overall economic policy which should consist of free, or preferential, trade between Empire members, and exclusive tariffs against the products of countries without the pale. To those who thought thus it was an entrancing picture and they were impatient with any who could not see it as they did.

Unfortunately for this scheme, however, the analogy between the Empire and any of the federations considered as examples was not a good one. The Empire consisted of the United Kingdom with its monarchy, its aristocracy, its traditions, and its habit of domination. Its interests were scattered all over the world. Next, were a group of relatively sparsely-settled Dominions of great potentiality, who had already gone far toward managing their own affairs. Then there were Crown colonies and dependencies of all sizes and degrees of independence and servility. How could all of these fit into such a scheme?

The responsible ministers of the self-governing Dominions were bound to consider what would be the situation if some time in the future the Empire should become embroiled in a conflict in which the United Kingdom believed its interests justified going to war, but in which the Dominions had little or no interest. And, conversely, as the Dominions increased in population and influence, they might easily embroil the Empire in conflicts contrary to the United Kingdom's best interests.

10

To begin thinking of possibilities such as these was to add argument to argument against Imperial Federation. It was all very well to appeal to idealism and a spirit of give and take, but the world was not operated on any such basis, and the British Empire would have to change in many important respects before its affairs could be so regulated. So, with Imperial Federation no longer an issue, the Dominions proceeded along the road toward greater freedom. And, as had been prophesied, the bonds arising out of their common interests and aspirations strengthened with the years. The friction and irritation unavoidable under a system of remote control lessened and largely disappeared as these controls were removed.

There were still some who dreamt of a far-flung Empire, and they would be heard from again.

CHAPTER XV

REAPING THE WHIRLWIND

THE fortunes of the Laurier government had reached their peak in 1904, when 139 seats in a House of 214 were carried. The complacency that comes with length of office and the slowing down caused by the inevitable incrustation of patronage barnacles had not yet begun to show. A few changes, some for the better, had occurred in the great cabinet of 1896. Sir Oliver Mowat had gone to Government House in Toronto; and Mr. Tarte, whose irresponsible ways had become a liability, had been asked to resign in 1902.

By 1908, although outwardly as strong, signs of decline were becoming visible. Some of the veterans had been superseded by younger and more vigorous men. In 1905, on the ground of ill-health (he died in 1944 at the age of 100!), Sir William Mulock had gone to the Ontario Supreme Court, and Rodolphe Lemieux, brilliant and capable, had succeeded him as Postmaster-General, after an interval by A. B. Aylesworth, who had become Minister of Justice. Sifton, although out of the cabinet, was still a member of the party; in fact, he managed the 1908 campaign in the West.

Superficially the results of the 1908 election were very favourable to a government in power for a dozen years. The Liberals carried 134 seats out of a total of 221; Ontario and Quebec combined showed a difference of only one seat as compared with 1904. In the Maritimes, the loss of six seats in Nova Scotia had been offset by gains in the other two provinces. Manitoba and British Columbia, both with vigorous Conservative governments, reflected provincial influences, while Saskatchewan and Alberta, for similar reasons, remained strongly Liberal. Perhaps significantly, since one of the chief campaign issues in the West had been the record of the Sifton administration, the single Yukon seat had gone to the Conservatives.

While part of the change in Manitoba could be attributed to the efforts of provincial Conservatives, another reason was undoubtedly to be found in revulsion against the Sifton machine, which for years had controlled everything political in the country. During his term as Minister of the Interior, Clifford Sifton had built up throughout the prairies an organization extremely loyal to him. He, in turn, 'looked after' those who served him; while for those who failed him his vindictiveness knew no bounds. He dispensed all political favours; in many constituencies, Liberal nominating conventions were but perfunctory affairs: Sifton's nominee became the candidate, and the machine usually elected him.

Nevertheless, the result in Manitoba was mainly due to causes far deeper than a revolt against Siftonism, as it was called. For many years the prairie farmers had complained against the disabilities under which they laboured. Theirs was almost entirely a wheat economy, governed by a few simple factors. First of these was the price they received for their product, set by world conditions over which they had no control. The next was the cost of transportation and handling in transit to market. This might be controlled to a certain extent, and they had done what they could to reduce both. In an effort to this end, some of them had organized co-operative selling agencies, and they continued to put pressure on the government to have transportation costs reduced. One project which they believed would reduce transportation costs for a large section of the prairies was a railway to Hudson Bay. In 1904, Sir Wilfrid Laurier himself had promised them such a railway, but little had yet come of it.

Another important factor in the economy of the grain growers was the cost of everything they had to buy, farm machinery, building materials, binder twine, clothing, and in fact, nearly everything they required. Almost to a man, they were persuaded of the injustice of a protective tariff which taxed them in order, as they believed, to put money into the pockets of eastern manufacturers.

Except for those whose political sympathies or prejudices outweighed their economic interest, prairie farmers had generally supported the Liberal party, the ostensible champions of low tariffs. But, despite frequent promises, Mr. Fielding's budgets had consistently maintained the protective principle; some had begun to grumble, and then a revolt had set in. This was reflected in the 1908 election results.

In the spring of 1910, about 800 western farmers 'marched' on Ottawa, demanding relief from these injustices. They were met, as usual, with promises and excuses, which only served to increase their dissatisfaction. There was much talk of a western political party, although for this they were not yet quite ready, but they increased their efforts in the direction of co-operative marketing.

Thus, when early in 1910 President Taft intimated to the Canadian government that his administration was prepared to consider a Reciprocity agreement such as Canadians had longed for since 1866, the Laurier government gleefully fell in with the idea. Negotiations began at Ottawa in October of that year and wound up in Washington the following January. Mr. Fielding and Mr. Paterson, the Minister of Customs, carried on the discussions on behalf of Canada. In its broad outlines, the agreement they reached provided for the entry into the United States free, or at low customs rates, of all the main natural products of Canada, as well as a number of manufactured articles which would be admitted at greatly reduced duties. In return, Canada was to allow American products in the same categories to enter the country at the rates of duty already applicable to the United Kingdom and other favoured-nation countries.

President Taft lost no time in pressing the measure through Congress, and by the end of July 1911, both the House and the Senate, not without some stiff opposition from those who believed their interests might be adversely affected, had confirmed the agreement and the President had signed it. The Liberals were jubilant: they had secured, almost without effort, an answer to their free-trade critics which did not require them to jeopardize their position with the manufacturers.

Mr. Fielding laid the agreement before parliament on January 26, 1911. The immediate response of parliament and country was one of satisfaction, except, of course, for the disgruntlement of Conservatives who felt they had been out-generalled.

The atmosphere that confronted me in caucus was not invigorating [Borden wrote in his *Memoirs*]; there was the deepest dejection in our party, and many of our members were confident that the Government's proposals would appeal to the country and give it another term of office. Foster was greatly impressed by the proposals and said that when they were presented his heart had gone down in his boots. The Western members were emphatic in their statements that not one of them would be elected in opposition to Reciprocity.

In Vancouver, for example, so slim did their chances seem that none of the leading Conservatives could be induced to run, which provided an opportunity for Harry H. Stevens, relatively unknown at the time.

Then, gradually, opposition developed. In some way, the railways came to the conclusion that free trade in natural products with the United States would interfere with their long-haul, east and west.

It must be remembered that Canada was still a long, narrow strip along the northern border of the United States. Very few yet knew anything of that great northern region whose minerals, timber, water-power, and other resources were soon to give Canada breadth as well as length.

Behind the ranks of the railways, stiffened the opposition of financial institutions with which they were associated. Manufacturers, not adversely affected by the agreement, were nevertheless persuaded that this was but a beginning, and that next time their turn would come, and they took up the cry.

In the past, the United States had been an ungracious neighbour, often contemptuous of the feelings or interests of the, to them, un-important people north of their border. The view most general in the United States concerning Canada was that, soon or late, it would be annexed. In fact, even before the Canadian parliament had a chance to consider the agreement, American public men and others gave evidence of this. Champ Clark, Speaker of the House of Repre-sentatives, declared that: 'We are preparing to annex Canada. . . . I am for the Bill because I hope to see the day when the American flag will float over every foot of the British North American possessions clear to the Pole.' Even the President incautiously referred to Canada's being at the 'parting of the ways'.

The Canadian Pacific Railway, on the political sidelines for some years, was now back in politics with everything it had. William C. Van Horne came out of retirement and, in characteristic fashion, declared he was 'out to bust the damned thing'. Doubtless Van Horne and his associates had persuaded themselves that the agreement would hurt their interests, but the action of the government in creating competitors to the Canadian Pacific had long rankled in their bosoms. And as late as May of that year the government had, unnecessarily, so it seemed to them, guaranteed the cost of the Canadian Northern's line from Port Arthur to Montreal, the final link in its transcontinental system.

What of Mackenzie and Mann and their Canadian Northern Railway? They, too, were lined up with the opponents of the agree-ment. This, however, was to have been expected, for already it was evident that more than an understanding existed between them and the Conservative Party. Originally, the fortunes of the Canadian Pacific and the Conservatives had been very closely linked; but after the Conservatives had gone out of office the Canadian Pacific's ardour cooled somewhat. Laurier's action in joining with the Grand Trunk might have thrown the C.P.R. back into the Conservatives' lap, but Mackenzie and Mann were already there, which, however, did nothing to improve the C.P.R.'s feelings toward the Liberals.

Even with these forces against it, the agreement might not have been defeated. The decisive factor was undoubtedly the defection of Clifford Sifton. It is probable that he was not greatly concerned, personally, one way or the other; but in the pull of forces it suited him best to oppose the measure. In the first place, although he had continued to support the Liberals, loss of his place in the cabinet still rankled.

A man of intense prejudices, the fires of his North Ireland forebears burned strongly within him, and he had a deep distrust of Catholics and their ways. This had thrown him without reservation into the fight over the Manitoba School question, in which he and Laurier had been unexpected political bedfellows. Despite his instinctive aversion to Catholics, he could work with Laurier as long as nothing occurred to stir his antipathies. Because Laurier was not afraid to challenge the bishops, Sifton was beguiled into thinking that perhaps he was different from other papists. But after, as he believed, Laurier had attempted, at the behest of the hierarchy, to impose separate schools upon the new prairie provinces, his confidence in Laurier was never quite the same.

Furthermore, in the interval, Sifton's business ramifications had become extensive, and his new associates were practically all among those who now opposed Reciprocity. But he had another compelling reason. As a student of government, he was well aware of the fundamental defect in the American congressional machinery which renders manipulation by pressure groups almost inevitable. He believed that any agreement made with the United States would be constantly at the mercy of strongly intrenched interests opposed to it. And, in addition to this, arising out of his experiences in connection with the Alaska Boundary Tribunal, he had no faith in American fairplay with respect to international affairs.

Although Sifton's power of logical analysis was keen, the pull of self-interest was always strong, but even stronger was the pull of his prejudices. In this case, all his compulsions tended in the one direction; and so, without hesitation, he threw himself into the campaign against Reciprocity.

The Canadian Pacific–Bank of Montreal group could be counted on to look after Montreal; but there was no equivalent group to head up the campaign in Toronto, where many of the leading financiers, although not politically active, were Liberals. With the assistance of Zebulon Lash, chief solicitor for the Mackenzie and Mann interests, Sifton organized the 'Revolt of the Eighteen', a group of Liberals prominent in Toronto financial circles.

But it was in the back concessions of Ontario that Sifton's campaign created most havoc. The Orange Lodges were still a potent political force, and it was never hard to start a crusade against popery among them, and Sifton knew how to get one going. Popery, of course, had nothing to do with Reciprocity, but Laurier had, and he was a Catholic, like Lavergne and others who would shoot holes in the Union Jack.

So much for Ontario; what about Quebec? The burning issue in that province was still the Laurier naval policy. Bourassa, who saw in the defeat of Laurier, whom he had come to hate, an opportunity to gain the leadership of Quebec, outdid himself in violence and passion. It is true he had always been opposed to any form of co-operation with Great Britain which might lead to Canada's involvement in British wars; and in 1911 no gift of prophesy was needed to envisage a day when Quebec youths might be dragged off against their will to fight in wars for England resulting from the failure of a foreign policy over which they had no control. Yet he must have known that the Conservatives, with whom he was now in league, were even less likely than Laurier to prevent this. He must have known that the course he followed was the one most likely to wreck the unity of Canada for which Laurier had worked all his life and for which, if he believed what he professed, he also should have been working.

On May 18, while the discussion raged outside, the House was adjourned for two months to allow the Prime Minister and other members of the government to attend the Imperial Conference. Meanwhile Mr. Borden toured the West, attacking the Reciprocity agreement without much apparent success. Parliament met again on July 18, but after ten days of obstruction by the opposition Laurier decided on an appeal to the people, and the House was dissolved.

Mr. Borden, in March, had weathered one of the periodical revolts against his leadership engineered by those who would have preferred the picturesqueness of British Columbia's Richard McBride or the implacability of Manitoba's R. P. Roblin. Undoubtedly he was as much surprised as anyone else at the fury of the campaign which soon developed. With Sifton, on the one hand, and Bourassa, on the other, he never quite caught up with the parade. Taking his cue from events as they occurred, he made a series of speeches at key points, leaving Quebec largely to his allies.

The newspapers in English-speaking Canada, with a few notable exceptions, swayed by the money which opponents of Reciprocity threw around, took up the cry: 'No Truck or Trade with the Yankees!' The agreement was represented as an attempt on the part of the Liberals to hand Canada over to the United States. Ratification would mean the end of British connection. Soon, like a prairie fire, the flames of unreason swept the country. (The *Manitoba Free Press*, although owned by Clifford Sifton, supported Reciprocity. Sifton's understanding with its editor, John W. Dafoe, was that the latter should control its editorial policy, and Dafoe had long been an ardent champion of Reciprocity.)

It seems in retrospect that the result should have been a foregone conclusion; and, of course, both sides made last-minute predictions of success; but, with few exceptions, when the votes were counted on the night of September 21, 1911, the result was as great a surprise to the winners as to the losers. The Laurier government had been defeated. The standing in the House was exactly reversed. The Conservatives and Nationalists had 133 seats to the Liberals' 88. Seven cabinet ministers, including Messrs. Fielding and Paterson, were defeated. In Quebec, the Liberal majority had fallen lower than in any election since Confederation—from 43 to 11; but it was Ontario that gave the allies the victory; out of 86 seats, the Liberals held only 14.

The new cabinet, when chosen, was representative of the factions that had joined to win the election. Mr. Borden received many suggestions concerning its composition. Van Horne wrote advising him to make his own decisions. He said that unfortunately George E. Foster had become 'besmirched' and suggested that E. B. Osler, though indolent, would be a good choice for Finance Minister. It was more than a coincidence that Osler was a C.P.R. director.

This, however, was not the C.P.R.'s day. For Finance Minister Borden chose W. T. White, of Toronto, one of the Eighteen, who represented financial interests associated with Mackenzie and Mann; another close to Mackenzie and Mann was Arthur Meighen, member for Portage la Prairie, who became Solicitor-General. It had been expected in some quarters that R. B. Bennett, of Calgary, who had helped set the prairie on fire during the campaign, might have a place in the cabinet, but his Canadian Pacific connection was not the sort of endorsement that counted at the moment.

Quebec Conservatives and Nationalists were represented by F. D. Monk, Louis Pelletier, Bruno Nantel, P. E. Blondin, who was selected as Deputy Speaker, and C. J. Doherty, who became Minister of Justice.

Old-guard Conservatives were represented by Robert Rogers, of Winnipeg, who secured the Public Works post, Col. Sam Hughes, who became Minister of Militia, George E. Foster, who because of the besmirching was forced to be content with the post of Minister of Trade and Commerce, and Dr. J. D. Reid, despite his being one of the ringleaders in the revolt against his leader in the spring, who became Minister of Customs.

The Naval Service Act of 1910 was now a dead letter. The new government took no steps to repeal it; neither was any effort made to put it into effect. Not till after Mr. Borden and three of his ministers had returned from a trip to England was parliament asked to vote $35,000,000 to pay the cost of three battleships to be presented to the imperial navy.

The opposition, though relatively few, contained a large percentage of experienced parliamentarians and debaters, and they decided to obstruct the new navy bill. The debate ranged afar, and every stratagem was employed to impede the bill's progress. Mr. Borden unwisely invited comment from Winston Churchill, then head of the Admiralty, whose letters only served to fan the opposition flame.

Finally, Conservative members declined to speak in their turn, leaving the Liberals to carry on the debate, if such it could be called, by themselves. On April 9, 1913, closure was applied, and the bill passed. The Senate, however, still—and for some time to come—filled with Liberals, killed it.

In the winter of 1912-13, the Prime Minister had been approached by Vilhjalmur Stefansson, recently returned from four years in arctic Canada and Alaska, where he had explored new territory and studied the ways of Eskimos, some of whom had not previously been visited by a white man. Stefansson, born in the Icelandic settlement on the shore of Lake Winnipeg, but brought up and educated in the United States, hoped to secure the backing of the Canadian government as part-sponsor of a more ambitious expedition. The American Museum of Natural History and the National Geographic Society had already pledged support.

After due consideration, Mr. Borden had informed Stefansson that since the proposed expedition would conduct its activities in

Canadian territory, if the American societies were willing, the government would assume the full cost of the expedition. The American societies, of course, were willing.

Stefansson's plans called for an expedition in two sections, one, which he would direct himself, to carry on exploratory work in the Arctic Ocean west of the Arctic Archipelago. In addition to the possible discovery of new lands, he hoped to prove that explorers could 'live off the country', independent of food from outside, while travelling on the sea ice as well as they could on land (which he had demonstrated on his recent expedition).

The Geological Survey of Canada saw an opportunity to undertake valuable investigations along the north coast, and a number of scientists were assigned from the Survey staff to constitute the second section.

The expedition sailed from Esquimalt, B.C., in June 1913, proceeding to the Arctic Ocean by way of Bering Strait. Shortly after rounding Point Barrow, the ship *Karluk*, heavily loaded with supplies and equipment, got caught in the ice pack, drifted a thousand miles to the west, and was crushed and sunk.

Despite this, Stefansson, with two companions and one dog-team, carried out an epoch-making trip during which he proved that properly trained explorers could indeed find food while travelling over the sea ice. During subsequent years (the expedition lasted five), new islands were discovered and claimed for Canada, and much valuable information was secured.

Stefansson's explorations were but the forerunner of a campaign to roll back the frontier and provide Canada with much-needed breadth. Aiding in this were agricultural scientists of the Dominion Experimental Farm at Ottawa, crossing strains to find grains which might safely be planted farther north than those in use.

Beginning as early as 1888, William Saunders, Director of the Experimental Farm, had conducted experiments toward providing a wheat which, while retaining high-grade bread-making qualities, should require a shorter growing season. When he retired, he passed the quest on to his sons, especially Charles E. Saunders.

The principal wheat grown on the prairies at the turn of the century was Red Fife, ideal in many ways. Endless experiments were conducted by Charles Saunders to find a wheat with Red Fife's bread-making qualities, but requiring a shorter growing season. In 1904 he found a strain which he called Marquis that seemed to possess all the requirements. A cross between Red Fife and an early-ripening wheat called Red Calcutta, its bread was superior to that of Red Fife, and it was early-maturing.

Several years were required before enough seed was accumulated to enable all tests to be made, but Marquis met the tests. Eventually, it superseded all others on the Canadian prairies and spread into the spring wheat regions of the United States. But, what was of greater importance, it pushed northward the wheat-producing area of the Canadian West. This one discovery has enriched the Canadian economy by many hundreds of millions of dollars. Following the discovery of Marquis, which, on the average, ripens about one week earlier than Red Fife, Charles Saunders, by further crossing, produced Ruby and Prelude wheats, maturing one and a half and two weeks earlier, respectively, than Marquis. Since then, Saunders' successors have produced other strains to meet varying conditions of growth on the prairies, and the end is not yet.

Meantime, the country had been plunging deeper and deeper into a depression. The great splurge of railway-building, which for a decade had provided employment for the hordes of immigrants, had largely stopped. The cities were filled with unemployed for whom no provision was made, and among whom there was much suffering. Wage-cutting was general. Commodity prices fell below the cost of production. Then it became apparent how great was the folly of refusing the Reciprocity offer. The government had no plan to suggest by which the country might be lifted out of the mire into which it was quickly sinking.

In the midst of all this, Mackenzie and Mann were on the government's doorstep; and they were not alone. With them were the bankers who had advanced them money; the contractors who were demanding payment; supply houses, themselves on the verge of bankruptcy; and, in the background, a motley array of camp-followers who, in one way or another, had an interest in the proceedings.

The government had already advanced money for the completion of the British Columbia section on which the McBride government had previously guaranteed the bonds ('The government will never be called upon to pay one cent of interest or capital'); and, in 1913, it had voted $15,640,000, said to be needed to complete the road. Now, in the spring of 1914, came the demand for a loan of $45,000,000, positively a last appeal!

Even with friends inside the cabinet, the chances of getting such a sum after all the money that had been poured into the Mackenzie and Mann hopper seemed remote. Yet the government could not very well allow the road to go into bankruptcy, since this would undoubtedly have grave repercussions upon the credit of Canada and further accelerate the depression. The Liberals were not in a position to criticize. Mackenzie and Mann had friends in their ranks also; they had friends in every part of the House.

Nothing like the lobby that now moved in had ever been experienced in Ottawa. The Canadian Northern Railway was largely the product of such lobbying of everything from town councils up. The pick of its expert lobbyists now converged on Ottawa, and the campaign they waged marked the culmination of a decade of high-pressure tactics which had not only resulted in a transcontinental railway, but had enabled the promoters to extend their interests into many other aspects of the national economy.

There were some in the House, however, who were not amenable to the lobbyists' lures. One of these was W. F. Nickle, Conservative member for Kingston, who mercilessly dissected the operations of Mackenzie and Mann and their railway, exposing their methods and calling upon the government to take over the enterprise.

But it was R. B. Bennett who spread upon the pages of *Hansard* the record, with all its ramifications, of the Canadian Northern and the 'shameless mendicancy' of Mackenzie and Mann. The House sat most of the time in awed silence as Bennett, a westerner with many years of experience as a railway solicitor, followed the devious trail of these two men and their associates. Nothing like it had ever occurred in the history of parliament.

That no love was lost between Bennett and Meighen was evident when Meighen more than once tried to interrupt. Momentarily checking the torrent of his invective to object to the 'impertinent interruptions of this young man', whom he called the 'gramaphone of Mackenzie and Mann', he continued his devastating indictment.

Bennett and Nickle left little more to be said, but the government was not yet prepared to take over the railway, nor to let it go into bankruptcy. The Prime Minister cracked the whip, or rather Meighen cracked it for him, and the House of Commons voted to make the 'loan'. This time, the Senate, though still largely Liberal, did not throw out the bill!

Meanwhile an event had occurred in southern Alberta which was to be the forerunner of developments, many years later, which would greatly affect the Canadian economy. In October 1913, a small flow of oil was struck in the Dingman well, in what was later known as Turner Valley, southwest of Calgary.

In the following May, a heavier flow was struck, and Calgary soon was in the throes of a first-rate oil boom. Oil companies were organized overnight. Brokerage offices were bombarded by people eager to rid themselves of their money. Rich and poor queued up in front of offices where oil shares were being sold, and mounted policemen were needed to keep them in line.

Clerks worked at top speed, writing receipts for money literally thrown at them, until, in some offices, wire waste-paper baskets, filled with cash and applications for shares, were piled on top of each other, almost to the ceiling. The outbreak of war ended the boom, and for the time being ended the search for oil.

CHAPTER XVI

TWO CULTURES CLASH

A S the summer of 1914 wore on, few observers in North America realized that the political rivalries of Europe, which a number of times during the previous dozen years had flared momentarily, would now end in armed conflict. In this connection, it is interesting to note the differing attitudes of Americans and Canadians as Europe, to borrow Sir Edward Grey's phrase, 'drifted into war'. Both populations consisted of European immigrants or their descendants, the United States probably having a greater percentage of those of more recent emigration.

President Woodrow Wilson immediately declared the United States neutral, and in this he was overwhelmingly supported by his people. The government of Sir Robert Borden (the title scarcely a month old), on August 1, cabled the determination of Canada 'to put forth every effort and to make every sacrifice to ensure the integrity and maintain the honour of our Empire'. This was done when parliament was not in session, and three days before the British government even knew whether or not it would intervene in the war.

Pending the meeting of parliament in special session, plans were adopted for the immediate raising of an army division of 22,500 men, and steps were taken to guard the frontier, for the control of enemy aliens, and for other precautions. Parliament, meeting on August 18 for a four-day session, ratified what had already been done, voted new taxes, and an appropriation of $50,000,000, a large sum in those days, yet only slightly larger than that voted to assist Mackenzie and Mann's railway.

Sir Wilfrid Laurier, in pledging his party's support, undoubtedly put into words the feeling throughout Canada.

I hasten to say [he declared] that to all these measures we are prepared to give immediate assent. . . . It is our duty . . . to let Great Britain know that all Canadians stand behind the mother country, conscious and proud that she has engaged in this war, not from any selfish motive, for any purpose of aggrandizement, but to maintain untarnished the honour of her name, to fulfil her obligations, and to save civilization from the unbridled lust of conquest and power. . . .

England is not engaged in an ordinary contest. . . . the allied nations are fighting for freedom against oppression, for democracy against autocracy, for civilization against reversion to that state of barbarism in which the supreme law is the law of might . . .

In the light of post-war disclosures, no serious student of history believes that World War I was fought for any such reasons, but Laurier unquestionably spoke that day for the majority of Canadians.

Sir George Foster (he had also been recently knighted) summed up the feeling in the House and country when he said: 'The last four days of this session have vindicated public life and parliamentary life for all time to come. They have shown that it is possible for us to forget all mean and petty things when our country and its liberties are at stake.' He, too, spoke under unusual emotional stress, but before very long, the 'mean and petty things' were to come sneaking out of their lairs.

Fifteen years later, while discussing the cynical diplomacy which preceded the war, and the 'petty rivalry of politicians, the unholy greed of territorial acquisitions, the crass incompetence of many military leaders', Sir George remarked on how 'this after-study and research into the preceding diplomacy and subsequent conduct of the war dispels our wartime illusions and lays bare the trickery and falsehood played upon our most sacred feelings of patriotism and willingness to sacrifice life and fortune for the fair cause of justice and liberty!' [1]

The political truce was fairly well maintained in the early part of the war, but the temptation to take advantage of situations as they arose proved too great for some. Colonel Sam Hughes, soon to become a major-general, a fanatical Orangeman, always a strong partisan, was determined that, so far as he could make it, the war should be an adjunct of the Conservative party. He, like most others at the beginning, believed the war would be a short one, and did not wish to share the glory of winning it with anyone else, especially the *Canadiens*, in his estimation, traitors, every one of them.

He gathered about him, as advisers and confidants, a group of congenial friends, among whom he distributed honorary military titles, and to whom he farmed out contracts of increasing value and importance. Typical of these friends was one 'Colonel' John Wesley Allison, to whom objection was taken by critics on both sides of politics, and on both sides of the Atlantic. After a number of fruitless efforts to persuade Hughes to get rid of his friends and modify his

[1] *Queen's Quarterly*, Summer, 1929, pp. 272-3.

egotistical behaviour, Sir Robert, in 1916, demanded his resignation. Naturally, during all this time, the Liberals had not been quiet, but until Hughes' vagaries had become such as to offend Sir Robert himself, they had not been able to get the government to take action against him.

Another member of the cabinet who was not above playing politics was Robert Rogers. The war had scarcely begun before he was urging his colleagues to ensure themselves a five-year lease of office by calling a snap election on the pretext that a mandate was necessary in order to carry on the war, and with some success. On September 2, 1914, Borden cabled Sir George Perley, in London: 'Please decipher this yourself. We are considering elections about first week November. Will wire further particulars within few days,' and again on September 27: 'All colleagues favour an election about end of November. McBride opposed.'

Until well into the following year, Borden actively canvassed opinion on the subject of an election. Some of those consulted were in favour and some were against. Lord Shaughnessey, at first, was for an election, but Sir Joseph Flavelle was decidedly against one. The Duke of Connaught, then governor-general, was very much opposed. On April 18, 1915, Borden cabled Perley: 'Not finally considered elections. Practically all members and ministers favour it immediately . . . elections probable about 7th or 14th June.'

Eventually, however, the end of the statutory term of parliament drew near, when an election must be held, unless, as had been done in England, an extension was agreed upon. To do this an amendment to the British North America Act would be required, which the British parliament would have to pass. It was not likely, however, that the British parliament would legislate without a reasonably unanimous request from the Canadian parliament. When the matter was broached to him by the Prime Minister, Sir Wilfrid, after a caucus of his followers, agreed to one year's extension, on the understanding that no contentious legislation should be introduced and that there should be no snap dissolution until that period had elapsed.

The controversy over the Ross rifle, mismanagement in the buying of shells for the British government, and the unchecked rapacity of profiteers, as well as repeated requests for handouts from Mackenzie and Mann, had conspired to lower the public estimation of the government. In ordinary circumstances, its chances in an election would have been more than questionable, but the alternative was to put Laurier in power, and this, English-speaking Canada, at least

11

a growing section of it, was unwilling to entertain. Was he not a French-Canadian? And were not French-Canadians letting down the war effort? Undoubtedly, Quebec was far behind some other parts of Canada in recruiting.

The reasons for Quebec's lack of enthusiasm for the war are given with fairness and restraint by Sir Robert Borden in his *Memoirs*, written years after the event, and help to explain a situation which to many English-speaking Canadians at the time seemed little less than treasonable.

The comparative failure of recruiting in Quebec was due, like most human events, to a variety of causes [wrote Sir Robert], and it would be difficult, in fact impossible, to assign to each cause its proportionate influence.

The Canadian of French descent is essentially a most desirable and useful citizen. He is devout, industrious, hardworking and frugal, thoroughly devoted to his people and his province and deeply attached to his family, his friends and his neighbours. To leave them for military service beyond the seas, to cross the ocean in unknown adventure made no appeal and seemed undesirable and indeed desperate. Naturally his vision was not very wide and sometimes it did not extend beyond the boundaries of his parish. He had an unbounded belief in the invincible power of Great Britain and regarded the co-operation of Canada as useless and futile as well as burdensome. It was no lack of courage that held back these people from enlistment. Those who went overseas proved themselves worthy of their descent from a fighting and heroic race.

One might suppose that the savagery of German warfare against the French people would have roused her kindred in Quebec, but the clergy had been alienated from their natural sympathy by confiscation of religious houses and property and by the growth of atheistic outlook and tendency in France. The Quebec peasant was sometimes told that the sufferings of the French people were just retribution for the unholy spoliation and humiliation of the Church in France.

Then, General Hughes' maladroit methods reached their highest point in his arrangements for recruiting among French-Canadians. He placed an English Protestant in charge of recruiting propaganda, and from time to time emphasized the foolishness of his action by more mischievous activities. He imagined that he was extremely popular in the Province of Quebec, but this was only one of many delusions from which I found him suffering on various occasions. The details of his activities in Quebec escaped me at the time and it can easily be understood that they were brought to my attention only after their unfortunate results had been made manifest.

Sir Robert might have added that the *Canadien* was a North American, like the people of the United States, and had a North American attitude toward events in Europe. There were some people in Canada who considered this attitude of Americans a reprehensible one, but not so many as those who considered the *Canadiens'* attitude even more reprehensible.

There was another reason. The government was unfortunate in its representation from Quebec. Messrs Patenaude, Pelletier, Nantel, Blondin and Sevigny had all been heaping fuel on anti-British fires kindled by Henri Bourassa in their attempt to defeat Laurier. They were therefore at a disadvantage in trying to persuade *Canadiens* to offer themselves to be shot at in support of what they had been assured was purely a British war.

Young people in Quebec marry early and tend to have large families, and men with families to support are not so likely to enlist as single men. Quebec was then still largely a rural province, with only Montreal having more than 500,000 people, and few other cities of any considerable size.

The western provinces showed the highest percentages of enlistments. There the ratio of single men to married men was higher than elsewhere in Canada, as was also the percentage of those who had recently come to Canada. The first Canadian contingent spoke largely with the accents of the British Isles, and in some units native-born Canadians were the exception. In fact, the likelihood of a man's enlisting was in inverse ratio to the length of time he or his ancestors had been in Canada.

The first Canadian troops reached France toward the end of February 1915, and had been in heavy fighting during the season at Ypres, St. Julien, Festubert, Givenchy and Neuve Chapelle. On September 14, a Canadian Corps of two divisions was organized under Lieut.-General E. H. Alderson.

In Canada, the number of recruits received up to the end of 1915 was reported as 212,690. But in a New Year's message the Prime Minister announced that Canada's contribution in men would be increased to half a million (authorized by order-in-council, January 12, 1916). All over the country factories working overtime were sending out an increasing stream of munitions and supplies, and the prairies harvested the greatest crop in their history, setting a record for volume which stood for thirteen years.

In 1916, Canadian troops were engaged at St. Eloi and Sanctuary Wood; and the Canadian Corps was increased to three divisions under command of Sir Julian Byng. At home, toward the end of that year, the needs of industry and the needs of the army began to clash. Over 400,000 men had joined the armed forces, while the factories were making ever-increasing demands on manpower. Although the recruiting agents had not taken so many from the farms as from urban occupations, farmers were already alarmed at the scarcity of help.

Since the beginning of the war, many people had been demanding conscription; and after it was adopted in Great Britain on January 24, 1916, their number increased and they became more clamorous in their demands. Canadians were assured, however, by the leaders of both political parties that conscription would not be imposed.

In order to discover exactly what its manpower resources were, the government, in September, established the National Service Board, of which R. B. Bennett shortly became the director. To allay fear of conscription and encourage registration under the scheme, Bennett more than once gave assurance that it was not the forerunner of conscription; and in this he was supported by the Prime Minister, who accompanied him on a tour of the country.

Since most of the available ablebodied men without obligations were already in the army, Bennett's strenuous efforts had but slight effect upon recruiting. There was the inevitable 'slacker', of course, but by this time all such persons had become immune to any influence short of physical compulsion.

Parliament reassembled on January 18, 1917, and in reporting on the manpower situation, Sir Robert Borden said:

The enlistments in the Canadian Expeditionary forces number . . . 392,647. Besides that, we have called out of the active militia 9,052 men who are now serving under arms, and we have a permanent force in Canada numbering 2,470 men, making a total of 404,169. In addition to that, we have enlisted from the citizens of Canada in the Canadian naval service 3,310 men, making a total of 407,479. We have done more than that; we have provided for the British naval service 1,600 men; we have provided for the Imperial mechanical transport 1,200 men and for munition work in Great Britain at least 3,000 men. . . . If you add these three items together you have 5,800, which, added to the previous total makes 413,279.

He said, further, that there also had gone forward from Canada, Russian and Italian reservists; and thus 'out of the manhood of Canada, not less than 434,529 have joined the Canadian colours or the colours of the Allied Nations'. Casualties to date, he said, were 70,263, including 10,854 killed in action.

On February 7, the Prime Minister moved that the House adjourn until April 19 to allow him to attend the meeting of the 'Imperial War Cabinet', of which with other Dominions ministers he had been invited to become a member. And it was while he was in England that, on April 2, 1917, the United States declared war on Germany. This, of course, changed the whole picture and made positive the success of the Allies. With the resources of the United States now to be drawn upon, the eventual supply of manpower was no longer a problem.

Nevertheless, something happened during the three months that Borden was in England to convince him that Canada must have conscription. There is no evidence that he had reached that conviction before leaving Canada. Yet within four days of his return he announced to parliament that conscription would be imposed.

During his absence—between March 7 and March 12—he had visited the front, where he had interviews with Generals Currie and Haig, and also inspected a sector recently captured by Canadians from the Germans. In his account of those few days, Sir Robert does not intimate that anything occurred which might lead to so momentous a decision. In his announcement to parliament, he said that immediate reinforcements were available for four divisions, but that they could not be maintained 'without thorough provision for future requirements'.

His speech was pervaded by extreme pessimism: 'I return to Canada impressed at once with the extreme gravity of the situation, and with a sense of responsibility for our further efforts at the *most critical period of the war* . . . if this war should end in defeat, Canada, in all the years to come, would be under the shadow of German military domination. . . .' This, in the circumstances, was an understandable exaggeration of a threat which, if correctly described, could not, however, have been averted by a handful of Canadian conscripts.

He then went on to declare that

the time has come when the authority of the state should be invoked to provide reinforcements necessary to maintain the gallant men at the front . . . I bring back to the people of Canada from these men a message that they need our help, that they need to be sustained, that reinforcements must be sent to them. . . . I have promised that this help shall be given. . . .

He did not say who it was that had given him the message, nor did he say to whom he had given his promise. With experience in another world war as a guide, it is now possible to understand how conditions at the front tend to dominate the thinking of all concerned. While civilian ministers presumably have the final word, they are guided by officers who tend to consider everything from a military standpoint. This inevitably results in plans calling for the largest possible military organization.

The larger the army, the greater the number of top-rank positions with equivalent pay and pensions. Consequently, when one division is completely organized, plans for a second, and then a third, and so on, are made, until either the war ends or the supply of manpower becomes exhausted. In both world wars, Canada's commitments were greater than they should have been, taking everything into consideration. And since most military men favour conscription, they are not inclined to consider military commitments as being beyond the country's capacity so long as conscription has not been enforced. Instead of allowing a safe margin for contingencies, they count on the supply of unconscripted men as a sufficient reserve.

This, toward the end, when manpower has become scarce, is a very risky thing to do, for if an unexpected increase in casualties occurs, they are bound to be caught short. This was undoubtedly the situation when Borden visited the front in 1917. Four divisions were in the field, but many units were reduced to skeleton strength, and sufficient replacements simply did not exist. Yet ambitious officers had planned a fifth division. This was not proceeded with, but even to maintain four divisions, Borden was faced with either insisting that existing units be consolidated, which would have been resisted all along the line, or promising to find replacements enough to enable the various units to continue as originally organized. There seemed no way to find the needed recruits but by conscription.

The Canadian forces had done well and their achievement was a matter of pride to Canadians. It was a natural desire to see them maintained in undiminished strength. A variety of reasons had led men to enlist, but whatever those reasons may have been, most men in uniform were in favour of compelling all others eligible to do likewise; their relatives were even more insistent. That is only natural. If, as Sir Robert intimated, failure to apply conscription might mean the difference between winning the war and losing it, there was little choice for anyone. But if that justification did not exist, and if, in order to secure these admittedly few men, he was prepared to rend the country asunder, to jeopardize the precarious national unity fostered with such care by Laurier and Macdonald, then the wisdom of imposing conscription was open to question.

On May 25, Sir Robert had an interview with Sir Wilfrid at which, after reciting the situation overseas and stressing the undesirability of a wartime election, he proposed a coalition government to enforce conscription, the new government to be composed of an equal number of Liberals and Conservatives, except for himself as Prime Minister.

Laurier replied that he was opposed to conscription, and did not desire office, but if the government should pass a conscription law he would do what he could 'to enjoin and maintain a respect for the law'. He finally promised to consult some of his colleagues, but on June 6 informed Sir Robert that he would not join a coalition government and reminded Sir Robert that he had previously told him that if his co-operation was desired he regretted that the invitation had not been made before the policy of compulsory service had been announced.

Borden then set about interviewing representative Liberals individually. One of these was Newton Wesley Rowell, Liberal leader in Ontario, who went to Ottawa at Borden's request. On July 6 Rowell refused to join a coalition government.

> I find myself compelled to conclude [he wrote] that no strong coalition government can be formed at this time [for reasons arising] out of opinions entertained in reference to the policy and administrative record of your government, and out of the views held by many of those who most strongly support conscription and the vigorous prosecution of the war, that they can render larger and more effective service to the cause by supporting these policies outside the government rather than inside. . . .

In his biography of Laurier (Vol. 2, pp. 516–17), Skelton writes:

> During these discussions Sir Wilfrid was visited by Sir Clifford Sifton. Sir Clifford was no longer in parliament, but he was still in politics, with close relations with eastern political leaders and wide-spreading business interests. They discussed the proposals. 'You are opposed to conscription,' his visitor summed it up; 'good. You are opposed to coalition; good. You are opposed to an extension of the term of parliament; no, you should agree to that.' Why? Sir Clifford would give no answer, other than the general consideration that the Liberal party would stand a better chance in an election a year later. The real reasons Sir Wilfrid could not fathom, though he believed they were connected with the desire to have an amenable parliament for the enactment of certain plans for meeting the approaching crisis in the affairs of the Canadian Northern and Grand Trunk Pacific. Once it was clear that his advice on the really vital one of the three points would not be taken, and that an election was inevitable, Sir. Clifford sought the same ends another way, seeking, it might be, a still more amenable parliament by supporting coalition and supporting conscription.

Although Sifton had a secretive and devious mind, Sir Wilfrid probably understood his way of thinking better than most of those who knew him, and since Skelton had the benefit of frequent consultations with Laurier, it is likely that the interview was as he has recorded it. Conversations with Sifton were usually very one-sided, but not in the way peculiar to many deaf people, who prefer to do most of the talking. Sifton used a speaking-tube, which he pushed toward his visitor, and then sat back and listened, making occasional short comments, but more often saying nothing.

On June 11, the Prime Minister introduced the Military Service Bill in a speech highly charged with emotion. 'My speech was well received by our men,' he wrote in his *Memoirs*. 'Sir Wilfrid said little and looked pale and wan'—and well he might! The Borden government was living on borrowed time, gained with the concurrence of the opposition and on the understanding that no contentious legislation should be introduced during that period. A few days later, on the third reading of the bill, Sir Wilfrid declared that 'we are face to face with a cleavage which, unless it is checked, may rend and tear this Canada of ours down to the very roots'. The Military Service Bill became law by a majority of 58, several of the government's Quebec supporters voting against it, but 22 Liberals supported it.

It was one thing to pass the bill, but quite another thing to enforce it. First, an election must be won; but before that a Union government must be organized to include conscriptionist Liberals, if they could be secured. The man to do this was Clifford Sifton, who had now swung in behind Borden. Although he did not neglect any opportunity in the East, his activities were directed more generally to the West, where his *Manitoba Free Press*, still under the editorial direction of J. W. Dafoe, had, for some time, been whipping up sentiment for conscription. On August 7, a large convention of Liberals was held in Winnipeg, which, while largely conscriptionist in feeling, denounced the Borden government and adopted a resolution expressing confidence in Sir Wilfrid Laurier.

This was not what Sifton had hoped for, but he did not despair. Working as usual from the sidelines, he concentrated upon a few western Liberals who could usually be counted on to follow Dafoe's lead, and who were already committed to conscription. These negotiations resulted in a code telegram from Winnipeg to Sir Robert signed by Sifton's elder brother, Arthur, Premier of Alberta, James A. Calder, Minister of Railways in the Saskatchewan government, Thomas A. Crerar, president of United Grain Growers Limited, and A. B. Hudson, a prominent Winnipeg lawyer, to the effect that they were in favour of a national government and the creation of a war council of six, but that a change of leadership was essential, suggesting either Sir George Foster or Sir Adam Beck, as Premier (although Sir Robert offered to retire, the Conservative caucus refused to consider it).

Meanwhile the ordinary (and extraordinary!) business of government must go on. In the latter category was the Military Voters Act introduced on August 13 by Mr. Doherty, providing that any British subject, male or female, who had served in any military, naval or air service, should be entitled to vote at a general election during the war or before demobilization. If, due to the nature of his service, the voter might not know the name of the particular candidate for whom he wished to vote, he could simply vote for the government, opposition, independent, or Labour candidate; and he could have his vote apply in any electoral district he indicated (or which was indicated to him).

Then, on September 6, Mr. Meighen introduced the Wartime Elections Act providing for the enfranchisement of female relatives of soldiers; the disfranchisement of all former citizens of Germany and Austria and all former citizens of other European countries whose mother tongue was German, who had become naturalized after 1902. Since large numbers of immigrants in western Canada had come from parts of Austrian and Russian empires, and were far from sympathetic toward their former rulers, it was assumed that they might be opposed to autocratic methods and less likely to support conscription. In no other country in the world which claimed to be democratic had such a measure ever (or since!) been enacted into law.

Also in the category of ordinary business of government was a further appeal from Mackenzie and Mann for assistance. By this time the government had received the report of what was called the Drayton-Acworth Royal Commission appointed in 1916 to study the railway problem. The majority report recommended the nationalization of the Canadian Northern as well as the other bankrupt railways, and this the government now proposed to do, ignoring, however, the commissioners' findings that the common stock was worthless, and proposing to buy it at a price to be determined by arbitration. The opposition, while agreeing that nationalization was unavoidable, made a strong fight against paying anything for the stock. The debate was shut off by closure on August 29.

With or without a Union government, the Wartime Elections and Military Voters Acts ensured the election for the government, but Sir Robert Borden was determined on having a Union government.

With singular persistence and amidst the countless distractions of government in wartime and other pressing matters, he continued his efforts to gain the support of a sufficient number of prominent Liberals to justify the term, and one by one, despite their previous refusals, a group of Liberals responded.

Only three of the incoming Liberals were members of the House of Commons—A. K. Maclean, of Nova Scotia, Frank B. Carvell, of New Brunswick, and Hugh Guthrie, of Ontario, none of whom had previously held office. From the provincial field came Rowell, Calder and Arthur Sifton; while Major-General S. C. Mewburn, of Hamilton, C. C. Ballantyne, a Montreal businessman, G. D. Robertson, an Ontario Labour representative, and T. A. Crerar were new to public life. The cabinet, when completed, consisted of 9 Liberals and 14 Conservatives. Albert Sevigny and Pierre Blondin were the only *Canadiens*.

The job of cabinet-making was completed on October 12, and election day was set for December 17. Then followed a campaign the like of which had never before been experienced in Canada. With ample money, with almost the entire English-language press, with high-priced speakers and writers, with newspaper advertisements, with the Protestant pulpit largely become an adjunct of the hustings, a steady barrage of abuse was rained upon Laurier and his supporters. From billboards in type 4 feet high, voters were warned that 'A Vote for Laurier is a Vote for the Kaiser!' and they were asked: 'How Would the Kaiser Vote?'

While it would be hard to equal the scurrility of a few of the Conservative newspapers, the Toronto *Globe*, that bulwark of Liberalism since the days of George Brown, outdid all the others. And two former friends of Laurier, one a particular protégé, seemed to derive a peculiar satisfaction from outrageously denouncing him.

Despite the fact that two Nationalists were members of the cabinet, and that Bourassa himself had been the ally of Sir Robert Borden's party in the recent Reciprocity election, Bourassa's most extreme statements were displayed as typical of those opposing conscription and Union government.

In the West, with its many immigrants, voter after voter, never dreaming of disfranchisement, was turned away from the polls because his mother-tongue had been German. At more than one meeting men strode to the platform and publicly tore their naturalization papers to shreds.

Two weeks before polling day, even with the aid of their two disreputable election Acts, the Unionist campaign managers were still not sure of success, and at a special council meeting (held on Sunday!) it was decided that farmers' sons—the largest group of possible recruits—should be exempted from the provisions of the Military Service Act. An announcement to that effect was made by General Mewburn, the Minister of Militia, and flashed immediately all over Canada by obliging news services.

Although just past his 76th birthday, Sir Wilfrid, after a strenuous campaign in the East, made a trip to the Pacific coast, braving sub-zero weather on the prairies, speaking several times in each of the principal cities. 'I have been called a traitor, and I have come across Canada to show you what a traitor looks like,' was his salutation to the great crowds who gathered to see and hear him. Election day occurred before he reached home, and news of his defeat was broken to him by friends who met his train at a stop in northwestern Ontario.

The result was as may have been expected. The government was returned by an overwhelming majority; the new standing in parliament, 153 to 82. The government had lost only 2 seats in the West, 1 in Alberta and 1 in Manitoba, while in Quebec it carried only 3 out of 65. The Maritimes returned 10 Liberals to 21 for the government, while in Ontario only 8 seats remained to the Liberals. Many more seats in Ontario and the West had been won by the Liberals which were lost to them by the manipulation of the soldiers' vote. In some cases the Liberal majority at home was greater than the total number of soldiers recruited in that constituency, but it was to meet such contingencies that the Military Voters Act had been framed, and it had not failed!

It is interesting to speculate upon what might have happened if the Canadian people had known the truth about the ghastly blunder which had cost 16,000 Canadians at Passchendaele only a few weeks before. Sir Robert Borden himself did not know the full facts until nearly a year later. In a letter from England, addressed to the Acting Prime Minister at Ottawa, he stated concerning Passchendaele that the offensive had no useful result, no advantage in position was gained, and 'the effort was simply wasted'. 'Currie reports', he went on, 'that the conditions in front of Passchendaele, when the Canadian Corps were ordered to take it, were simply indescribable.'

On December 6, 1917, the *Imo*, a Belgian relief ship, collided in Halifax harbour with the *Mont Blanc*, a French ship loaded with explosives, causing an explosion resulting in the deaths of upwards of 2,000 people and property loss estimated at about $20,000,000.

A great part of the city of Halifax, especially the northern portion, was totally destroyed, for a time almost putting the busy port out of commission. The federal government made an immediate contribution of $500,000 toward relief, and other contributions poured in from all over Canada, the United States and Great Britain. Haligonians were especially grateful to the people of Massachusetts, who rushed a delegation of relief workers to the stricken city with cash and supplies. Heavy snowstorms on the days following the disaster added to the misery of more than 25,000 who had lost their homes, and to the difficulties of those engaged in searching the ruins for the dead and injured.

CHAPTER XVII

AFTERMATH

WHEN it was all over, what did the Military Service Act accomplish? Despite a vigorous attempt at enforcement, it failed to produce an appreciable number of men beyond what might have been secured by much less effort, if expended wisely, in the direction of voluntary enlistment. Out of 117,000 Quebec registrants in the first class, unmarried men from 20 to 24, for example, 115,000 claimed exemption on one ground or another; and, out of 125,000 Ontario registrants in the same class, 118,000 claimed exemption. And so it went in other parts of the country. By March 31, 1918, what with exemptions and desertions, the drag-net had dredged up only 26,000 who were available for military duty. Mayor Tommy Church of Toronto, a supporter of Union government, declared: 'The Military Service Act will cost the country millions and is getting very little results. If the government had spent one-quarter of the money in voluntary recruiting, they would have got more men.'

In order to tap the largest reservoir of unrecruited young men—those on the farms—the government, on April 19, cancelled all exemptions granted to men of 20, 21 and 22 years of age. This enraged the farmers, whose sons had been especially exempted on the eve of the election. Farmers in Ontario and the West had been quite content to conscript other people's sons, but when the chickens came home to roost, they were furious. On May 14, a deputation of several hundred (someone told Sir Robert Borden there were 5,000!) made a descent on Ottawa, demanding the rescinding of the order, but received little sympathy. They wanted to meet the government in the parliament buildings as in 1910, but were forced to gather in a theatre, where Sir Robert met them.

The exasperated farmers went home determined to make their influence felt in the only way possible; and in the next three years—Ontario in 1919, Alberta in 1921, Manitoba in 1922—provincial governments which had nothing to do with the Military Service Act fell to the fury of their onslaughts, and a new federal party had been organized which, in 1921, sent sixty-five members to Ottawa.

In the fall of 1918, in common with many other countries, Canada was swept by a wave of influenza which cut a wide swath among the young and the vigorous from whose ranks the war had already taken its grisly toll. Many looked upon the visitation as a judgment upon a sinful world, but it could equally as well have been explained in terms of cause and effect without the aid of the supernatural.

Then, in November, the country was swept by another wave, this time of unutterable joy as word of peace flashed across the land, not entirely dispelled by the warning that the news was premature, for it was felt that the real armistice could not be long in coming. The world was to experience other peace-days, but none to compare with that first one, when all still believed that peace was possible.

The Union government was responsible for much useful legislation, some long overdue. Among other things, it gave the vote to women. Possibly the fact that some had voted in the recent elections suggested that perhaps the time had come to give all women a vote, especially since they already had the right in five of the provinces. It might be noted that nearly all the Quebec members were opposed to this act of justice.

An income tax was first imposed in Canada in 1917, as a war measure, remaining thereafter as part of the tax structure. On incomes greater than $1,500 in the case of unmarried persons and widows and widowers without children, and on incomes over $3,000 in the case of other persons, the tax was 4 per cent. Graded supertaxes were imposed on incomes in excess of $6,000. Companies were taxed 4 per cent on incomes over $3,000.

Another matter which the new parliament, not, however, initiated by the government, dealt with, was the conferring of titles. The discussion was started by W. F. Nickle, he who had, a few years earlier, delved into the doings of Mackenzie and Mann. Sir Wilfrid Laurier, when Prime Minister, had had occasion to complain of the granting of titles by the governor-general (Lord Minto) without his being consulted; and as recently as 1916, Sir Robert Borden had complained of similar action by the Duke of Connaught. Information concerning these complaints was not divulged by either Sir Wilfrid or Sir Robert at the time, but in discussing Nickle's motion Sir Wilfrid said:

Why I accepted it [his title] with the views I hold now, will be going into a matter of personal history which I do not care to bring forward. But at all events I may say that: I see here a little class of titled people, knights commanders of this order or that order. If they will make a bargain with me, I am quite prepared if we can do it without any disrespect to the Crown of England, to bring our titles to the market-place and make a bonfire of them. . . . The time will come—and perhaps soon rather than late—when all titles will be held to be of no value in this country, and the only title which will be accepted will be that of a citizen of Canada and a British subject.

Sir Robert Borden informed the House that the matter had been discussed and that an order-in-council had already been passed requesting the British government to confer no further titles upon Canadians, except for services in the present war, without the approval of the Prime Minister of Canada; and that in future no hereditary titles should be granted at all. But when an amendment was moved to extend the definite prohibition to non-hereditary titles as well, Sir Robert surprisingly declared that if the amendment carried he would resign, and the matter was allowed to stand as it was.

Shortly after, Sir Robert and three of his ministers sailed for England on the *Melita* to attend a meeting of the 'Imperial War Cabinet'. 'In our convoy', he wrote in his *Memoirs*, 'there were thirteen ships all crowded with United States troops. No less than twenty-five hundred were aboard the *Melita*.' He does not mention, however, that these thirteen ships probably carried a greater number of men than his Military Service Act had produced, and that there were more where those came from.

On February 17, 1919, Sir Wilfrid Laurier died. He died as his great predecessor Macdonald had died. On the previous Saturday, while alone in his room in the Victoria Museum, where parliament had met since the destruction of the original building by fire in 1916, he had suffered a slight stroke, but was able to make his way home unaided. He had a second stroke the following morning, and death came quietly the next day.

With two such examples as 1911 and 1917, he must often have felt that he had failed in the cause to which he had devoted his life. Yet a more dispassionate estimate than he was able to make of the difference in Canada's status at his entry into politics and that which it had attained at his death must credit him with the greater part of the advance that had been achieved. And much of the advance that has since been gained, as well as the increase in national unity, has been built on foundations laid by him.

The Liberals immediately began preparations for a national convention to select his successor, and the date was later set for the first week in August. Never before in the history of Canada had a national convention been called for such a purpose. In 1893, the Liberals had held a nation-wide convention, but to adopt a platform. The party at Laurier's death consisted almost exclusively of those who had followed him in 1917. A few who had differed on the conscription question, such as Fielding and George P. Graham, still considered themselves Liberals, and the latch-string was out for any other wanderers who cared to return.

Naturally, when the delegates met in Howick Hall at the Ottawa fairgrounds, the spirit of Laurier hung over the gathering. On the wall, back of the platform, hung a huge portrait of the dead leader, while all eyes frequently turned to the gallery where, much of the time, Lady Laurier sat. At such conventions, the proceedings usually consist of speeches lauding the party's achievements and condemning the opposing party and all its works, and this was no exception (Lapointe: 'A Tory is a Tory because he hates someone or something; but a Liberal is a Liberal because he loves someone or something!').

Overshadowing everything else, however, was the question: Who will be the new leader? Many names were suggested, but always the talk narrowed down to two: W. S. Fielding, veteran of Laurier's great cabinet of 1896, and William Lyon Mackenzie King, Minister of Labour for a short time before the debacle of 1911, who had been defeated again in 1917. Many of Fielding's former associates were working hard for him, and practically all the Liberal provincial premiers (then numbering eight) and their cabinets. But, in the opinion of the rank-and-file who had borne the heat of battle in 1917, Fielding suffered from one irreparable disability: he had not been with Laurier in that dark day. For that reason observers who understood the depth of this feeling were confident that King would win, and so it happened.

On August 7, Mr. King was elected over Mr. Fielding by a vote of 476 to 438. Credit was given by some political writers to the speech delivered the previous evening in which King had greatly outshone the less-spectacular Fielding, but it is doubtful if the speeches changed many minds. In fact, in view of the prevailing sentiment, it was a tribute to Fielding that he polled so many votes.

In the meantime, conditions in Canada had been going from bad to worse. Munitions plants and others producing war supplies had either shut down or were attempting a shift to products for which new markets must be developed, resulting in men being thrown out of work, often with little prospect of another job. The cost of living, rising steadily throughout the war, now reached an all-time high (sugar, 21 cents a pound). Housing was scarce, and rents had increased even beyond the general level of swollen prices. Naturally, in cities like Vancouver, Winnipeg, Toronto, Hamilton and Montreal there was much industrial unrest, and consequently much hardship for which practically no provision was being made.

Soldiers, once described by Sir Robert Borden as 'silent, grim, determined men', were coming home, some not so silent, and many grim, but nearly all determined to re-establish themselves in civil life. Most of them had neither the time nor the inclination, as once suggested, to 'put Quebec in its place'. Their great desire was to get out of uniform, resume their interrupted education, occupation or profession, and do what they could to recover something of the years they had lost. A few, dissatisfied with the slowness of demobiliza-tion, had begun rioting in England, in which they were not alone, for in every country that had known war similar disturbances occurred.

Trouble occurred at Winnipeg in May 1919, when for six weeks the city was tied up in the only general strike in Canadian history. At the time, people not involved personally in the issues at stake, but whose ways of life were being seriously affected, were easily convinced that it was a revolutionary attempt to sweep all workers into the ranks of the One Big Union.

Undoubtedly, some firebrands and near-revolutionaries had in-filtrated into some of the unions, but the issue which precipitated the strike was a dispute between the machinists, most conservative of workers, and their employers, who resented being 'dictated to' by the union and had decided that this was a good time to have a showdown.

The cost of living was high in Winnipeg, and, as elsewhere, wages had not kept pace with it, while, day by day, the financial pages of the newspapers announced company profits greater than ever. The contrast caused feelings of bitterness which it was nobody's business to do anything about.

Thus, when it was announced that the employers had locked out the machinists, other unions, not knowing when it might be their turn, also downed tools and walked off the job. In a matter of days, an epidemic of strikes had swept the city; workers seemingly content

12

today walking out tomorrow, to the amazement and consternation of their employers.

In order to maintain essential services and prevent complete anarchy, a 'Strikers Committee' was set up without whose authority no service could be performed by any member of a striking union, and many others as a matter of convenience applied for permits, which made the whole thing seem very arbitrary and dictatorial.

To protect themselves, and also to oppose the strike, a 'Committee of One Thousand' came into being, composed chiefly of people drawn from the so-called 'white collar' classes. The city police had voted overwhelmingly to join the strike, and consequently the streets were patrolled by volunteers, untrained and in some cases unfitted for police duty.

Since the newspapers were considered too partisan, the *Strike Bulletin*, edited by J. S. Dixon, M.L.A., was published to keep strikers informed of the course of events and to assist in maintaining morale.

Although other factors were also involved, the strike was finally broken by the action of the Canadian government. Parliament was in session, and an amendment to the Immigration Act was rushed through all stages at a single sitting, authorizing the Department of Immigration to deport any immigrant, British or otherwise, irrespective of the length of his Canadian domicile, without trial by jury or other process of law.

An amendment to the Criminal Code was also passed, the notorious Section 98 which, until it was repealed by the King government, hung like a sword over the head of any person whom the police chose to suspect of subversive behaviour.

The strike leaders were arrested in the early hours of the morning and whisked away to Stony Mountain Penitentiary, where, at first, they were held without bail, pending early deportation proceedings. This, however, attracted widespread attention and protests poured in which caused the authorities to hesitate about deportation. Instead, the arrested men were charged with conspiracy, sedition, seditious libel, and the like. Dixon and Rev. J. S. Woodsworth, who had succeeded him as editor of the *Bulletin* after his arrest, were charged with seditious libel.

The feelings aroused by these events resulted in the first and only riot during the strike, but it was a serious one. A messenger boy was killed and hundreds of people were injured, one man so badly that he died later.

After the lapse of nine months, the trials began, lasting for nine weeks, the most remarkable series of trials in Canada's history up to that time. Dixon's brilliant speech to the jury won his acquittal; and when it was discovered that Woodsworth's alleged statements were verbatim quotations from the Prophet Isaiah, the case against him was withdrawn. Alderman A. A. Heaps, who pleaded his own case, was also acquitted, but seven others went to gaol for a year each.

The most significant verdict, however, was rendered a short while later when four of the convicted leaders—J. S. Dixon, Rev. Wm. Ivens, George Armstrong and John Queen—were elected to the Manitoba legislature. All but Dixon were in gaol at the time, and on their release walked from one public institution to the other and took their seats. Dixon, elected by one of the largest majorities ever given a candidate in Winnipeg, was already there.

Subsequently, John Queen served several terms as mayor of Winnipeg. In the 1921 federal election, J. S. Woodsworth was elected for a Winnipeg constituency, which he represented till his death; and, in 1925, A. A. Heaps carried the adjoining constituency.

During 1918 and 1919, Sir Robert Borden was absent in England a great deal of the time, attending meetings with British and Dominions ministers in connection with arrangements for the Peace Conference. Borden was insistent that the Dominions should be signatories, but the British government was at first inclined to the view that while the Dominions might be consulted, the final responsibility was one that it could not share; and some of the allied countries looked upon the Dominions' demands as a scheme to secure additional British votes. Eventually, Borden won his point 'that there should be distinct representation for each Dominion on the same basis as was to be accorded to the smaller nations of the Allied Powers'.

On June 28, 1919, at Versailles, the treaty of peace with Germany was signed on behalf of Canada by Sir George Foster and Mr. Doherty.

In the meantime, the Union government had been ploughing through heavy seas. Although Sir Thomas White did his best as Acting Prime Minister, the administration suffered from absentee leadership. It had been created for the one purpose of imposing conscription, and to that end free traders, low-tariff men, and high protectionists, autonomists and imperialists had come together. Now, with the war over, and conscription something to be forgotten, the issues which divided people before the war resumed their old urgency.

But was conscription forgotten? T. A. Crerar, who had joined Union government as Minister of Agriculture, resigning before the 1919 budget was introduced, did not go back to the Liberals immediately but took a seat on the 'cross-benches', where he was joined by a number of other former Liberals from the West.

Throughout the country, the farmers were seething. In September, a relatively unknown farmer named O. R. Gould was nominated to contest a federal by-election in the Saskatchewan constituency of Assiniboia. By an ironical circumstance Gould's only opponent was W. R. Motherwell, who was largely instrumental in organizing the Territorial Grain Growers Association in the early days of the century. He had not followed the farmers into politics, but had remained a Liberal, holding the office of Minister of Agriculture in the Saskatchewan government. Motherwell was snowed under by Gould, who won by a majority of over 5,000. Then, in November, the crusading farmers carried a federal by-election in New Brunswick by an even larger majority; and, before the year was out, they had won two other federal by-elections, both in Ontario constituencies.

For two years past, Sir Robert Borden's health had been giving him and his friends considerable concern, and more than once his doctors had warned him that, if he wished to live, he must retire from public life. Furthermore, his frequent absences in search of rest, and his longer absences in pursuit of the wider affairs of state, were having an adverse effect upon the government's fortunes. Deciding finally to retire, he announced his intention at a caucus of Unionist members, advocating at the same time a continuance of the Union government and the formation of a new political party to be known as the National Liberal-Conservative party. The idea of the new party was well received, but genuine regret was felt concerning Sir Robert's retirement. In order to assist Sir Robert in selecting his successor, the members were asked to send in ballots indicating their choice.

Sir Robert's own choice was Sir Thomas White, who was also the first choice of nearly all his cabinet colleagues, but a majority of the members' ballots favoured Arthur Meighen. Thus, when White declined the honour, Sir Robert and Mr. Meighen called on the governor-general, whom Sir Robert informed of his impending resignation. Mr. Meighen was then asked to form a government, which was sworn in on July 13, 1920. Newton Wesley Rowell and A. K. Maclean, former Liberals, declined to serve, leaving only Hugh

Guthrie, James A. Calder and C. C. Ballantyne of the original nine.

The most important matter facing the new government was the railway situation. Like the Old Man of the Sea, it sat on the neck of every government. In 1915, the government had transferred the National Transcontinental, 1,800 miles, to the Department of Railways, already operating the Intercolonial, 2,187 miles, and a number of other lines which, from time to time, had been left on the government's doorstep. Then, in 1918, the government had taken over the Canadian Northern's 9,900 miles of lines. It was now decided that this large aggregation of railways should no longer be operated by the Department of Railways, and a board of directors, free, as Sir Robert Borden promised, from political influence or interference, was appointed to manage them, with D. B. Hanna, former vice-president of the Canadian Northern Railway, as chairman.

Later, the Canadian National Railways was incorporated by parliament under which all the government-owned railways were to be operated in future. Mr. Hanna continued as president with a somewhat larger board of directors chosen according to regional and other considerations. The first duty of the new board was to bring order out of chaos by reorganizing, consolidating and integrating the whole system, now aggregating some 14,000 miles.

In addition, the Canadian National Railways had been given the task of bringing about a certain measure of co-operation with the Grand Trunk Railway; but it was not till May 1921 that the government gained actual control of the Grand Trunk, although still operated by a separate board of directors.

When Arthur Meighen became Prime Minister, the die had already been cast insofar as nationalization of railways was concerned; the various railways had already become so integrated that their unscrambling might have been a very difficult matter if it had been desired to return them to private ownership. This, however, was impossible for quite another reason: neither the Canadian Northern nor the Grand Trunk Pacific could have been operated without the expenditure of large sums of money for betterments and operational deficits, and no aggregation of private capital could have been found to undertake such a risk.

On the other hand, the Grand Trunk System, relieved of its obligations in connection with the Grand Trunk Pacific, could conceivably have continued under private ownership; and the directors of the road were very anxious to try. Many leading railway authorities believed that such a course should be followed. They claimed that the troubles of the Grand Trunk were largely due to its having been drawn into the expansion schemes of the Laurier administration, but there was no gainsaying the fact that the Grand Trunk management had gone in with its eyes open. In fact, there was some doubt as to who pushed whom.

Since the decision to adopt public ownership had been reached, the government had taken the stand that the taxpayers, already compelled to assume large burdens because of the failure of over-ambitious railway promoters, could not fairly be expected to assume only the unproductive lines, leaving in private hands those that might have a chance to succeed. Unperturbed by the gloomy prognostications of those who, for one reason or another, opposed the government's policy, Mr. Meighen introduced a measure into parliament for the acquisition of the Grand Trunk. The road was virtually bankrupt, and the principal question to be decided was which of its many classes of debentures should the government assume, and which should be written off as worthless.

On the eve of the final vote, Lord Shaughnessey, chairman of the board of the C.P.R., undoubtedly an outstanding railway authority, released a statement to the press in which he attempted to show that the government's course, if persisted in, would endanger the financial fabric of Canada. He advocated, as an alternative, the continued operation of the Grand Trunk under private control. The Liberal opposition, now led by Mackenzie King, who had recently found a seat, while more or less indefinite about public ownership, professed to be impressed by Lord Shaughnessey's arguments and urged the government to give the matter further consideration, claiming that information asked for by the opposition had only recently been received. It was past midnight, the House was tired, but Mr. Meighen, explaining that Lord Shaughnessey's proposals had been considered—and rejected—cracked the whip over the heads of his unenthusiastic followers, and the vote was taken. The national system was rounded out and a course charted admitting of no return.

There was no other course, in the circumstances, but it is doubtful if, with all the forces arrayed against him, there was any other man in Canada who had the combination of qualities to proceed that night as Arthur Meighen had done.

Meanwhile, things were not going so well in the provinces—so far as the fortunes of the Meighen government were concerned. In addition to the by-elections already mentioned, the Conservative government in Ontario had been defeated in the fall of 1919, by a combination of organized farmers and urban labour, and E. C. Drury, long associated with farm organizations, had become Premier.

On June 27, 1921, a federal by-election was held in the Alberta constituency of Medicine Hat to fill the vacancy left when Arthur Sifton had joined the Union government in 1917. The Conservatives had a strong candidate, a former member of the legislature. The United Farmers of Alberta nominated a local farmer, Robert Gardiner. The Liberals stayed out. After an intense campaign which was watched by all Canada, Gardiner was elected by a majority of 9,765, never before or since equalled in that constituency.

While the tariff was undoubtedly a factor in this election, as it was in the by-election in Assiniboia in 1919, a large part of the farmers' irritation could be traced to still-smouldering resentment at the government's repudiation of exemption for their sons from military service.

Prairie farmers had an added reason. During the war, the price of wheat had been controlled in the interest of the war effort and the consumer. With the prospect of a return to a free market in the post-war years, the farmers began agitating for a floor-price to protect them against a disastrous decline, and the government had met their demand by organizing the Canada Wheat Board, which had set a minimum price for the 1919 crop. With the lapsing of the government's wartime authority went its power to fix prices and the farmers were frantic as the bottom fell out of the market in 1921. Most of them believed that the government might have done something to relieve their distress, which was made no easier to bear by the realization that, in the past, they had been the chief exponents of a free market for the products of others.

Against this background, the Liberal government of Alberta, now headed by Charles Stewart, a farmer among other things, decided to appeal to the electorate. The government had seemed strong at the time that Arthur Sifton resigned the premiership, but when, within three weeks of polling day, the Medicine Hat by-election indicated the strength of the insurgent farmers, the Liberal leaders at Edmonton were filled with foreboding. On July 18, the farmers, plus a smattering of politicians formerly of more orthodox leanings, carried 38 out of the 61 legislature seats.

The man chiefly responsible for the result, Henry Wise Wood, resolutely declined to accept the premiership, and Herbert Greenfield, equally inexperienced with the majority of his following, became Premier. As with farmers' administrations in other provinces, filling the office of Attorney-General, practically always held by a lawyer, was a problem. In this case, a young Calgary lawyer, J. E. Brownlee, who had been acting as solicitor for the United Farmers of Alberta, was chosen and a seat was found for him. When, in a short while, Greenfield resigned, Brownlee succeeded him.

In the federal field, T. A. Crerar and the group who had followed him out of the Unionist party had been busy organizing the Progressive party, drawing its strength mainly from the prairie provinces, but also from Ontario, and to a much smaller extent from the Maritimes and British Columbia. Quebec was not interested in agrarian politics.

Then, of course, there was the Liberal party under its new leader, the untried Mackenzie King. He was not taken very seriously by his opponents (who continued for the next thirty years to make the same mistake!). It was conceded that he would hold his Quebec following, for no one was simple enough to expect that Quebec would so soon have forgotten 1917; and it was conceded that he might retain his following in the Maritimes, even adding slightly to it. But Ontario and the West! There the successor of Laurier would find little support.

Parliament was dissolved on October 4, and election day was set for December 6. The campaign was hotly contested, but lacked the bitterness of the two previous ones. Mr. Meighen attempted to scare Easterners by creating a bogeyman out of Henry Wise Wood, whom he represented as an American edition of Lenin and Trotsky, but without much success, as was evident on election day.

Mr. King, with 118 seats, although failing a majority, had the largest group. Mr. Meighen, defeated himself in Portage la Prairie, led a compact group of 50 Tories (and a few former Liberals). But, perhaps not so surprising, Mr. Crerar's Progressives numbered 65, including parliament's first woman member, Miss Agnes Macphail, elected as a representative of the United Farmers of Ontario.

There was, of course, Mr. J. S. Woodsworth, from Winnipeg, who, with William Irvine, from Calgary, formed the nucleus of the Labour party. (Irvine used to say that Mr. Woodsworth was the leader and he was the party.)

Mackenzie King

CHAPTER XVIII

UNEASY INTERLUDE

A T 46, Arthur Meighen had been the youngest Prime Minister in Canada's history, and William Lyon Mackenzie King was but a year older when he assumed office on December 29, 1921. The King cabinet, consisting of veterans of former Liberal cabinets, men without administrative experience and others whose experience had been gained in the provincial field, was fairly representative of the party as it then stood. In the first group were William S. Fielding, again Minister of Finance, George P. Graham, Charles Murphy, Henri S. Beland and Jacques Bureau. Prominent among the tyros were Raoul Dandurand, Ernest Lapointe and James A. Robb. The three from the provincial field were Sir Lomer Gouin, former Premier of Quebec, Charles Stewart, former Premier of Alberta, and William R. Motherwell, one-time Minister of Agriculture for Saskatchewan. All but Fielding, Graham and Stewart had stood firm for Laurier in 1917.

No man in the annals of Canadian politics has been so consistently under-rated as Mackenzie King was during the greater part of his political career. It is perhaps natural that he should have been disparaged by his opponents, but he was also discounted by many in his own party. And while it is true that some of his successes were due in large measure to the ineptitude of his opponents, recognition of his genius came slowly, and in many cases grudgingly. At first, the opposition press professed to believe that he was not master of his administration, and persisted in suggesting that Sir Lomer Gouin was the real power behind the government. This allegation could not be sustained, however, when in due course Gouin retired, leaving no appreciable gap in the administration.

In fact, if Mackenzie King danced to anyone's tune it was to the pipes of Thomas Alexander Crerar and his block of Progressive members, for King was minus a majority, dependent upon the support of the western agrarians who, in the main, preferred his policies to those of the protectionist Conservatives. Consequently the Liberal legislative program was designed to appease the Crerarites, while attempting at the same time to placate the eastern wing, inclined to look with suspicion upon all crusading agrarians.

It was therefore with one eye on the West and the other on the East that Mr. Fielding framed his budget proposals in the spring of 1922; and while they contained little that was pleasing to either extreme, his words, when he addressed the House, were definitely aimed at the Progressives. So obvious was this that Sir George Foster twitted the Minister of Finance on his attempt to 'woo' the agrarians. 'And, Mr. Speaker,' he said, 'as my right honourable friend wooed them, and wooed them, and wooed them, I felt like kissing someone myself!' Mr. Fielding and the Progressives looked properly bashful, and the House roared.

Except on the tariff, most of the Progressives differed very little in their views from the Liberals, and it was therefore natural that, during the early years of King's ministry, many should have returned to the Liberal fold, while a few others remained aloof to provide the seed for the next protest movement.

The first major problem which the government had to face was hard times. The inflated prices that had prevailed at the close of the war, and which continued for a while afterward, had slumped badly under the deflationary policies of the British and United States governments, and Canada's foreign markets were shrinking.

The average price of No. 1 Northern wheat at Fort William during January 1921 was $1.99¼ a bushel, while in December of the same year it had dropped to $1.16¼ a bushel.

The average price of good 1,000–1,200-lb. steers on the Toronto market in January 1921 was $9.55 per cwt., while in December it was $6.15; select hogs were $15.53 in January, and $10.33 in December.

In 1921, the total amount of creamery butter produced in Canada was 122,776,580 pounds, which had a market value of $45,893,088, as compared with 111,691,718 pounds in 1920, which, however, had a value of $63,625,203. Quantity had increased by 10 per cent, but value had dropped 28 per cent.

The estimated gross agricultural revenue for all Canada in 1920 was $1,961,715,000, while in 1921 it had shrunk to $1,396,233,000. Fortunately, the people could not see what was ahead of them in the lean thirties!

While the economic pulse beat more slowly, the twenties saw a quickening in other directions. In 1921, a group of writers, among whom were B. K. Sandwell and John Murray Gibbon, gathered at Ottawa to organize the Canadian Authors Association. About the same time a number of landscape painters, later known as the Group of Seven, chiefly centred in Toronto, had their eyes suddenly opened to the fact that the flavour of Canadian scenes could not be captured by the techniques of another day and another land. And just as the men of science were becoming aware of the wealth locked within the rocky fastnesses of the Canadian Shield, so did the painters see new glories in the vast vistas of rock, water, timber and muskeg. Elizabeth Wyn Wood, a young Toronto sculptor, had begun a series of modelled northern landscapes in a variety of materials; and before the twenties were done, Mazo de la Roche was to write the first of the Jalna stories.

In the field of scientific research, what has been described as the most important medical discovery in Canada's history, and one of the most important in medical history, was announced by Dr. Frederick G. Banting in the March 1922 issue of the *Journal* of the Canadian Medical Association.

Working under Dr. J. J. R. Macleod, in the physiological laboratory of the University of Toronto, with C. H. Best as his assistant, and after long and careful experimentation, Dr. Banting had succeeded in extracting from secretions of the pancreas a substance called insulin, essential in the digestion of starch and sugar, lack of which was found to be the cause of diabetes.

Later, with the aid of Dr. J. B. Collip, a practical method of producing synthetic insulin was evolved, thus making relief possible for the millions whose lives would otherwise have been greatly handicapped and in many cases definitely shortened. Dr. Banting immediately turned over all rights in the discovery to the University of Toronto for the benefit of the medical profession and the general public. Honoured by leading medical societies the world over, he was awarded the Nobel Prize for medicine, which he shared with his colleagues in the research.

On January 6, 1922, the International Joint Commission, by unanimous decision, reported favourably on the practicability of the St. Lawrence–Great Lakes Waterway, which it had had under consideration since January 21, 1920.

The report, an exhaustive one, recommended that the governments of Canada and the United States should enter into an agreement for the improvement of the St. Lawrence between Montreal

and Lake Ontario at a cost of $252,000,000. Money expended by
Canada on the Welland Canal, then nearing completion, should be
credited as part of Canada's share. The cost of 'navigation works'
should be apportioned on the basis of benefits received by each; but
works for the production of power should be divided equally, as
should also the power.

On May 17, the United States Secretary of State, Charles E.
Hughes, through the British ambassador, notified the Canadian
government that the Harding administration was prepared to begin
negotiating a treaty for the construction of the waterway. The
Mackenzie King government, however, was not in a position to
comply. Montreal, backed by the Quebec government, was violently
opposed, and other parts of Canada, remote from the Great Lakes
area, were indifferent. The government replied, according to a statement made in the House by Mr. King, that 'the present is not an
opportune moment to take the matter up . . . and that for the time
being, considering the magnitude of the project and the expenditure
involved, the matter should be allowed to remain in abeyance'.

It is not by any means certain that the Harding administration
could have passed a treaty through the Senate, but in view of subsequent criticism in Canada of delays caused by the United States,
Canadians might remember that theirs was the original postpone-
ment.

Every government since Confederation, and before, has had its
railway problem to face, and the King administration was no exception. Before it took office the irrevocable decision had been taken to
include both Canadian Northern and Grand Trunk railways in the
nationally-owned system, which then aggregated 22,114 miles. Most
of the government-owned lines except the Grand Trunk were operated under a board of directors headed by D. B. Hanna, but the
Grand Trunk was still operated by a separate board.

The government now decided to consolidate the two systems,
and in making the announcement Mr. King said:

We intend to give government ownership of the national system . . . the
fairest treatment and under the most favourable conditions it is possible
for a government to secure. So far as it is possible for the government to
demonstrate what can be done under government ownership, it is our intention to see that it is done.

Believing that the system would have a better chance if given
entirely new leadership, the government made an effort to secure

W. L. MACKENZIE KING

an outstanding railway executive, and at length the choice fell upon Sir Henry Thornton, an American by birth, who had learned to operate railways with the Pennsylvania Railroad, had become General Manager of the Great Eastern Railway, in England, and Inspector-General of Transportation for the British Expeditionary Forces.

With the lessening of the depression, and an increase in production, conditions improved throughout Canada. The unavoidable deficits of the first years of the administration were overcome, the budget was balanced, some 'nuisance' taxes were reduced or removed, and duties were lowered on implements of production in the agricultural, mining and lumbering industries, which tended further to increase production.

Mr. King was soon to have a chance to show where he stood in the matter of Canada's national status, and was to make clear, in connection with the Chanak incident (September 1922), that he was not willing that the Canadian people should be used as pawns in the game of power politics. Mr. Lloyd George, then Prime Minister, in a quarrel with Turkey, the details of which are now unimportant, attempted to impress the Turks by enquiring publicly of the Dominions whether, in the event of war, they would be willing to stand behind the United Kingdom. Instead of replying 'Ready, aye, ready; we stand by you!' as Mr. Meighen insisted, Mr. King refused to get excited and asked for further information. This, of course, was not what Lloyd George wanted, and the threatened war ended before it began. It is hard to say, however, what might have happened had Canada sprung to attention and blindly pledged support.

For years, Canadian governments had been hampered by what British diplomatists called 'maintaining the solidarity of the Empire' in their efforts to deal direct with other governments. After much effort, Canadian officials had been permitted to carry on their own negotiations, and could even sign what are called 'conventions', but they could not sign a treaty. For a treaty, the signature of the appropriate British functionary was necessary.

In 1923, Ernest Lapointe, as Minister of Marine and Fisheries, had concluded a treaty with the United States concerning halibut fisheries in the Pacific, and he saw no reason why he should call in the British ambassador to give it the final stroke. In this he was supported by Mr. King, but stubborn resistance on the part of

British officialdom had to be overcome before Lapointe was permitted to sign.

Mackenzie King's attitude toward such questions was not a new one. It was in line with the policy initiated by Sir Wilfrid Laurier and consistently followed by him. Both Laurier and King, as well as many others, had been influenced by the writings and advice of John S. Ewart, who since 1904 had published a steady stream of pamphlets dealing with the entire field of Canada's constitutional relations.

Ewart, a nephew of Sir Oliver Mowat, after practising law in Toronto, had gone to Winnipeg while it was still a frontier community. He had established a successful practice there, and had occasion to extend his knowledge of constitutional questions as chief counsel for the Catholics in the long-protracted litigation over the Manitoba School question. Retiring with a comfortable income at a relatively early age, he moved to Ottawa, where he continued to act in Supreme Court and Privy Council cases, and undertook the self-appointed task which was to claim his attention till his death in 1933. For years his mailing list often reached 12,000, and the cost of printing and mailing came out of his own pocket.

The status which Ewart advocated for Canada differed only in degree from that envisaged by Sir John Macdonald when he suggested the title: Kingdom of Canada, and which was finally attained in 1931 by the passing of the Statute of Westminster. Ewart was particularly insistent that Canadian ministers should avoid being drawn into consultation in matters concerning British foreign policy, because consultation would lead to advice, and advice to responsibility for results. This was not advisable since Canada could have no effective share in the formation of British policy, over which only British electors had control.

Ewart's writings, later published in book form, are an invaluable aid to the student or writer of Canadian history, but they have been largely ignored because, although practically no one now disagrees with the implications of Canada's status, Ewart, who advocated it for years, is still looked upon by many as having been of doubtful loyalty. Loyalty to what is not clear.

For some years, three of the Protestant denominations had moved toward amalgamation. In a country like Canada, consisting of many sparsely-settled areas and small communities, it was patently a waste of money and energy, and a limitation upon effective service, for congregations having so much in common to maintain separate establishments throughout the country. There was nevertheless considerable opposition to union, some on traditional or sentimental grounds, others on matters doctrinal, but gradually the advocates of union won over most of the dissidents. They were so successful with respect to the Methodist and Congregational churches that these went in without a division of membership. But in the case of the Presbyterians, opposition was so great that a large minority, including among them Mr. Mackenzie King, continued under the old name. It was necessary, in their case, to divide the assets and property of the Church, which might have been a difficult thing had not the division been conducted in a spirit of tolerance and fair dealing. The Church Union compact was ratified by act of parliament and became effective on June 10, 1925. Its subsequent success has more than justified the faith of those who worked so long and so hard to bring it about.

Governments are usually chary about having to fight with their backs to the wall, and generally pick what seems a favourable moment for an election, well in advance of their statutory time-limit. Consequently, while still having more than a year to go, the Liberals decided to try a test of strength with Mr. Meighen, but they miscalculated. For much to their discomfiture, on October 29, 1925, Mr. King and eight of his ministers were defeated and they ended with fewer seats than the Conservatives. The latter had 116, the Liberals 101, the Progressives 25, Labour 2, and there was 1 Independent. Although the party was in a minority, Mr. King still hoped to carry on, as in the past, with the aid of the Progressives.

His situation was not greatly different from what it had been during the past three years. Although he then needed less support from the Progressives, he had always been dependent upon them for his majority, but during that time Mr. Meighen had never been able to secure their support for any of his policies. King believed there was no reason to suppose he could do so now.

Clearly, Mr. King was entitled to face parliament and let it decide whether it wished to continue under his leadership. Nevertheless, the unexpected verdict was a great shock to him and appears temporarily to have shaken his self-confidence. What happened is a controversial point, but there seems to be no doubt that he promised the governor-general, Lord Byng, that if he could not command a

13

majority of the House he would advise him to call on Mr. Meighen to form a government. He need not, of course, have given any such promise. He was still the King's minister, and it was his duty to advise the King's representative, not to bargain with him.

After securing seats for himself and other defeated ministers, King still had a formidable task ahead of him because of the inherent nature of the Progressives upon whose whim the fate of his government now hung. They were divided into two principal groups, the larger of which consisted of those referred to by Mr. King as 'Liberals in a hurry', whose background was Liberal and who differed only slightly from the majority of official Liberals. Crerar himself was one of these, as was his successor in the leadership of the group, Robert Forke. Chiefly from Manitoba and the East, they had objected for a long time to the dominance of eastern financial interests in the affairs of both the old political parties. They were not radicals, and did not wish to change the basis of society, but they did hope to correct some of the economic disabilities under which they believed agriculture had suffered for many years.

Generally, this group subscribed to the political and economic views of J. W. Dafoe, editor of the *Manitoba* (later *Winnipeg*) *Free Press*, undoubtedly the most outstanding journalist in Canada at the time, and one of the greatest editors the country has yet produced. For a generation, from his modest editorial room, this burly man with the rumpled, tawny hair had kept a discerning eye on Canadian affairs, both external and domestic, especially as affecting the prairies. In 1911, he had thrown the support of the *Free Press* into the fight for Reciprocity in opposition to the stand taken by its owner, Clifford Sifton; but in the contest over Union government and conscription, he and Sifton had fought together, and his influence had been largely responsible for the defeat of Laurier candidates on the prairies.

The second group of Progressives followed another and a different type of mentor. They were chiefly from Alberta and their prophet was Henry Wise Wood, in his own way as remarkable as Dafoe. In order to understand the viewpoint of the people of Alberta, and to a lesser degree, Saskatchewan, at that time, it must be remembered that a considerable part of the farm population consisted of immigrants from the middle-western states who had been subjected to a variety of radical economic philosophies arising out of dissatisfaction with conditions in the farming communities, which they blamed on protective tariffs and the control of government by eastern financial interests. They had come to have a distrust of political parties and of the existing system of representative government, believing that members elected to state and federal legislatures should act as delegates of those who elected them, subject to recall if they failed to do so.

Wood had been influenced by such ideas. Born in Missouri and educated for the ministry in the Campbellite sect, he had become a farmer, although, on occasion, filling in as a lay preacher. Politically, he had been active in movements such as the Farmers' Alliance and the Populist party, developing a distrust of the farmer in politics, preferring co-operative action at the economic level.

When Wood emigrated to Alberta, in 1905, and settled on a farm at Carstairs, a few miles north of Calgary, he was already 45 years of age, tall, rugged, with a massive domed head, almost completely bald. He was a ready speaker, careful in his choice of words, but when he warmed to his subject, capable of a high degree of homely eloquence. He quickly gained a place of influence among the farmers, and by 1916 was president of the United Farmers of Alberta. Since the movement was still non-political, he had been a nominal Liberal, but had refused to run for office, preferring to confine his activities to the farm movement.

Wood's political and economic thinking led him to the belief that in human society two principles were in conflict, competition and co-operation; that the former was destructive, and the latter, constructive. He believed that the farmers must organize co-operatively, sending rigidly-controlled representatives to the provincial and federal parliaments to contend as best they could with the representatives of other organized interests, already in control.

Widely read as he was in economics, he was probably familiar with Marx's writings, and many saw in his group ideas a similarity to the theory of the class struggle which obsessed the Marxists, but it is doubtful if he was ever much impressed by the dialectics of communism. If there was any respect in which he could be compared to the communists, it was in the evangelical fervour with which he promoted his ideas. Without personal ambition, he was a perfect example of the 'incorruptible man'.

It was therefore natural that the group of U.F.A. members (who, by the way, were chiefly of British origin) in the House should form a cell within the larger group with whom they co-operated or not as the spirit moved them. They refused to be bound by the decisions of caucus, playing hob with the plans of the whips, finally absenting themselves altogether. As is often the case, despite their emphasis upon the merits of co-operation, they were strong-willed individualists, each with a pet theory of his own; yet when they did combine on an issue, they fought with the ferocity of tigers.

CHAPTER XIX

DAYS OF DERELICTION

D URING the session which began in January 1926, the government led a precarious life, holding on to office by the slimmest of margins. Despite this, it was able to carry the Address and the Budget by majorities of 9 and 13, respectively, and to conduct the ordinary routine of business. King's right to govern had been demonstrated, and his promise to the governor-general, if ever made, had been fulfilled.

It was during this time that J. S. Woodsworth and A. A. Heaps (Irvine, who had previously constituted Woodsworth's 'party', had been defeated in Calgary, but Heaps had been elected in Winnipeg) saw their chance to advance the cause of Old Age Pensions, which Woodsworth had been urging since entering the House. They addressed the following letter to the Prime Minister:

DEAR MR. KING:

As representatives of Labour in the House of Commons, may we ask whether it is your intention to introduce at this session legislation with regard to (a) Provision for the unemployed; (b) Old age Pensions.

We are venturing to send a similar enquiry to the leader of the Opposition.

Mr. King hastened to reply that it was the intention of the government to introduce an Old Age Pensions measure, but Mr. Meighen's answer was considered unsatisfactory by the Labour members. In his speech on the Address, Mr. Woodsworth, after reading the replies from the two leaders, promised that 'so long as the government is prepared to bring down legislation which commends itself to our judgment we must continue to support it'. When eventually introduced, it provided less than Woodsworth desired, but at least a start had been made.

What finally brought down the government was a scandal, ostensibly involving the Customs Department. In reality, it involved much more than the Customs Department: it involved both political parties, in the provinces as well as federally, but this was not known until much later. The strategy of the opposition was to pin it firmly upon the Mackenzie King administration. If they could do this, they might have a chance to defeat the government.

Nearly every serious political scandal in Canada can be charged to the corrupting influence of campaign funds. This does not mean that the soliciting or contributing of funds for political purposes necessarily leads to corruption, for in many cases no such implication is justified. But every so often a situation arises in which some particular group requires a favour or a concession out of the ordinary; and in such cases contributions are hard to distinguish from bribes.

Before Confederation, and down to the second decade of the twentieth century, railways and railway promoters were the chief sources of campaign funds. But after most of the railways had passed into government hands this source largely dried up. By this time, however, other interests were ready to bid for favours; and since the outs of today are often the ins of tomorrow, contributors were careful to subsidize both parties indiscriminately. Chief among these new sponsors were the organized liquor interests.

Since the early days of the Dominion, the liquor interests, from distillers and brewers to tavern-keepers, have had to contend with a resolute band of temperance reformers. Before World War I, by means of propaganda, lobbying and stressing the social and economic consequences of drinking, the temperance forces had gradually lessened the area in which liquor could legally be sold. Furthermore, they had created a public attitude toward the use of liquor which was hard to counteract. With many members of the evangelical churches, the liquor question was definitely a moral matter. The liquor trade was on the defensive, and seemingly had little defence to offer.

In 1900, Prince Edward Island, after being partly dry, became totally dry; and in Nova Scotia, New Brunswick and Ontario, county after county had exercised its option under the Canada Temperance Act to exclude the sale of liquor. World War I completed what the temperance forces had begun. Saskatchewan, in 1915, Ontario, Alberta, Nova Scotia, Manitoba, New Brunswick and British Columbia, in 1916, passed prohibition laws; while, in 1918, Quebec fell into line with its sister provinces. To round out the picture, in December 1917, the Union government, by order-in-council, prohibited the importation and manufacture of liquor anywhere in Canada.

In the meantime, the United States, by constitutional amendment had gone dry. Thus, for a time, from the Mexican border to the polar seas, no oasis existed where alcoholic liquors could be legally sold.

The Union government's order-in-council of December 1917 had been passed under the authority of the War Measures Act, but when the war was over, the government decided that it no longer had a right to intervene in a matter of exclusive provincial jurisdiction, and consequently, on December 31, 1919, the order was rescinded.

There had always been a certain amount of bootlegging; and after the United States had gone dry whisky-running across the line grew to large proportions. But with the rescinding of federal restrictions upon the exportation of liquor, whisky-running became big business. Large stocks of liquor were on hand, which its owners were determined to dispose of as quickly as possible.

The greater part of the Ontario–United States border consists of international waterways, which made smuggling relatively easy, especially if the connivance of customs officials on both sides could be secured. And since the traffic was extremely profitable, money was available for the purchase of connivance.

That being so, it was an easy matter for the smugglers to load with liquor at some Canadian point, declare a fictitious destination— Havana or Buenos Aires—and sail ostensibly for such destination, often repeating the process the next day. In many cases, the cargo was landed somewhere on the Canadian side, to be bootlegged to thirsty Canadians.

This traffic went on for years, and was known to almost everybody. The newspapers knew all about it; customs officers undoubtedly knew all about it; legislators knew all about it. The whole thing was looked upon as a joke.

Brewery and distillery companies, some of which were controlled by men prominent in the financial and business life of Canada, became active partners with bootleggers and others engaged in this illicit trade. They paid bonuses to those who exceeded their sales quotas, and when runners were occasionally caught, the liquor companies paid their fines, fraudulently entering the amounts so paid in their accounts as 'travelling expenses', 'sales promotion', 'malt consumption', etc., ultimately claiming income-tax exemption.

Profitable as this traffic was, those engaged were hungry for added profits, and soon were deep in two-way smuggling. Water-craft, from row-boats to steamers, as well as all sorts of land equipment, loaded with liquor, made regular runs to points in the United States, returning with a variety of merchandise for smuggling into Canada. Numerous articles, particularly electrical appliances, some kinds of textiles, cigarettes and many other things, are cheaper in the United States than in Canada, and large profits were possible in smuggling them across the border.

While Canadian customs officers might have been inclined to turn a blind eye upon liquor smuggling by free-handed whisky-runners, it was another matter to wink at the smuggling of goods into Canada; but money induces myopia; and before long the service was honeycombed with near-sighted officials.

In this, however, the smugglers over-reached themselves. Canadian manufacturers and retailers became alarmed at the quantities of smuggled merchandise flooding various parts of Canada, some of it obviously stolen. They complained to the government, and they also briefed the opposition.

The liquor companies, coining money out of illicit trade, spent immense sums in propaganda, and in contributions to political parties, all such payments charged in their books to less incriminating accounts. This campaign, and the social chaos which resulted, had its calculated effect; beginning with Quebec in May 1921, the various provinces, one by one, repealed their prohibition laws and established government-operated sales stores, and, in some provinces, beverage-rooms for beer by the glass, and eventually cocktail bars.

These new outlets provided legitimate markets for liquor; but, having tasted the fruits of illicit trade, the liquor interests were not satisfied. Since excise taxes were not imposed on liquor for export, they conspired to cheat the government by consigning shipments to fraudulent addresses outside the country, short-circuiting the liquor back into Canada for sale by bootleggers in opposition to the government liquor stores.

For many months previous to the election of 1925, Mackenzie King had known that all was not well in his Customs Department, and had ordered an investigation. When he became aware of how serious matters really were, he asked for the resignation of the Minister, Jacques Bureau, but, believing him uncorrupted, although complaisant and easy-going (he had quashed convictions at the behest of lawyer-members on both sides of the House), had transferred him to the Senate. George Boivin, a promising young Liberal, was appointed in Bureau's place, charged with the almost hopeless task of cleaning up the Department.

It is not likely that King was aware of how deeply the Liberal party was implicated in the whole sorry mess, for he had always been careful not to know more than he could help about the sources of campaign contributions. This was a sore point with party officials whose duty it was to collect the money, for King might unwittingly pass a heavy contributor in the Commons corridors with an absent-minded nod when the donor expected at least a smile of recognition. Of greater consequence, King did not know that, through a leak, evidence of the situation was in the hands of the opposition, who were awaiting the right moment to spring the trap.

That moment came early in February, when Harry Stevens rose in his place and let loose a damning indictment against the Customs Department, its ex-minister and the government. Although evidence of what had been occurring was plain to be seen on every side, Stevens' charges created a sensation. Knowing that much of what he said was true, the government moved for a select committee of four Liberals, four Conservatives and one Progressive, to 'investigate the administration of the Department of Customs and Excise', and the committee immediately entered upon its labours.

The committee's unanimous report,[1] tabled on June 18, shocked the people of Canada. It disclosed a deplorable situation, recommended the retirement of the deputy minister, the dismissal of six officers of the Department, and a general clean-up. This, however, did not satisfy critics in House and country.

H. H. Stevens moved as an amendment to the formal motion for concurrence in the Report that it be referred back to the committee with instructions to add clauses implicating both the ex-minister and the government. He castigated the ex-minister for 'perverting his opportunities of service to the state to the distribution of indulgences to his favourites . . . High officials, with a long career of faithful service to the country, were debauched by him and must now pass out of the picture under a cloud more or less of shame.' These facts, he declared were 'well-known to the Prime Minister and his associates. Yet he [the minister] was allowed to resign his seat and his position as minister and he was rewarded with a seat in the Senate while his puppets have been driven out of the service in shame.' He declared further: 'It is high time for this unholy partnership between the government of Canada and a gang of bootleggers to be dissolved.'

Stevens started the debate on Tuesday, June 22, and it continued

---

[1] Statements in this chapter are based on information contained in the committee's report, and that of the succeeding Royal Commission.

till the following Saturday morning at 5.15. During that time, the really significant events were two subamendments to Stevens' amendment, the first by J. S. Woodsworth, on Wednesday, the second by William R. Fansher, a Saskatchewan Progressive, on Friday. In between, round and about, the debate raged, involving endless digressions while points of order were discussed, the Speaker's rulings accepted or reversed.

Woodsworth wanted to see the charges thoroughly investigated and the corruption cleaned up, but he did not believe the Prime Minister was implicated, and was not prepared to see the government defeated. His subamendment was supported by the Liberals, declared out of order by Meighen, and, after the Speaker had ruled it in order, was defeated by a margin of two votes.

Fansher's subamendment called for a judicial investigation, but, by implication, condemned the government. It was declared out of order by the Liberals, who were supported by the Speaker, but his ruling was reversed by two votes, after which, now accepted by the Liberals, it was carried without division.

Two motions to adjourn were moved during the final night, both by Liberals; the first was defeated, but the second carried by a single vote.

The Liberals had voted with the majority only once; three times they had been in a minority; but since none was a government motion, the government, technically, was not defeated.

At adjournment, the Stevens amendment, as amended, was before the House.

Since King seemed unable to command a majority in parliament, and, in his opinion, no other party leader could, he called on Lord Byng, the governor-general, and advised a dissolution. This advice the governor-general refused to accept, on the ground, it was alleged, of King's promise eight months before. On the following Monday (June 28), after again advising His Excellency that in his opinion the public interest would best be served by a dissolution, and his advice having again been ignored, King tendered his resignation.

At two o'clock, that same day, he informed the House of the circumstances.

May I make my position clear? [he said]. At the present time there is no government. I am not Prime Minister; I cannot speak as Prime Minister. I can speak as only one member of this House and it is as a humble member of this House that I submit that inasmuch as His Excellency is without an adviser, I do not think it would be proper for the House to proceed to discuss anything.

If the House is to continue its proceedings, some one must assume, as His Excellency's adviser, the responsibility for His Excellency's refusal to grant dissolution in the existing circumstances; and until His Excellency has an adviser who will assume this responsibility, I submit that this House should not proceed to discuss any matters whatever.

In that statement Mackenzie King indicated the course he proposed to take in the coming contest. By refusing to grant a dissolution, the governor-general had acted on his own initiative, which Mr. King was to contend he had no right to do. The defence would be that the governor-general was but exercising the King's prerogative, the answer to which was that not in recent times had the King exercised his prerogative in this manner. With a sensitiveness to the trend of public opinion that was to characterize his future career, King instinctively felt that on such an issue he might have a chance to win. At any rate, it offered a hope, which an attempt to defend his Customs Department did not.

Yet, if most political observers had been asked to decide which party was likely to win, one having for campaign material all the unsavoury details of the Customs scandal, or one compelled to campaign on the niceties of the King's prerogative, they would have been unanimous that the scandal would win hands down.

Mr. Meighen, having been called upon to form a government, promptly did so, and since that constituted acceptance of an 'office of emolument under the Crown', he was compelled to vacate his seat until he should pass through the ordeal of a by-election. Since every minister appointed by him would be in a similar situation, and it was obvious no government could carry on with all its members out of the House, Mr. Meighen's fertile mind hit upon a variation of the 'double shuffle' invented by the resourceful Macdonald. He appointed seven ministers without portfolio who were to fill all the cabinet offices as acting-ministers. It was a desperate expedient, but he hoped it would bridge the period till dissolution could be secured.   Sir Henry Drayton was deputed, in the meantime, to lead the House.

King waited until the House was in Committee of Supply the following evening, and then proceeded to question the ministers, one after the other, as to their right to administer the departments they presumed to head; and when they admitted that they had not been sworn to any of the offices they claimed to hold, he rounded upon them.

This country [he declared in ringing tones] to-day is being governed with all the great responsibilities of government, by a cabinet in which there is not a single minister of the Crown in parliament and in which there is no Prime Minister with a seat in the House. With such a sequence of events I say that if ever a Prime Minister was justified in tendering advice urging that the conditions demanded dissolution, I have been justified in this instance.

All evening until a late adjournment, and all the next afternoon and evening, King kept up the grilling, piling argument upon argument, quoting one authority after another, in support of his claim that the 'ministers' were acting in violation of the constitution. It was two o'clock in the morning of July 1 when, by a majority of one vote, the House adopted a motion that

the actions in this House of the honourable members who have acted as ministers of the Crown since June 29, 1926, are a violation and infringement of the privileges of the House for the following reasons:

1. That the said honourable gentlemen have no right to sit in this House and should have vacated their seats therein, if they legally hold office as administrators of the various departments assigned to them by Orders-in-Council;

2. That if they do not hold such offices legally they have no right to control the business of government in this House and to ask for supply for the departments of which they state they are acting-ministers.

To mark the occasion as memorable, and to provide material for endless discussion and speculation, the vote which gave the opposition its majority of one was cast by T. W. Bird, Progressive member for Nelson (Manitoba), who afterwards admitted that he should not have voted because he was paired with another member. His explanation came too late to save the Meighen government; but in the circumstances, the government could not have been expected to weather many such attacks.

The following day, Mr. Meighen advised the governor-general to grant him the dissolution he had so recently refused Mackenzie King.

CHAPTER XX

PAPER-PROFIT CHASE

IN the campaign that took place in the summer of 1926, the Conservatives did their best to keep the Customs scandal uppermost, but the Liberals persisted in evading the subject, continuing to enlarge upon the seriousness of a situation in which a governor-general had refused to act upon the advice of his Prime Minister. This argument, the Conservatives, especially Mr. Meighen, attempted to answer, but the weight of sound precedent was against them. Not that precedent counted for much with electors more concerned with 'keeping the governor-general in his place'.

Conservative argument was: (1) King had sought a second dissolution in order to avoid defeat in the House, thus flouting the authority of parliament; (2) he had been properly refused a dissolution since a reasonable expectation existed that an alternative government could be formed; and (3) cases could be cited in support of such arguments.

The Liberals answered that: (1) King had demonstrated his ability to govern, and what he asked for was not a 'second' dissolution; it was the Prime Minister's right to advise, the governor-general's duty to accept such advice; (2) none of the precedents cited was applicable because they all concerned Crown colonies—the only legitimate comparison was with practice in the United Kingdom, where no dissolution had been refused in over 100 years; (3) dissolution had not been sought in order to avoid defeat in the House, but even if it had, the Ramsay MacDonald government, in 1924, had secured a dissolution *after* being defeated in the House and other similar precedents could be cited; and (4) an appeal to the people could not properly be considered as 'flouting' parliament—the electorate is the highest court of appeal.

Mr. Meighen made a valiant effort to rally protectionist support by accusing Liberals of selling out eastern industrial interests for party purposes to gain the support of western agrarians. But that, too, seemed of little interest to voters who had become strangely persuaded that the real issue was whether a governor-general should or should not act upon the advice of his Prime Minister. The constitutional niceties of the question bothered the average voter very little; though few of them realized it, they had been caught up in the wave of national self-consciousness engendered by Canada's part in War and in Peace, and while they had no desire to break up the Empire, they were disposed to resent what they believed to be an unwarranted interference on the part of an appointee, however distinguished, of the British government in the domestic affairs of Canada.

Thus, King snatched victory out of defeat. Although only 116 Liberals were elected in a House of 245, the presence of 9 Liberal-Progressives and 13 Progressives assured him of a working majority, without having to depend upon the support of 11 members representing the United Farmers of Alberta. The Conservatives had elected only 91, of whom Mr. Meighen was not one. He had again suffered personal defeat; and until his successor was appointed the opposition would be led in the House by Mr. Guthrie.

The Meighen government's term had been but an interlude in the administration of Mackenzie King. The Meighen ministers, with an election on their hands, scarcely had time to become acquainted with the chiefs of their departments before the triumphant Liberals came trooping back. Mr. Bennett, who was defeated in Calgary by a single vote, had the distinction of being the only Minister of Finance since Confederation who had never brought down a budget.

The interval, and especially the election, gave Mr. King an opportunity to strengthen his cabinet. Sir Lomer had retired from politics in 1924 and Mr. Fielding in 1925. In Fielding's place he put James A. Robb, an English-speaking member from Quebec. Charles A. Dunning, former Premier of Saskatchewan, who had been elected in Regina, became Minister of Railways. James L. Ralston, though defeated in the recent election, became Minister of Defence, and a seat was found for him. James Malcolm, a furniture manufacturer from Kincardine, Ontario, brought business experience and an engaging personality to the cabinet. But the man King relied upon above all others was Ernest Lapointe, who had succeeded Gouin in 1924 as Minister of Justice. Lapointe, who entered the House from the backwoods district of Kamouraska in 1904, and for years was a back-bencher, unable to speak English, had since become a fluent bilingual speaker. Representing the old Rouge element of Quebec, he was personally unambitious and loyal, and in time came to command the respect of the people of his province in a manner seldom if ever equalled.

By winning the election, King established his domination over the Canadian political scene which was to endure, with but one interval, for the next two decades. But, more than that, his victory made extremely unlikely that ever again would a governor-general presume to undertake an official act contrary to the advice of his constitutional adviser.

The new government was installed on September 25, and one of its first acts (September 28) was the appointment of a Royal Commission to continue the investigation of the Customs Department and other irregularities brought to light by the parliamentary committee. The commission consisted of Sir Francis X. Lemieux, Chief Justice of the Superior Court of Quebec, chairman; Hon. James T. Brown, Chief Justice of the Saskatchewan Court of King's Bench; and Hon. William H. Wright, of the Supreme Court of Ontario. Later, Sir Francis Lemieux resigned and Hon. Ernest Roy was appointed in his stead, Mr. Justice Brown becoming chairman.

The commission held public hearings in every province and gathered an immense amount of evidence, but by the time its report was issued on October 15, 1927, the public had largely lost interest in the matter. The report constitutes a damning indictment of the activities of the liquor trade and its allies.

The Duncan Royal Commission, appointed in the spring of 1926 to enquire into the grievances of the Maritime provinces, had continued its labours throughout the summer and reported two days before the King government resumed office on September 25. The commission, consisting of Sir Andrew Rea Duncan, Hon. W. B. Wallace, and Professor Cyrus Macmillan, investigated a great variety of complaints and listened to numerous suggestions. The report contained many recommendations, but the two principal measures of relief were: increased subsidy payments and reduction of freight rates.

The outstanding fact, it seems to us [the commissioners reported], is that the Maritime Provinces have not prospered and developed . . . as fully as other parts of Canada. We are unable to take the view that Confederation is, of itself, responsible for this fact. . . .

Even within Confederation there has been such a measure of responsibility resting on each province for its own development that much at least of what has happened within the Maritime Provinces must be related to their responsibility and not to the responsibility of the Dominion. We

are far from saying that the Dominion, within its sphere of control, has
done all for the Maritime Provinces which it should have done.

The commissioners found that 'the Maritime Provinces have
satisfied us that they have a genuine claim to a readjustment of the
financial arrangements that exist between the Dominion and themselves'. While, pending a more thorough survey of all factors involved, they could not make final recommendations in this field,
they recommended interim lump-sum increases, as follows: Nova
Scotia, $875,000; New Brunswick, $600,000; and Prince Edward
Island, $125,000.

With respect to transportation, they recommended an immediate
reduction of 20 per cent in all rates on traffic originating or termina-
ting within the Atlantic Division of the Canadian National Railways.
In addition, they recommended the establishment of statutory
harbour commissions for both Halifax and St. John.

Immediately after he had seen his new cabinet installed, King
prepared to attend the Imperial Conference to which he had looked
forward since 1923, and especially since his controversy with Lord
Byng. Consequently, it was to be expected that in view of what had
happened in Canada, the Conference should go on record that:

it is an essential consequence of the equality of status existing among the
members of the British Commonwealth of Nations that the governor-
general of a Dominion is the representative of the Crown, holding in all
essential respects the same position in relation to the administration of
public affairs in the Dominion as is held by His Majesty the King in Great
Britain, and that he is not the representative or agent of his Majesty's
government in Great Britain or of any department of that government.

This made necessary the appointment of a High Commissioner to
act as a channel of communication between the government of the
United Kingdom and the Canadian government.

This and other changes that had already taken place were recognized in the Balfour Declaration in which the Dominions were said
to be 'autonomous communities within the British Empire, equal in
status, in no way subordinate one to another in any respect of their
domestic or external affairs, though united by a common allegiance
to the Crown, and freely associated as members of the British
Commonwealth of Nations'.

The declaration did not mention the relationship of the respective
Dominions to the United Kingdom, which could not yet be said to
be 'equal in status, in no way subordinate'. In practice, that was the

case, but some time must yet elapse before it had become a reality in law as well.

In October 1919, Sir Robert Borden had forwarded a despatch to Lord Milner, at the Colonial Office, in which he urged that an arrangement should be made for the appointment by the Canadian government of a minister at Washington as part of the British Embassy establishment to be the sole channel of communication between the Canadian government and that of the United States. This proposal was eventually agreed to by the British government with the further suggestion that the proposed minister might take the place of the ambassador when absent. Although announcement of the arrangement was made in the House on May 10, 1920, nothing had been done in the interval to appoint such a minister.

This Mr. King now proceeded to do, not, be it observed, as part of the British Embassy set-up, but in an establishment entirely Canadian. As the first minister to the United States he appointed Vincent Massey, member of a family that had been engaged in the manufacture of farm implements in Ontario since 1847. After completing his education at Oxford, Massey had taught modern history at the University of Toronto for a few years before entering the family business, eventually becoming president. In 1925, although Massey was without political experience, and despite the handicap of a name synonymous with the tariff-protected implement industry, King had taken him into the cabinet as minister without portfolio. He had run in Durham County, long associated with the family name, but had been defeated. The choice of Massey for the Washington post was to prove a wise one, and was eventually to lead to a much more important field of service for him.

Following his defeat, like other party leaders who had failed, Mr. Meighen offered to resign the leadership. Judged by his subsequent political activities, it is probable that he would have remained had he been sufficiently pressed to do so. But, realizing Meighen's ability as a debater and parliamentarian, and naturally convinced of the superiority of their political philosophy, and having a low opinion of the abilities of Mackenzie King and the adequacies of Liberal policy, the Conservatives could only attribute Meighen's continued failure to defects within himself. Besides, they now had a suitable and willing substitute. Consequently, in October 1927, the Conservatives gathered at Winnipeg for their first national convention and Richard Bedford Bennett was chosen leader.

14

A New Brunswicker by birth, Bennett had gone to Calgary in 1897, where he had since lived and practised law; yet he had never really become a Westerner. Although Calgary when he arrived had hitching-posts along the main street, it is doubtful if he ever had thrown a leg over a horse. The West provided him with a large fortune, yet to the end of his days he remained uncontaminated by the social and economic currents which coursed through that country. In accepting the Conservative leadership, he dedicated his health, strength, talents and 'the fortune that God has been good enough to give me, to the interests of the great party to which I am privileged to belong'.

With characteristic energy, Bennett lost no time in turning an oratorical barrage upon Mackenzie King and the Liberals which, by itself, might have succeeded, even had not other forces greatly assisted in ousting King. Three years must elapse, however, before this would occur.

During the session of 1928, a discussion arose over the control of radio, and a number of proposals were made, but no action was taken. Then, on December 6, an order-in-council was passed appointing a Royal Commission 'to examine into the broadcasting situation in the Dominion of Canada and to make recommendations to the government as to the future administration, management, control and financing thereof'.

The commission consisted of Sir John Aird, president of the Canadian Bank of Commerce, chairman; Charles A. Bowman, editor of the Ottawa *Citizen*; and Augustin Frigon, director of the Polytechnic School, Montreal. At the first meeting of the commission, Donald Manson, of the Radio Branch of the Department of Marine and Fisheries, was appointed secretary.

In January 1929, the commissioners, including Manson, sailed for Europe, where they spent two months visiting Great Britain, the Irish Free State and several continental countries. Upon their return to Canada, they departed for the Pacific coast to begin a series of public hearings across Canada.

Before the commission's report was acted upon, many things were to happen, which was also to be the case with another matter which the King government had under consideration during the latter part of 1928, and the early part of 1929. This was an application by the Beauharnois Heat, Light and Power Corporation for approval of its plans to construct a canal for the development of power on the south shore of the St. Lawrence, between Lakes St. Francis and St. Louis, with a power-house at the Lake St. Louis end capable of generating 300,000 horsepower, which could be expanded to generate 500,000 horsepower. The company had already secured the power rights from the Quebec legislature, but approval by the federal government was also required because of its control over navigable waterways. After considering a number of objections, and examination of the proposal by government engineers, the Minister of Public Works, J. C. Elliott, announced on March 8, 1929, that the cabinet had sanctioned the proposal, but with certain stipulations designed to safeguard navigation.

The middle twenties were the days of 'Coolidge Prosperity', when the people of the United States were assured that economic laws applying elsewhere were specially abrogated in their favour. The stock-market boomed, and there was no way for stocks to go but up. Europe was an economic desert of inflated currencies and bread-lines, but the United States refused to forgo collection of its loans and reparations, even though new loans must continually be advanced out of which interest and principal payments might be paid. Signs of disaster were plain to be seen, but neither the people nor the government heeded the signs.

Canada followed in the trail of its big neighbour like a wabbly-kneed puppy after a Great Dane. Canadian stock-exchanges did proportionately as much business as those in the United States. Most of the issues traded in were those favoured by speculators across the line. As an instance of this aberration, one of the favourites of the time was a taxicab company! One day, it was this stock, the next, it was something else. Everybody made money, on paper, because stocks always went up.

Despite all this, much sound development occurred in Canada. The proving of the Horne mine by Noranda Limited marked the opening of a most productive mining region in Quebec whose possibilities have not yet been fully explored. In northwestern Manitoba, the Hudson Bay Mining and Smelting Company Limited had succeeded in solving the metallurgical problems which previously had held back the operation of the great copper-zinc-gold-silver mine at Flin Flon. And about the same time Consolidated Mining and Smelting Company of Canada Limited had also solved its metallurgical problem at the Sullivan mine, in southeastern British Columbia, which has since developed into such a remarkable enterprise.

Industrial production, which had continued the upward trend begun in wartime into the postwar years, had declined after the peak gross value of $3,772,250,057 had been reached in 1920. Following a temporary slump, production had gradually gained until a gross-value production of $3,769,850,362 was attained in 1928, reaching a peak of $4,063,987,279 in 1929.

Agricultural production had remained relatively high during the same period, reaching its peak in 1927 and 1928, a record prairie wheat crop of 544,598,000 bushels in the latter year helping to maintain the level, which swiftly declined thereafter.

Then, at the end of October 1929, came the day of reckoning. In Canada, the disaster, though bad enough, was not so great as in the United States. While all lost their paper-profits, and those who held shares in even the most stable and well-managed concerns saw their equities dwindle almost to nothing, not many were completely ruined as was the case in the United States. A revulsion of feeling followed on the part of speculators unwilling to accept the consequences of their folly, and half a dozen Toronto stockbrokers, guilty of practices at which the authorities had winked for years, became convenient scapegoats, serving terms in the penitentiary.

Thousands of office and factory workers were thrown out of work, in most cases to swell the rapidly-growing ranks of the unemployed. Few remembered the depression following the panic of 1893, which had lasted for nearly three years; the panic of 1907 had been sharp, but recovery was rapid; the depression following the defeat of Reciprocity and the advent of the Borden government in 1911 had been curtailed by World War I; and the depression that began in the early twenties had soon given way to the recent wave of prosperity.

For this reason, the general impression was that the present 'recession' was but a temporary aberration of an economic system which few understood but which by most, like any other system based on faith, was believed to be fundamentally sound. This belief was put into high-sounding platitudes by leaders of finance and industry in their year-end pronouncements.

Those thrown out of work were soon in desperate circumstances. Few could get jobs. As their meagre savings were spent, they borrowed from friends little better off than themselves. Others appealed to charitable or social agencies, which were soon swamped by demands. Municipal governments, besieged by applicants for help, in most cases had neither the money nor the machinery to meet the need. They, in turn, went to the provincial governments, which, for a while, cushioned the shock; but soon they, too, found their resources inadequate. Inevitably, the problem arrived at the door of the federal government.

In ordinary circumstances, the care of the needy is a matter strictly within the jurisdiction of the provinces; but, since the depression had assumed the proportion of a national disaster, and the provinces were unlikely to protest against such an invasion of their jurisdiction, the obligation of the federal government was clear. (These jurisdictional niceties resulted, at about the same time, in the Hoover administration's ruling that federal funds might be used to feed mules but not people!)

Since most of the provincial governments were now Conservative, even Nova Scotia having recently been lost to the enemy, Mr. King forgot his habitual caution and made a statement which, in the months to come, would return to haunt him. Reiterating his claim that the problem was primarily municipal and provincial, he declared in the House that he might be prepared to go a certain length in meeting the needs of one or two of the western provinces that had progressive premiers, but he would not give a single cent to any Tory government.

This produced an uproar from the Conservatives, which stung King to further elaboration:

May I repeat what I have said? With regard to giving moneys out of the federal treasury to any Tory government in this country for these alleged unemployment purposes, with these governments situated as they are today, with policies diametrically opposed to those of this government, I would not give them a five-cent piece!

A portent of things to come was the attempt of Robert Gardiner, leader of the U.F.A. group, to suggest that something might be wrong in connection with the Beauharnois application for approval of its power plans. A letter, dated October 14, 1926, from R. O. Sweezey, president of Beauharnois, to J. Alderic Raymond, of the Windsor Hotel, Montreal, had come in some unexplained way into his hands, and he read it to the House. One significant paragraph was as follows:

Enlist with our syndicate two or three individuals, who in addition to providing some cash as their fair share, can assist us in getting our rights extended or enlarged so as to develop the entire available flow of the St. Lawrence at this point. As the whole situation is entirely within the

Province of Quebec, our influence has to be exerted only in Canadian political circles—that is, at Ottawa and at Quebec.

Charles A. Dunning, becoming Finance Minister in 1929, was a pledge to the West that Liberal budgets would not, as often charged, be entirely dictated by Ontario and Quebec interests. The famous Dunning budget of 1930, among other things, extended the preference on imports from Commonwealth countries. 'We do not intend', Dunning said, 'to meet the other countries of the British Commonwealth of Nations in a spirit of petty bargaining, but rather in the broad spirit of willingness to become in ever-increasing measure good customers of those who treat us in like manner.'

Depending on the budget, the Liberals went to the country in the summer of 1930. But the people, smarting over speculative losses, or the loss of a job, with thousands on the dole, were in no mood to listen to dissertations on the merits of a preferential tariff. To most, such discussions lacked a sense of reality, especially in the light of Mr. King's expressed intention not to contribute a five-cent piece toward their relief.

On the other hand, Mr. Bennett boldly announced that if elected he would end unemployment. As to the tariff, he declared that he would use it to 'blast' his way into the markets of the world. That was the sort of talk people wanted to hear! As Bennett, with boundless energy, ranged the country from coast to coast, he became infected by his own eloquence and something of his own confidence carried over to his listeners. Here was no politician mouthing platitudes. Was he not a successful man of business, a millionaire who had by his own efforts piled up a fortune? Many believed that he could do as he promised. Mr. King, never very effective on the defensive, was particularly ineffective in attempting to follow in the wake of such a verbal tornado.

The electors spoke on July 28. The Conservatives won 137 seats, significantly securing 24 in Quebec (without the aid of Bourassa!), while the Liberals were reduced to 88, only 5 more than in the debacle of 1917. The Liberal-Progressives and Progressives between them numbered only 5, but the United Farmers of Alberta were almost in full strength. Woodsworth and Heaps were back, and with them, Angus MacInnis, of Vancouver; but William Irvine, Woodsworth's former 'party', was now interned within the rigid ranks of the United Farmers of Alberta. In addition, there were 2 'Independents'.

CHAPTER XXI

WANT IN THE LAND OF PLENTY

M R. BENNETT, in selecting his cabinet, contented himself mainly with the material that had floated in on the election tide. He did not call in provincial leaders or outsiders from the ranks of business, industry or the sciences. He did, however, bring Arthur Meighen back to public life, appointing him to the Senate as government leader, with a seat in the cabinet as minister without portfolio. Bennett himself undertook the two important posts of Finance and External Affairs. The electors of Vancouver Centre had rejected Harry Stevens, but he was made Minister of Trade and Commerce and a seat was opened for him in Kootenay East. Hugh Guthrie became Minister of Justice, and Dr. R. J. 'Bob' Manion, Minister of Railways and Canals. As for the rest, the level of mediocrity was unrelieved.

Bennett's first onslaught upon the depression consisted of cutting expenses. Not yet had he learned that in such times a wise government spends money. He saw no difference between a government and a private citizen. In his own case, if his income were to drop, he would cut his spending, even though it might mean drastic reduction in his scale of living. So with governments. He accordingly issued instructions to all departments to carve their estimates to the bone; and after this had been done, with his own blue pencil, he slashed them again.

The civil service was drastically curtailed. Many a public servant, entitled by years of faithful service to security in his job, learned from the newspapers that he had been retired. Consternation stalked the corridors of government buildings. But, since many people believe that civil servants are highly paid, do little work, and have received their places through favouritism, the cries of anguish that ascended to the Ottawa skies went largely unheeded.

Parliament met in special session on September 8, 1930, and passed three acts designed to relieve unemployment: (1) to provide $20,000,000 for aid to provinces and municipalities in undertaking desirable public works; (2) to increase the tariff on a wide range of products, including British imports, in the expectation that their exclusion might result in increased employment; and (3) to provide for the revision of existing regulations concerning 'dumping'.

Then in order to implement his own views concerning empire trade, Mr. Bennett decided to take advantage of the Imperial Conference scheduled to meet in London on October 1; but his views met with a cool reception from delegates representing the United Kingdom and the other Dominions. Mr. Ramsay MacDonald, head of the Labour government, curtly replied that 'we cannot do it', while Mr. J. H. Thomas was blunt enough to characterize the proposals as 'humbug'. None but a person so economically naïve as Bennett would have expected any other response to the warmed-over ideas of Joseph Chamberlain.

Nothing daunted, Mr. Bennett proposed that a further conference, devoted entirely to economic matters, should be held in Ottawa within twelve months. His invitation was accepted, but it was found later that the time was too short, and it was not till July 21, 1932, that the conference met in the parliament buildings at Ottawa. In the interval, Mr. MacDonald's Labour government had given place to Mr. MacDonald's National government, which contained a large leaven of Conservatives. Thus, to Ottawa, heading the United Kingdom delegation, came Mr. Stanley Baldwin, whose economic views were capable of a considerable amount of adjustment, and Mr. Neville Chamberlain, younger son of the redoubtable Joseph, who, at least, might look with favour upon his father's repeatedly-rejected proposals.

Judged by the amount of work done, the agreements negotiated and signed, the press releases handed out (through the ingenuous Dr. Manion, obviously quite mystified by the proceedings), and the spate of congratulatory speeches with which the conference ended, the affair was a huge success; but from the standpoint of increased trade and employment it was scarcely worth the amount of labour and effort involved.

The constitutional status of the Dominions had also received attention at the 1930 Imperial Conference, which, in that respect, was very successful. The Balfour Declaration of 1926, which affirmed that the Dominions were the equals of one another, had said nothing about the relationship of the Dominions to the United Kingdom itself, which still held them in colonial ties, especially with respect to the Colonial Laws Validity Act, under which certain British legislation was still operative in the Dominions, and the method by which governors-general remained as agents of the United Kingdom government. The conference decided that the disabilities caused by the Colonial Laws Validity Act should be removed, and that, in future, governors-general should be appointed only on the advice of the respective Dominion governments.

Accordingly, on June 30, 1931, an address was adopted by the Canadian House of Commons, and subsequently approved by the Senate, requesting the parliament of the United Kingdom to enact the Statute of Westminster removing the remaining legal limitations affecting the autonomy of the Dominions. In compliance with this address and others from the Dominions, the parliament of the United Kingdom passed the statute. Royal assent was given on December 12, 1931.

The Liberals, interested mainly in allowing the Bennett government to wallow itself out of sight in the quicksands of the depression, and concerned only with whatever might contribute to that end, suggested little in the way of alternatives to the government's policies. And, during this time, the most effective opposition, in some respects, was offered by those who came to be known as the 'Ginger Group', consisting of U.F.A. members, J. S. Woodsworth, Agnes Macphail, and others. With no immediate hope of attaining office, and with no past sins for which to atone, they were free to enter on paths that did not invite the feet of the official opposition.

As a matter of fact, they let in the light on one issue that the Liberals would have preferred to let lie. In 1929, Robert Gardiner had tried to draw attention to possible irregularities in the application of the Beauharnois Light, Heat and Power Company Limited for federal approval of its plans for developing power on the St. Lawrence. In the meantime, he had gathered further information and, on May 19, 1931, informed the House that he could produce evidence of serious irregularities in connection with that application. He alleged that campaign contributions had been made to both the old parties; and that persons close to the Liberal party had been 'greased' in order to secure the necessary approval.

A parliamentary investigation followed, disclosing a web of widespread intrigue and financial manipulation. According to the evidence of R. O. Sweezey, promoter of the project, a total of $864,000 had been handed over in campaign funds, most of which had gone to the Liberal party. Senators Andrew Haydon and Donat Raymond had received over $600,000 for the benefit of the Liberals. Senator Haydon, high in the counsels of the party, and the chief architect of the 1919 convention, was further involved. His law firm had received a fee of $50,000 contingent upon the success of the company's application, and promise of an annual retainer of $15,000 for three years.

As a by-product, it was learned that a contribution of $125,000 which the promoters of Beauharnois believed they were making to the campaign funds of the Conservative government of G. Howard Ferguson, in Ontario (the government was a customer for power), had not reached its destination. The federal Conservative party had received only about $30,000, a larger donation having been declined on instructions from the Prime Minister himself.

Among other disclosures, it appeared that Mr. King, while Prime Minister, had made a trip to Bermuda as the guest of Senator Wilfrid Laurier McDougald, an old friend, whose connection with the enterprise was in part due to his political influence. There is no doubt that Mr. King was absolutely unaware of any of these goings on, and he was greatly mortified to discover that men whom he trusted had used their positions, and especially his friendship, for such sordid purposes. Rising in his place in the House, he made an abject speech in which he declared that he and his party were in 'the valley of humiliation'. It was something new for a politician to do, and certainly would not have been approved by caucus, the usual procedure in such cases being to brazen the thing through.

Following receipt of the report of the Royal Commission on Radio Broadcasting by the King administration in 1929, the question had come up as to whether radio was under federal jurisdiction, and the subject had been referred to the courts. On February 9, 1932, by a decision of the Judicial Committee of the Privy Council, federal jurisdiction was confirmed; and on February 16, Mr. Bennett announced his government's intention to proceed with a measure for the control of broadcasting.

The question was first referred to a parliamentary committee, with instructions: (1) 'To consider the report of the Aird Commission'; (2) 'To advise and recommend a complete technical scheme for radio broadcasting for Canada so designed as to ensure from Canadian sources as complete and satisfactory a service as the present development of radio science will permit'; and (3) 'To investigate and report upon the most satisfactory agency for carrying out such a scheme'.

The committee held 27 meetings, heard a large number of persons, and on May 9 tabled its report. It recommended the creation of a national broadcasting system controlled and operated by a commission to be known as the Canadian Radio Broadcasting Commission, consisting of three members who should hold office for ten, nine and eight years, respectively. This commission should be vested with complete control of broadcasting.

Regarding financing, the committee did not support the recommendation of the Aird Commission concerning contributions by parliament, but stipulated that the system should be self-sustaining, deriving its income from licence fees and advertising.

The report was adopted by parliament and the Prime Minister introduced legislation to implement its recommendations. In the autumn of 1932, Hector Charlesworth, former editor of *Saturday Night*, was appointed chairman, with Thomas Maher, of Quebec, as vice-chairman, and Col. W. A. Steele, of Ottawa, as the third commissioner.

Meantime, Bennett's efforts at economy had swept across the country, causing a wave of deflation, leaving distress and ruin in its wake. The attempts of financial leaders and others to assure people that the worst was over, and good times just around the corner, were as futile as they were silly. The ranks of the unemployed rapidly swelled, and breadlines grew longer. The government joined with the provinces in attempting to provide money for relief, the amount needed increasing from day to day and week to week. By the end of 1930, the federal government had spent on relief alone a total of $17,728,000, which then seemed a large amount of money, but in reality was only the beginning. That Canada was caught in a world-wide depression made the situation no easier; in fact, it was the worldwide feature that hit Canada the hardest. Since agricultural and forest products were Canada's chief items of export, the drying-up of foreign markets was a serious blow.

In 1932, the price of wheat dropped to the lowest point in 300 years, and other agricultural prices were not much better. At a retail price of 24 cents a pound for butter, it did not pay farmers to milk cows, but semi-destitution was better than complete want, and they continued.

In June 1932, the United States imposed a duty of 4 cents a pound on copper, which sold on December 6 at 5 cents a pound, an all-time low; and on December 29, silver reached a record low of 24.5 cents in New York. These prices caused some Canadian base-metal mines to close down, but the position of the gold mines was relatively improved.

During the boom, the pulp and paper industry had been too widely extended, and now, with advertising revenue shrunk to new low levels, newspapers, cutting their editions and losing circulation, were using much less newsprint. Pulp and paper plants were closing down, throwing mill and woods workers out of their jobs; and before some of them were to resume operations the huge stacks of pulpwood awaiting the idle choppers and grinders would rot away.

To make matters worse, the severest drought in the country's history settled upon the western plains, especially in the southern portions of Saskatchewan and Alberta. Throughout the spring and summer, day after day, the sun beat down upon the parched land. Dry, hot winds caught up the powdery earth which the roots of tumbleweed and sow thistle could not bind, producing the only clouds that veiled the sun's fierce glare.

Farm people, reduced to the lowest extreme, no longer able to buy gasoline, hitched horses to their idle motor-cars and called them 'Bennett buggies'. Many who lived through those years on the prairies could not, in after years, explain how they did it; and it is likely that archaeologists in ages to come will find its indelible mark in the bones of those who went through the Great Depression and Drought on the Saskatchewan plains.

Years before, the grain-growers had organized elevator companies which had effected savings in the handling of their products, but these, in the course of time, had come to differ very little in their objectives from the privately-owned elevator lines; both were primarily concerned with earning returns upon invested capital. During the twenties, rising costs and declining prices had caused the growers to take further steps toward reducing their marketing costs. In 1923, farmers in each of the three prairie provinces had begun the organization of co-operative selling pools, with a central selling agency, in an effort to eliminate the speculative element in grain-marketing.

Members were bound by five-year contracts to deliver all their wheat to the pool. On delivery, payment was made in part, the balance becoming due after the entire crop was sold and costs of handling ascertained. By 1927, the pools had 140,000 members, comprising well over half of all prairie grain-growers, and returns to members were, on the average, several cents a bushel greater than those received by non-pool growers.

But, following the 1929 crash, when the price of wheat dropped to an all-time low, the pools found themselves facing bankruptcy. The initial payment on account of the 1929-30 crop had been greater than the final selling price. In an attempt to force higher prices, the pools had withheld wheat from the market, with the result that the elevators were glutted with their wheat, unsalable except at the risk of further depressing the price.

The provincial governments, unwilling to allow the pools to fail, came to their assistance with guarantees, but this was not enough. The federal government then assumed control of the central selling agency, appointed its own general manager, and attempted both to 'stabilize' the market and to dispose of the accumulating wheat stocks.

This situation led to the Canadian Wheat Board Act, 1935, under which the government, through a board of grain commissioners, provides a 'floor' price for wheat. The pools, however, have continued as voluntary agencies and, as such, have become permanent features of the prairie economy.

Meanwhile, instead of lightening, as the government hoped, the depression picture grew darker. In 1929, gross agricultural revenue for all Canada was $1,631,081,000; by 1932, it had shrunk to $766,794,000; and by 1933, to $762,302,000. The three prairie provinces had a total gross agricultural revenue in 1929 of $642,022,000, which by 1932 had shrunk to $299,080,000, and, in 1933, to $271,109,000.

In manufacturing, the situation was much the same. In 1929, the gross value of Canadian manufactured goods was $4,209,371,340, but in 1932 that total had shrunk to $2,126,194,555, and in 1933, to $2,086,847,847.

The cities, especially the larger ones, such as Vancouver, Winnipeg, Toronto and Montreal, became the repositories of hopeless men. Thousands of self-respecting workmen, bricklayers, stonemasons, carpenters, machinists, and other artisans, who had not done a stroke of work for years, sat at home while their wives made the dreary pilgrimage to the 'pogie'. Young men and women left school discouraged because, for them, there was neither prospect of jobs nor marriage.

In the run-down sections of the cities—and these were rapidly encroaching upon the once-considered better-class districts—desperate men congregated. It was easy for those wishing to stir up trouble to goad some of these into acts of violence. It is strange that so few responded.

Relief camps which the federal government had organized to provide board, lodging and a semblance of occupation for unattached men (twenty cents a day in addition!) were fertile fields for trouble, some of the most troublesome of which were in British Columbia, filled with idle woods-workers. More than once, Woodsworth and his colleague, Angus MacInnis, member for Vancouver East, warned the government of the unwisdom of keeping young men interned indefinitely with no prospects for the future.

On May 21, 1935, MacInnis drew the Prime Minister's attention to a statement by the mayor of Vancouver, as reported in the press, to the effect that a condition existed in Vancouver which required the intervention of the federal authorities. In reply, after describing the situation in British Columbia, for which he put most of the blame upon communist organizers, Mr. Bennett concluded:

There can be no trifling with anarchy; there can be no playing with chaos; and so far as this government is concerned, they propose within the ambit of their power to be always ready and willing to assist those who are charged with that responsibility if they find themselves unable to do so. But mob violence, mob threats, mob law will not be the means by which to deal with matters of this kind between the province of British Columbia and the Dominion of Canada.

A few weeks later, an 'army' of relief-camp strikers, under the leadership of one Arthur Evans, began a 'march' on Ottawa, travelling as uninvited passengers upon Canadian Pacific freight trains. Numbering between 800 and 1,000 when they left the Pacific coast, their ranks were swelled by other camp-deserters along the way, until by the time Regina was reached they had almost doubled. Here, especially-recruited forces of Canadian Mounted Police removed them from the trains and attempted to herd them into camps provided for their care until they could be sent back to where they had come from.

The men refused to go into the camps, thus providing a problem for the city and provincial authorities. A deputation of eight, including Evans, proceeded to Ottawa to interview the government. Giving an account in parliament of this interview, Mr. Bennett declared that: 'Evans was the only Canadian-born of the eight. He himself has a criminal record. . . . The delegation made certain demands upon the government which I think beyond question it was realized were incapable of being granted by any government, in whole at least. . . .'

Eventually the inevitable clash occurred. Late in the afternoon of

Dominion Day, the men were holding a meeting in the Regina market square which both the city police and the R.C.M.P. attempted to disperse. A city detective was killed and two R.C.M.P. constables so seriously injured that they were taken to hospital. In the House next day, Mr. Bennett charged Evans with the responsibility, quoting him as having said, according to the press, that 'blood would flow in the streets of Regina'.

In the debate that followed, Mr. Woodsworth pointed out that these young men had already been interned for nearly four years and that the alternatives offered them were to continue in the camps in idleness, to starve or to become criminals. Harry Stevens, no longer a minister of the Crown, asked if it would not be infinitely better to send a messenger to 'these young men offering them some hope for the future, some hope of getting employment and earning a living?'

Every phase of the national economy was affected by the depression, and naturally the railways were hard hit. At the end of the railway-building era, Canada had more railways than its restricted population and development could support. Too large a percentage of railway mileage lay through unsettled territory, which little or nothing had been done in the meantime to develop.

Now, with reduced agricultural and industrial production, with curtailment of both foreign and domestic trade, railway revenues dropped disastrously. The Canadian National Railways, so largely serving sparsely-settled territory, not yet fully co-ordinated and consolidated, was naturally hardest hit, but the well-established C.P.R. also felt the strain.

In 1929, gross earnings of all steam railways in Canada were $534,106,045, which, by 1931, had shrunk to $358,549,382. The dividend rate of the C.P.R. was dropped from 10 per cent to 5 per cent for the second and fourth quarters of 1931. Net operating revenue for the Canadian National, which in 1929 had been $41,864,705, had shrunk to $1,192,167, while interest on its funded debt was $55,587,145, to say nothing of $32,643,624 due the government for loans made from time to time in the past.

There was much talk of amalgamating the two great systems. E. W. Beatty, president of the Canadian Pacific, was the leading advocate of this course, but not many connected with either railway were in favour of the idea. It was felt in some quarters that Mr. Bennett and Mr. Beatty were of like mind in the matter, perhaps because of Mr. Bennett's long association with the Canadian Pacific, but Bennett made a speech opposing amalgamation and recommending a co-operative arrangement, summing up with the slogan: 'Co-operation Ever, Amalgamation Never!'

Against this sombre background of pessimism and disappointed hopes was played the final scenes in one of the most dramatic episodes in Canadian history. The Canadian National Railways System, from its inception, had incurred the inveterate hostility of powerful interests, both political and financial. Financial hostility centred chiefly in Montreal, springing quite naturally from rival railway interests. Politically, the Canadian National had come to be identified with the Liberals and inevitably became the object of attack by the Conservatives.

When the Liberals came to power in 1921, nationalization had already become an established policy which they were disposed to accept without question. Having decided to give the system a chance to justify itself, they counted themselves fortunate in securing the services of Sir Henry Thornton as president and chairman of the board of directors.

Thornton, a giant of a man, in his early fifties, came to Canada with an established reputation. An engineer who thoroughly understood the technical side of railroading, he was also an adept in dealing with people. Of an expansive, outgoing nature, he easily attracted people to him, holding them in loyal attachment. A man of vision and imagination, he was fired by the opportunity to share in the development of a country with such great possibilities as Canada. Mr. King offered him a free hand and he threw himself into the task with enthusiasm.

When Thornton assumed control of the Canadian National Railways System late in 1922, it still consisted of disintegrated units of formerly rival railways. Its roadbed was generally in poor condition, and much of its rolling-stock was antiquated and obsolescent. The morale of its officers and men was at a low ebb. Public confidence was lacking; the constituent railways had been the butts of jokes for years.

Thornton soon brought about a change. Except for a relatively few whose positions had been adversely affected by Thornton's changes, the formerly dispirited staff gained new confidence and self-respect, efficiency improved all along the line and business increased. Thornton became a familiar and popular figure in every part of Canada, and Canadians, not any too confident of themselves or their country, were flattered and reassured by the optimism of the dynamic personality who had come among them.

As traffic and revenue increased, Thornton felt justified in spending money on further business, and in this he had the support of his board of directors and of the government. Among other things, he was a pioneer in the development of the diesel-electric locomotive. Not only did he spend the system's money with a lavish hand, but he spent his own. Drawing a salary of $75,000 a year, which his critics contended was double that amount with expense allowances and other perquisites, he lived to the full extent of his income.

Competition was keen between the two great systems. Every innovation instituted by one was quickly followed and exceeded by the other. It was a new experience for the staid Canadian Pacific to go out after business; during most of its career business had come to it. Although never so efficient as when spurred by the competition of its rival, Canadian Pacific officers, shareholders and supporters complained bitterly at having to spend ever-increasing sums in competition with a government-subsidized rival.

Then came the crash, for which Sir Henry and the Canadian National were less prepared than most. Sir Henry, the optimist, had looked forward to many years of growth and development, and was unable at first to appreciate or cope with the situation which now confronted him. Refusing to believe that it was more than a temporary panic, and with characteristic loyalty to those who worked with him, he refused to sanction the wholesale dismissals that were becoming the rule with other companies, until forced to shorten sail by dropping revenue and relatively rising costs.

As the Liberals had become more and more the champions and defenders of Thornton and the Canadian National, it was but natural that the Conservatives should be driven into the role of critics; and Thornton's spectacular methods, unavailing in the changed circumstances, frequently gave them good reason for criticism.

Others, not connected with either politics or railways, were critical too. Thornton's manner of life had left him open to criticism; he worked hard, played hard and drank hard. Occasionally, he appeared in public in a condition which caused tongues to wag. As long as times were good, people were willing to overlook these aberrations, but now they were not so tolerant, and Thornton lost support that might have been of value to him.

With the crash came a change of government. Now his friends were out and his critics were in the driver's seat. The railway

committee of parliament, which had formerly cast a lenient eye over
Canadian National affairs, now became a court of inquisition, in its
ranks some who bore Thornton and the railway no good will. The
committee sat almost continuously throughout the sessions of 1931
and 1932, and every action, every dollar spent, by the system during
the previous nine years was combed over.

In the temper of depression days, expense accounts not exceptional in days of prosperity seemed grotesquely out of proportion.
Dr. Peter McGibbon, Conservative member for Muskoka-Ontario,
R. B. Hanson, Conservative member for York-Sunbury, and F. R.
Macmillan, Conservative member for Saskatoon, were the chief
inquisitors. Dr. McGibbon, especially, seems to have had a deep
antipathy to Thornton and his questions were fine examples of the
art of innuendo.

McGibbon usually preceded such a question by an assurance of
his own disbelief; he had heard on trains, in hotel lobbies, and elsewhere, this thing or that thing said, and he merely wanted to know
if it was true. He was one of the originators of what has since come to
be known as 'the smear', not previously, nor since, employed to any
great extent in Canada. Nevertheless, the statements which he 'did
not believe' never failed to appear in the headlines of the hostile press,
as when he declared that 'they' were saying all over the country that
'the Canadian National Railways is a fertile field for graft'.

'Personally,' he repeated, 'I do not believe that. I do not mind
telling you that the public are saying that.' And so they were as soon
as the press agencies had flashed his words across the country.

There could be only one end to all this. Sir Henry, broken in
health, broken in fortune and in reputation, was finally forced to
resign by the Minister of Railways, Dr. Manion, whose attitude
toward him and the railway had been covertly antagonistic from the
first.

Thornton resigned on July 19, 1932, and within a year was dead.
Never in the history of Canada had any man been so relentlessly
pursued. True, he had left himself open to attack; but, after the lapse
of two decades, in considering the magnitude of his accomplishment,
and making full allowance for his failings and his weaknesses, it can
be said that he towers above most of those who hounded him to his
death.

In one of his appearances before the committee, Sir Henry had
recommended the appointment of a Royal Commission to study the
railway situation in the light of circumstances then existing, and to

examine claims by Beatty of the C.P.R. that some 5,000 miles of excess trackage could be torn up. On November 20, 1931, Mr. Bennett appointed a Royal Commission consisting of Chief Justice L. P. Duff, chairman; Sir Joseph Flavelle, Toronto financier; Lord Ashfield, a British railway man; F. L. Loree, president of the Boston and Maine Railroad; Beaudry Leman, Montreal financier; Dr. W. C. Murray, president of the University of Saskatchewan; and J. C. Webster, M.D., of Shediac, New Brunswick.

The commission's report, which followed an exhaustive examination of the whole subject, was submitted in September 1932, and put at rest, for the moment, at least, the agitation for amalgamation. Instead, it recommended a policy of close co-operation between the two systems, with reduction of duplicate or purely competitive services.

As a result of the commission's recommendations, an act was passed by parliament, effective May 23, 1933, under which the board of directors of the Canadian National Railways was replaced by three trustees. In order to bring about economies, the Canadian Pacific and the Canadian National were directed to devise co-operative measures wherever practicable; and by arrangement with their employees to provide for a fair and reasonable apportionment of employment in connection with any co-operative measure.

Mr. Justice Fullerton was later appointed chairman of the board of trustees, and S. J. Hungerford continued as chief operating officer, with the title of president.

In 1934 and again in 1935, Mr. Bennett saw fit to revive the practice of granting titles, discontinued since 1919. While it was generally admitted that if titles must be granted at all, those who received them were, in most cases, worthy of recognition, nevertheless, except for a relatively small number of sentimental traditionalists, it was felt that in restoring titles Mr. Bennett had consulted his own wishes rather than those of the majority of the people in whose name he presumably acted.

For many years the establishment of a central bank had been advocated, principally by the Labour and agrarian groups, but the idea had been frowned upon by those of orthodox financial views. But, in 1934, the Bennett government introduced legislation to establish the Bank of Canada. The new bank was to serve as the fiscal agent of the government, maintain the flow of credit and capital, and, in short, to make possible that managed currency which had previously been the subject of so much orthodox scorn. Eventually, it would be the only bank to issue notes for general circulation.

The Bank of Canada, however, was not to be owned by the government. Its $5,000,000 capital stock was offered for subscription to the public. The bank was to be directed by a governor, deputy governor, assistant deputy governor, and a board of seven directors. The first executive officers were to be appointed by the government, after which they would be appointed by the directors. (Some of these provisions were changed after the Liberals returned to power.) The bank, of course, does not accept deposits from private persons; its customers, aside from the government, are the chartered banks, which are required to maintain a reserve of not less than 5 per cent of their deposit liabilities in notes of the bank.

The Farmers' Creditors Arrangement Act, 1934, was one which, under other circumstances, a government headed by a man of Mr. Bennett's views could never have considered; but the depression had shattered the preconceived ideas of sterner men than Bennett. The purpose of the act was to enable farmers to retain their homes, even though liable to foreclosure through arrears of principal and interest. Provision was made for the scaling-down of the indebtedness, the amounts so reduced not to remain as continuing liabilities.

Another act, in connection with the depression, for which the Bennett government was responsible, was the Prairie Farm Rehabilitation Act, which received royal assent on April 17, 1935. It provided, by means of tree culture and water conservation, for the rehabilitation of lands, subject to soil drifting or drought, in Manitoba, Saskatchewan and Alberta.

Unfortunately, the obsession for 'economy' which had marked the Bennett regime had prevented such an obviously desirable project as the damming of the Saskatchewan river, to provide water for irrigation and other purposes, which, after twenty years, still remains to be done.

CHAPTER XXII

RISE OF THE SPLINTER PARTIES

MR. KING'S claim that only under Conservative governments did third-party movements develop in Canada was more than borne out during the Bennett regime. The revolt against the two-party system which had produced the Progressives when Borden and Meighen were in power, and had kept the cross-benches more or less tenanted ever since, now, under Bennett, produced not merely one, but three new parties.

In 1921, the editor and publishers of the Ottawa *Citizen* had become converts to a plan of fiscal reform advocated by Major C. H. Douglas, a British engineer, which was based in part on the thesis that in boom times the investment of capital tends more and more to concentrate in the production of plant and equipment, and that the portion of the national income available for consumer-spending becomes correspondingly less. This results in restricted buying, the slowing-down of production, and the laying-off of workers until a balance is reached between production and consumption. In this way, Douglas attempted to account for the recurrent slumps and booms of the capitalist system.

Douglas was no socialist; he believed in the capitalist system. Control of credit and currency was the thing he wished the government to assume. As circumstances required, purchasing power could be increased simply by issuing it, or, as some of the advocates of the scheme termed it, 'by a scratch of the pen'.

One of the methods suggested by Douglas to put purchasing power into the hands of the consumer was to distribute the difference between the national income and the available amount of purchasing power equally among the people through a 'national dividend'.

It was argued, as justification for such a distribution, that the community, as such, also plays a part in the productive process, and consequently is entitled to a share of the proceeds. He contended that so long as the amount of purchasing power did not exceed the value of available consumer goods there could be no inflation.

Social Credit, as it is called, did not at first make many converts in Canada, but William Irvine made a number of speeches in and out of the House advocating ideas derived from Douglas. He later succeeded in having Douglas' proposals referred to the Standing Committee on Banking and Commerce when a revision of the Bank Act was being considered, and was instrumental in having Douglas appear as a witness.

After the disintegration of the Progressives, the Alberta members, soon to become known as the 'Ginger Group', had found themselves more and more thrown into association with Woodsworth and his Labour associate, or associates, of the moment, generally supporting the same things, seconding one another's motions, and, as a rule, finding themselves members of the same minority in divisions.

Although Woodsworth was a socialist, many of the things he advocated could have been supported by any advanced non-socialist. His arguments often constituted an indictment of the existing economic order, but so did those of the Alberta group, although not all professing socialism. There was no great difference between Wood's co-operative groups and Woodsworth's co-operative society, except that Woodsworth would include everyone, while the Albertans wished to confine their co-operation to people of like economic interest.

In the end, Woodsworth's views and their own became indistinguishable, and in May 1932, at a meeting held in Woodsworth's room in the House of Commons, it was decided to attempt the formation of a national organization. Each member, after discussing the matter with the organization he represented, agreed to attend a later meeting in Calgary to which representatives from other congenial groups would be invited.

At this meeting, held in August, a provisional national council was appointed, of which Woodsworth was elected chairman; plans for a nation-wide organizing campaign were drawn up; and a date was tentatively set for a national convention in Regina the following year. The name chosen for this new political organization was: the Co-operative Commonwealth Federation, or C.C.F., as it shortly became known.

The original idea was that the C.C.F. should be a federation of existing organizations, such as the United Farmers of Alberta, the United Farmers of Canada (Saskatchewan section), various provincial Labour parties, and other groups holding similar ideas. In Ontario, despite their recent unfortunate experience in politics, the

United Farmers of Ontario, at their annual convention, decided to throw in their lot with the C.C.F. Small Labour groups in a number of the larger cities also quickly joined; but at a mass meeting held by Woodsworth in Toronto in November, more than 1,000 men and women having no occupational affiliation signed cards signifying their desire to join.

Since no provision had been made for individual membership, units called 'C.C.F. Clubs' were formed, generally one to a federal riding, into which these recruits could be enrolled. The first C.C.F. Club was organized in Toronto on December 22, 1932, and within three months about 100 had come into being throughout Ontario. Thus the C.C.F. quite early departed from its original basis, and it was possible for a person to be a member without belonging to any occupational group.

The depression was now nearing its climax; dissatisfaction with the existing economic system was widespread. From the Ottawa river to the Pacific, varying with the locality, people flocked to the C.C.F. Its progress was watched with interest by all and with fear by many old-line politicians. In July 1933, as arranged the previous year, a national convention (attended by delegates from six provinces) was held in Regina at which a 14-point manifesto was adopted and Woodsworth was confirmed as chairman.

James Shaver Woodsworth was a remarkable man. He was born at Islington, near Toronto, the same year as Mackenzie King and Arthur Meighen, with whom he was to sit in the House of Commons for so many years. In 1882, his father, a Methodist minister, moved to a mission field in Manitoba, and James grew up in the prairie communities of Portage la Prairie and Brandon. Educated at Wesley College, Winnipeg, Victoria College, Toronto, and Oxford University, he entered the Methodist ministry and began mission work in Saskatchewan, later holding the position of associate minister of Grace Church, Winnipeg.

While at Grace Church, he came to doubt the effectiveness of the Church as an advocate of Christian principles, as he saw them; he believed that it should take more active steps toward the creation of a Christian social order. He therefore offered his resignation, but the Conference declined to accept it. Then followed six busy years in the heart of North Winnipeg as superintendent of All People's Mission, where he worked among the immigrants being poured into Winnipeg by the trainload.

Woodsworth was secretary of the Canadian Welfare League at

the outbreak of World War I, and by 1916 had become director of the Bureau of Social Research, maintained in Winnipeg by the three prairie provinces, when an issue arose which touched deep springs within his nature. Instinctively hating war, and believing it to be contrary to the principles of Christian living, he wrote a letter of protest to the *Manitoba Free Press* concerning the National Registration scheme then proposed by the Borden government. 'This registration is no mere census,' he wrote. 'It seems to look in the direction of a measure of conscription. As some of us cannot conscientiously engage in military service, we are bound to resist what—if the war continues—will inevitably lead to forced service.'

That was the end of his job. With Mrs. Woodsworth and their young children, he moved to the Pacific coast, securing a small church at Port Gibson, a few miles from Vancouver, where they were happy; but his support of a co-operative store, operated in competition with the most influential member of his congregation, brought his ministry to a close. This time he insisted on his resignation being accepted.

Then, to support his family, this frail man, in poor health, worked on the Vancouver docks as a longshoreman. This led to his becoming a member of a union and finally a writer and lecturer for the trades union movement. Invited to undertake a speaking tour of western Canada in 1919, he found himself back in Winnipeg during the general strike. This sequence of events ended two years later by his being elected to the House of Commons.

The C.C.F.'s first chance to measure its strength with the two old parties was in 1934, when elections occurred in Ontario and Saskatchewan. Although candidates were nominated in the principal towns and cities of Ontario, only one member was elected against the victorious sweep of the Liberals under 'Mitch' Hepburn, who defeated the Conservative administration in office since 1923. In Saskatchewan, where five seats were won, the C.C.F. became the official opposition.

In the meantime, the ideas of Major Douglas, having failed to stir anyone to political action in Ontario, had blossomed forth in Alberta, whose people had sought for a long time without success to find a formula that would lead them out of their troubles. The words may have been the words of Major Douglas, but the voice, day in and day out, was the voice of William Aberhart. A schoolteacher, he had a way of combining biblical injunctions with economic philosophizing that appealed to the people of Alberta, especially farm folk.

In 1921, Alberta farmers had hopefully elected a government chiefly composed of their fellow-farmers, but these it seemed were no better than the representatives of the old parties whom they had already kicked out. Powerless to arrest the drift of the terrible depression, which had taken its toll of everyone, they had also failed to break the grip of eastern financiers, whose control was now tighter than ever. Then, to make matters worse, leaders of the Farmers' government had become implicated in scandals involving women, which shocked the farm folk, in whom there is a broad puritanical streak, and they were now in the proper frame of mind to respond to the seductive radio voice.

When the Farmers' government called an election in 1935, William Aberhart and his Prophetic Bible Institute had already awakened new hope in the breasts of the distrustful farmers. For those to whom a dollar looked slightly larger than a cartwheel, the promise of dividends running perhaps to twenty-five dollars a month seemed almost too good to be true, but the advocates of the new, exciting philosophy explained how it could be done.

Did not the banks, for the benefit of the big interests, create credit merely by the scratch of a pen? Why could not the government, acting for the people, who produced the country's wealth, do likewise? The radio voice said it could be done.

It could not be denied that in this land of vast resources, which for years had produced crop after crop of the finest wheat and shipped top-quality beef and pork to market, the people, neither lazy nor shiftless, were mortgaged to moneylenders from whose grasp there seemed little chance of deliverance.

Ah, yes! There was a chance of deliverance. And on the 22nd of August, the farm people of Alberta flocked to the polls and voted out the Farmers' government which they themselves had elected with such hopes fourteen years before. William Aberhart, who had never sat in a legislative assembly of any sort, became Premier.

Aberhart's task was a hard one, and he soon found that his stock of political ideas would not fit into the realities of the established order; Alberta was not by any means an autonomous community. Especially the control of money and credit, so important in the Social Credit program, was entirely within the jurisdiction of the federal government, which was very jealous of any infringement upon its authority. Nevertheless, in view of the difficulties which beset him,

William Aberhart faced his task with high courage and displayed no little capacity for public affairs.

What with the C.C.F. and Social Credit parties already having gained a foothold within legislative halls, Mr. King's contention was well enough sustained, but there now appeared another new party, one formed from a rib of the Conservative party itself.

Some time during the latter part of 1933, Mr. Bennett had agreed to be the speaker at the annual meeting of the National Shoe Retailers' Association to be held in Toronto on January 15, 1934. He had accepted with the usual stipulation that if he were not available on that date some other minister might speak in his place. And that is how it came about that Harry Stevens, Minister of Trade and Commerce, kept the appointment instead.

Stevens had received various complaints from manufacturers about the treatment they claimed to be getting from department and chain stores. Among other things, they alleged that these organizations, possessed of immense purchasing power, were in the habit of beating them down to the lowest possible price before placing an order. This led to sweat-shop conditions in a number of industries. Furthermore, having secured an advantageous price, the mass-buying organizations would then sell the product at prices just under what small retailers must secure, thereby rendering it impossible for the latter to compete.

Mulling over the implications of such practices, Stevens, once a small retailer himself, decided that this might be a good subject to discuss with the shoe retailers. His success was greater than he dreamed. Not only were the shoe men interested, but when the newspapers and press agencies had reported his remarks, an avalanche of letters, telegrams and telephone calls almost overwhelmed him. Overnight, Stevens had become the hero of the thousands of little merchants across the country who lived in fear of the oncoming chain-store menace.

Not all the response was favourable. Those criticized were not slow in making themselves heard, and for a time Bennett's telephone buzzed with calls from Toronto and Montreal. Stevens offered to resign, but Bennett would not hear of it. He could be independent when the notion seized him, and he was more pleased than otherwise with the furore stirred up by his colleague. On February 2, he himself moved for the appointment of a select special committee with wide powers to enquire into the spread between prices received by producers and those paid by consumers; the effect of mass buying by chain and department stores; labour and wage conditions in these industries; the marketing of livestock and other farm products; and other similar matters.

The committee, consisting of six Conservatives, with Stevens as chairman, four Liberals and one U.F.A. member, immediately undertook the task, and soon its proceedings overshadowed those of parliament itself. People from all over Canada flocked to Ottawa. The precincts of parliament and the Chateau Laurier were thronged with lawyers and public relations counsel, representing clients on all sides of the controversy. Not since the days of the Canadian Northern lobby had there been such a concourse of special pleaders in Ottawa. As the investigation dug deeper into the hitherto hidden details of mercantile life, everyone connected with it, except the small retailers and manufacturers, wished heartily that it had never been begun.

On June 29, in order to sit during the parliamentary recess, the committee was converted into a Royal Commission, with no change in membership.

Some time later, Stevens addressed a study club of Conservative M.P.s on the subject of the investigation, and multigraphed copies of his address were made available. Copies reached some of those criticized—unfairly, they claimed—and complaints were again made to Bennett. Stevens, on his way to Vancouver, was reached by telephone at Winnipeg, but was able to satisfy his chief that the pamphlet was meant only for private circulation. Publication early in August of the text of the pamphlet added further fuel to the flames.

Bennett, however, was on his way to a League meeting in Geneva, and it was not until after his return that the subject came up again for discussion. At a cabinet meeting, Bennett and other ministers complained to Stevens about misstatements in the pamphlet, suggesting that he make some public explanation and suitable correction. Apparently Stevens did not agree with this, for the following day, October 26, he resigned both the chairmanship of the commission and his post in the cabinet.

Stevens' resignation led directly to the formation of a new political party, called the National Reconstruction party, with Stevens as its leader. Its membership consisted largely of those engaged in various kinds of business as well as some who had not found a congenial place in the other parties.

In ordinary circumstances, an election would have been held in 1934, but the time did not look propitious to Bennett, and he held off. It was therefore not till August 14, 1935, that parliament was dissolved and the elections set for October 14. The campaign was one of the strangest in Canadian history. Never had the electors such an array of parties from which to choose.

The great unknown was the C.C.F. Born of the depression, it had made the cause of the jobless its own. In some provinces it was allied with the organized farmers, and with Labour in nearly every province. Its leader, with a record of devotion to the cause of the oppressed and the unfortunate, was known as an able speaker and parliamentarian. Among C.C.F. candidates across the country were an unusual proportion of teachers and other professional men and women, including many with experience in municipal affairs.

On the other hand, the tide had already begun to ebb for the C.C.F. During the depths of the depression, people in all walks of life had turned to it, but it had also attracted an aggregation of crack-pots and opportunists whose doctrinaire pronouncements and continual bickering caused many to doubt whether it could be effective if it should attain office. Furthermore, it had become infiltrated with both Stalinist and Trotskyist communists who used it as a battle-ground for their own internecine warfare. In addition, there were some who joined it for the purpose of advancing the interests of one or other of the old parties to whom they still held allegiance.

The National Reconstruction party, on the other hand, had all the advantages of a crusade still in its first flush. It, too, had attracted its share of opportunists and others not satisfied with the appreciation they had received from the older parties; but, in general, its candidates, although lacking in parliamentary experience, were men and women of consequence in their respective communities.

The wrongs they wished to right, however, touched only a small portion of the people; and, to those experienced in elections, the main question, insofar as the Reconstruction party was concerned, was to what extent it would contribute to the defeat of the Conservatives.

Undoubtedly, the battle was between the two old parties. Both were well organized, well financed, and both carried on a strenuous campaign. As in 1926, it became a duel between rival leaders.

By now, Mackenzie King's political personality had become well established, although even yet, to most people, somewhat vague in outline. A small and seemingly insignificant man, he apparently did nothing to overcome that appearance. Nevertheless, he more than any other public figure of his time was more truly representative of the average Canadian. While the tendency of his mind was not radical, he had no fear of change; what he wanted to know about a new proposal was whether it was too far ahead of the people's thinking.

King's critics, among his followers as well as his opponents, accused him of always keeping his ear to the ground. This was true, but King never forgot that, in a democracy, the people have the final word; and he knew that the leader who could best gauge the public mind would be most likely to remain longest in power. King's career provides eloquent testimony to his sagacity in this respect.

Bennett, on the other hand, and Meighen, to a greater extent, were more concerned with moulding the people to their own will; and, if they could have done so, they would have put into effect policies which a majority might be against, if they themselves believed in them. Such a course was impossible to King.

In the House, King feared Meighen, and was never comfortable while he led the opposition. By temperament, as well as by experience, King had developed a circuitous approach to every problem, leaving himself ample opportunity for later modification should the need arise. Meighen could always see through these circumlocutions and with merciless logic expose them.

Bennett, on the other hand, while having as great a memory for details as Meighen, or King, was more superficial than either; instead of avoiding commitments, as King always tried to do, he walked into one after another without any apparent concern for the consequences; and his own words, like chickens, continually came home to roost.

King had a fairly consistent set of political doctrines which, however, fitted into no known system of economics. This he had put into his book, *Industry and Humanity*, published in 1918, and his economic thinking had changed very little in the interval.

Bennett had never written a book; if he had, he might have been the gainer. Ideas which seem sound in casual contemplation are seen for what they are when spread over the pages of a book. Bennett had become imbued with the political maxims common during the latter part of the nineteenth century, and although he had lived on the prairies for nearly forty years, and, for most of that time, had been involved in business and politics, his views had not materially changed.

Therefore, as the year 1935 opened, Bennett confounded both friends and foes by a widely-heralded political conversion, going on the air with a series of talks in which he outlined a program 'more comprehensive, more far-reaching, than any scheme of reform this country has ever known'.

Many of his hearers were frankly sceptical, attributing his action to a rather indecent anxiety concerning the coming elections. Others believed he had been persuaded of the virtues of the welfare state by his brother-in-law, W. D. Herridge, whom he had appointed Canadian ambassador at Washington, and who was supposed to have imbibed such views from Franklin Roosevelt's New Deal.

Bennett's 'fireside talks' were given over a radio network of thirty-eight stations, beginning on the evening of January 2, and continuing at intervals till January 11.

This is a critical hour in the history of our country [he began]. . . . In the last five years great changes have taken place in the world. The old order is gone. It will not return. . . . Your prosperity demands corrections in the old system, so that, in the new conditions, that old system may adequately serve you.

He then turned to a discussion of conditions as they were when his government took over in 1930, and the picture he gave was not very flattering. If that was what they wanted, he warned his listeners, 'you and I hold contrary and irreconcilable views. *I am for reform* . . . And in my mind reform means government intervention. I nail the flag of progress to the masthead. I summon the power of the State to its support.'

In a particularly moving passage, he declared that 'Canada on the dole is like a young and vigorous man in the poorhouse. The dole is a condemnation, final and complete, of our economic system. If we cannot abolish the dole, we should abolish the system.' Many of his hearers would have agreed with him, but they could not forget that for five years he had been the one person in whose hands lay the power to change the very conditions of which he now complained. And perhaps in anticipation of this objection, he declared that 'unwise or untimely action might well have been disastrous', but he did not attempt to explain just how.

In his second speech, on January 4, he reiterated his belief in the 'need of reform of the capitalist system', and went on to demonstrate his fitness to criticize that system. 'From the days of my early manhood,' he said, 'I have watched the ways of capitalism.' As a lawyer, as a director of large financial corporations, and in other ways, he had had opportunity to study the iniquities of the capitalist system, and he repeated that 'the economic system must be reformed . . . capitalism must change to meet the changed conditions of this new world if it is longer adequately to serve you'. Reform seemed to be the refrain of his song.

Elaborating, he declared that 'I think there is, from all worth-while points of view, an inequality in the distribution of income, and I think . . . there must be devised . . . a better balance. . . . For I doubt if the present disequilibrium can indefinitely continue without serious injury to our whole economic system.'

In the third talk, on January 7, he discussed the economic system as it affected the farmers, stressing what he had already done to mitigate the condition of the farm community by his Farmers' Creditors Arrangement Act, outlining further legislation which he proposed to enact.

The fourth talk, on January 9, consisted mainly of justification of his past policies; and in this connection he declared that 'the results of the Ottawa Conference were the first and in some ways the most important of our recovery measures'.

Then, on January 11, he remembered the existence of the Liberal party and told his hearers exactly where the Liberals stood with respect to reform. They were against it. Once, a long time ago, the Liberal party had been a forward-looking party, but it had degenerated. What was its present attitude? Why, 'at a time when your government were fighting for the life of this country, we were handicapped and embarrassed and opposed by a party which seemed to think far more of getting back into office than it did of you'.

He really felt sorry for the decrepit old Liberal party, with its sights so twisted. 'When young Liberals come to ask, "What did the Liberal party do in the Great Depression?" I am glad that someone else will have to answer them,' he said sadly.

In resting his case with the jurors, in his best defence-attorney style, he said: 'My case you know. Reform or no reform; action or reaction; progress or stagnation; equality, justice; the people before all else. The decision is for you to make.'

In the Speech from the Throne at the opening of parliament a week later, the government announced that it would introduce measures to correct some of the evils of which Bennett had complained:

Action will be taken to ameliorate the condition of Labour . . . to safeguard the consumer and primary producer against unfair trading practices and to regulate, in the public interest, concentration in production and distribution . . . measures to provide the investing public with means to protect itself against exploitation . . .

Unfortunately, the courts later found much of this legislation beyond the jurisdiction of parliament.

One still-born measure was a tariff-reducing agreement (shades of 1911!) which Bennett had negotiated with the Roosevelt administration, but which had not been signed when the sands ran out on his government. Mr. King gleefully signed (and took credit for) it shortly after returning to power.

King, and especially Woodsworth and other C.C.F. speakers, treated Bennett's deathbed repentance rather irreverently. King, feeling the drift toward newer economic ideas, had begun himself to criticize the sacred cause of capitalism; he, too, insisted that the only road to salvation lay in its reform. Woodsworth, on the other hand, had for years been preaching that capitalism had outlived its usefulness; that it could not be reformed; that, basically, it was a system of organized selfishness, and nothing else would do but its replacement by a system based upon the 'production and distribution of goods and services for the general welfare'.

King, his ear to the ground, was confident that a groundswell favourable to the Liberals had set in. When he had gone out of office in 1930, most of the provincial governments were in Conservative hands; but since then, British Columbia, Saskatchewan, Ontario, and Nova Scotia had returned to the Liberal fold. At a mass meeting in Toronto a week before election day, by means of a nation-wide radio hook-up, the voices of eight provincial premiers were heard in support of Mackenzie King and the Liberal party. All this, to a seasoned campaigner like King, seemed to augur well for the Liberals.

On election night, Mackenzie King stood vindicated. His party had carried 171 seats, by far the greatest number ever won by the party; while the Conservatives, with but 39, were at their lowest in history. The National Reconstruction party carried only one seat, that of Stevens himself which, by rights, might have been included in the Conservative column. The C.C.F. had 7 seats, and among those elected in Saskatchewan were M. J. Coldwell, destined to be a future leader of the party, and T. C. Douglas, who was to head the first socialist government in Canada.

As remarkable, in its way, as any other result, was the winning of 15 of the 17 seats in Alberta (and 2 elsewhere) by the Social Credit party. Such stalwarts as G. G. Coote, Robert Gardiner, E. J. Garland, William Irvine, D. M. Kennedy and Alfred Speakman had fallen in the fray, never again—with the exception of Irvine—to reappear in parliament.

The unfairness of the prevailing system of voting was never better exemplified than in this election. The Liberals polled 1,955,727 votes to gain their 171 seats, while the Conservatives, with 1,311,459 votes, had won only 39. Social Credit, with only 182,767 votes, had won 17 seats, while the National Reconstruction party received 384,215 votes, but could only claim one seat. Or, in other words, to elect one member, Social Credit needed to poll 10,751 votes; the Liberals 11,437 votes; the Conservatives 34,909 votes; the C.C.F. 56,694 votes; and the Reconstruction party 384,215 votes.

The Liberals, in 1919, had endorsed proportional representation, and in the interval, while out of office, had more than once paid lip-service to it, but when in office had never shown any disposition to adopt it. In 1935, it would have reduced their standing in the House, but the result would have been much more representative of the country at large. That, however, is one of the last things political parties are concerned about. A smacking majority is what they want, but when this occurs they often have cause to regret it.

CHAPTER XXIII

ONCE MORE THE SCOURGE OF WAR

ALTHOUGH upwards of a million people were on the dole when King resumed office on October 23, 1935, Canada had begun to emerge from the miasmic mists of despondency that had settled over the country in the dark days of '32 and '33. Canada was emerging in the same way that it had plunged into the depression—in the wake of the United States. That country, under the hypnotic spell of Franklin Roosevelt, had now regained its courage and self-confidence. Canadians were getting the benefit of this new attitude and the better times that resulted from it.

The cabinet contained a few new members, and, on the whole, was an experienced and able group of men to face with King the exceedingly great problems of which they were yet happily in the dark. Mr. King himself took the post of Minister of External Affairs, and his loyal friend Lapointe was back as Minister of Justice. Dunning was again Minister of Finance; Cardin was Minister of Public Works; Crerar, Minister of Mines (and three other departments); and Ian Mackenzie, of Vancouver, Minister of National Defence.

Among the new men were Norman McLeod Rogers, member of a brilliant Nova Scotia family, previously one of King's secretaries, who became Minister of Labour; James L. Ilsley, another Maritimer, Minister of National Revenue; Clarence D. Howe, a professor and engineer, Minister of Railways, little realizing what lay before him; C. G. 'Chubby' Power, who, despite his name, was counted a French-speaking member of the cabinet, Minister of Pensions and National Health; and James G. Gardiner, former Premier of Saskatchewan, Minister of Agriculture.

While the Canadian people were mainly preoccupied with their own affairs, they were becoming increasingly aware of the shadow hanging over Europe. During the twenties, in common with most of the world, they had experienced a revulsion against war. They had read Remarque's *All Quiet on the Western Front*, and had flocked to see Sherriff's *Journey's End*. They had largely ceased to hold the old gentleman living quietly at Doorn, Holland, responsible for the world war; but, after reading Beverley Nichols' *Cry Havoc* and George Drew's *Salesmen of Death*, were inclined to throw the blame on the munitions-dealers. The new villains were Zaharoff, Krupp, and other high-class ironmongers. Peace pledges had been signed by millions who applauded the efforts of those seeking by international agreement to outlaw war.

Canadians had not yet seen, in the dramatic appearance of a dictator in Italy, the outward evidence of a desperate people's attempt to extricate itself from the slough of humiliation and despair into which it was sunk. Mussolini, to most, was but a 'Sawdust Caesar', an amiable jackanapes who, nevertheless, could make the trains run on time, and had no patience with socialists, trades unionists and other trouble-seekers.

Even when Hitler emerged, the significance of what was about to happen was not apparent. From the first, his behaviour plainly marked him as a paranoiac, with such typical characteristics as delusions of persecution and delusions of grandeur. His was an extreme case of over-compensation arising out of feelings of frustration and inferiority afflicting the whole German nation.

What more natural, then, that the German people should respond to his call? While it was still possible to prevent his rise by correcting in another way the evils from which the Germans were suffering, the countries concerned—Great Britain, France, the United States, and, farther down the list, Canada—failed to read the signs. And when the portents became clear it was too late: only force remained.

It is commonly supposed that the part played by its troops in World War I gained for Canada a place among the nations of the world, but this had little to do with the question. In the first years of the war, Canada's contingents were, as a matter of course, part of the British army, and even when the Canadian Corps was eventually organized as a separate unit, it was still commanded by a British general. Only after Canadian troops, and especially General Currie, had been measured against the troops and leaders of other countries did it become evident to Sir Robert Borden and his ministers that Canada should manage its own affairs, in war as in peace.

By the same process of reasoning, Sir Robert Borden insisted that Canada should be represented at the Peace Conference, and should sign the Peace Treaties. He also insisted on Canada's right to independent membership in the League of Nations.

From the first, Canadian delegates had advocated the repeal of Article X of the Covenant, which pledged members 'to respect and preserve as against external aggression the territorial integrity and existing political independence of members of the League', leaving to the Council of the League the decision as to what action should be taken in cases of aggression.

At the General Assembly meeting in 1922, Mr. Lapointe had proposed an amendment to Article X, the purport of which was that 'no member shall be under obligation to engage in any act of war without the consent of its parliament, legislature or other representative body'. On the vote, 29 countries had supported the amendment, 22 had abstained, and one had voted against it. As a result, the president did not declare it lost, but merely 'not adopted', which seems a distinction without a difference.

The attitude of the Canadian government was at least clear. Having established the right to participate or not as it saw fit in British wars, Canada, as a North American nation, in no way responsible for Europe's dissensions, refused to be drawn, willy-nilly, into Europe's wars.

During the Bennett regime, the regular delegate to the League was G. Howard Ferguson, onetime Premier of Ontario, High Commissioner in London since 1930. With the change in government on October 23, 1935, Ferguson had been replaced by Dr. Walter A. Riddell, an officer of the Department of External Affairs, who had represented Canada on the International Labour Organization, a division of the League. Riddell had come to be a firm believer in the League's mission, and, like many others, was convinced that in its hands lay the power to prevent future wars.

This conviction was not peculiar to people in the League's official family; many in Canada and in other countries felt the same way. Some of the most ardent League supporters in Canada had been consistent advocates of Canadian autonomy for whom membership in the League was a further step. For this transference of allegiance they had no feeling of disloyalty, for was not the Commonwealth, as it was now called, also part of the League? The League became merely the object of a higher loyalty.

Although Canada's part had been a minor one all along, events during the autumn of 1935 were about to bring it unexpected and undesired prominence. The Italian dictator had determined to add Ethiopia, also a member of the League, to his dominions. All summer he had been conducting propaganda toward that end, accompanied by appropriate diplomatic activity. On October 2, Italian troops with high explosives, poison gas and aircraft advanced against the defence-less Ethiopians. This was a direct affront to the League, but an inevitable outcome of the existing conditions of European politics.

The League was the handmaiden of the Treaty of Versailles, designed to enforce the penalties imposed upon the vanquished; but the treaty had set in motion forces which the League was powerless to control. The dictators were the spawn of the war and the peace; and no power which the League could invoke would prevent them from weaving to the end their woeful destiny.

It is safe to say that no country in the world favoured Italy's action, the United Kingdom and France least of all. But both had had an unfortunate history in North Africa. As far back as the mid-eighties of the nineteenth century, the United Kingdom, in order to have a free hand in Egypt and the Sudan, had agreed not to interfere with France in Tunisia and Morocco. Then, in 1906, when both were blocking Germany's attempt to gain a foothold in North Africa, Italy's support was secured by recognition of its claims to territory in those parts of Africa in which England and France were not inter-ested, and, in 1911, Italy had advanced into Tripoli. Italy's claims were confirmed by the Treaty of London in 1915, when that country entered the war on the side of the Allies; and again in 1925 by an exchange of notes between the United Kingdom and Italy which recognized Italy's 'special interest' in Ethiopia.

In the meantime, England, France, Italy and Ethiopia had be-come members of the League, pledged 'to respect and preserve as against external aggression the territorial integrity and existing politi-cal independence of members of the League'. And although peace lovers had pinned their hopes to the good faith of countries sub-scribing to the League Covenant, only the very naïve believed that international morality had undergone a change.

The smaller nations took comfort in the thought that, if they were attacked, the mightiest nations in the world (outside of the United States, which was not a member) would rally to their defence. These small nations constituted a sort of conscience for the League, and by the power of world opinion were able at times to keep some of the larger ones in the path of rectitude.

Although not quite in the same category, Canada was frequently aligned with the other small nations. Canada's population was small, but its wealth and industrial capacity more appropriately placed it among the larger nations.

This was the situation, then, when Mussolini moved into Ethiopia. The Canadian people, engaged in deciding which of several New Jerusalems they would have, were too busy with the elections to bother much about what was happening in Ethiopia. But Dr. Riddell, at Geneva, was greatly concerned. At the moment, he was probably the freest agent there. He was almost a man without a country: the Bennett government had been defeated, and the King government had not yet fully taken over.

Riddell cabled for instructions, but received no reply. Meantime the League had declared Italy an aggressor (which King, in a press release, had approved), and moved toward the imposition of sanctions. In the opinion of Riddell and others who thought as he did, the proposed sanctions would prove ineffective unless oil, coal and iron and steel were included.

Riddell was a member of the Committee of Eighteen, considering the sanctions question. The feeling among committee members was unanimous for additional sanctions, but no one was willing to propose the necessary motion. Riddell therefore decided to do so, cabling Ottawa for concurrence.

The question was reached on the agenda before Riddell's reply came, and, taking a chance, he proposed the motion. The Committee approved the motion, and its report was unanimously accepted by the Co-ordination Committee, consisting of representatives of all League members except those involved in the dispute.

When the news went out to the world, it was reported that Canada had moved to impose the oil sanction on Italy, and the fact that the resolution was unanimously approved by the Committee received much less prominence. In Canada, the news was received with mixed feelings. Those who had wanted a League with 'teeth' were delighted; others were proud that Canada was taking such a leading part in League affairs; but many were fearful that Riddell's action would involve Canada in the sort of entanglements that successive governments had sought to avoid.

Opposition came from Quebec, some from autonomists, who feared entanglements, and some from sympathizers with the Italian cause. Mackenzie King had departed on a holiday in the United States, taking along Dr. O. D. Skelton, Deputy Minister of External Affairs, leaving Ernest Lapointe to act as minister during his absence. When the implications of Riddell's action became apparent, Lapointe issued a press statement explaining that Riddell had acted on his own authority, and not in accordance with the views of the government.

That was the end of sanctions. The result would have been the same in any event. The big powers, as shown by the Hoare-Laval agreement, almost immediately afterward, were not prepared to intervene in the Ethiopian affair, and would have found other means to evade the League's edict. The Canadian government was castigated by the Winnipeg *Free Press*, and other newspapers and individuals who had erected a League to suit their hopes. Overlooking the League's failure to check Japan in 1931, and later evidences of its futility, these enthusiasts accused Canada of scuttling the League, some even going so far as to blame Canada for the Second World War.[1]

Mr. King's policy, in the face of the rising storm in Europe, was typically North American. In 1936, the United States, to prevent possible involvement in a European war, had passed a neutrality act. Mr. King, on his part, adhered to the policy of 'no entanglements'. If the United Kingdom were to become involved in a war of consequence, no one expected Canada would remain neutral; but Mr. King maintained the right of parliament to decide each case on its merits when the time came. (If he could control his Liberal majority, Mr. King could, of course, control parliament.)

Canadians, in common with the rest of the western world, became delirious over Munich, and followed in revulsion when hopes then raised were shattered by the conquest of Czechoslovakia. Mackenzie King, the optimist, like a prudent mariner, watched the international barometer, and began to batten the hatches against the possibility of a storm.

During the Bennett regime, plans for the mobilization, if necessary, of Canada's manpower had been drawn up by General Andrew McNaughton, then Chief of the General Staff. In 1935, Bennett, who did not entirely agree with McNaughton's views, transferred him to the National Research Council, as its head, for McNaughton was also a scientist. Upon King's return to office, the McNaughton plan once more became the official blueprint.

The plan called for a highly mechanized corps of two, possibly three, divisions, and appropriate extensions of air and naval services. McNaughton, who in World War I had been an artillery commander, had been imbued with the need for the maintenance of forces completely under the control of the Canadian authorities. Furthermore, he placed more emphasis upon mechanized equipment than upon

[1] For an exposition of this point of view, see Riddell, W. A.: *World Security by Conference*, Toronto, 1947.

foot soldiers, and believed that, in a future war, Canada could serve its allies best as an arsenal for munitions and other war materials and supplies, as well as food. With these views, the Mackenzie King administration, in the main, agreed.

Although the United States was seemingly determined to sit the next war out, its interests and those of Canada touched at too many points for either country to overlook the implications of a war in which Canada might be a belligerent. Despite the Neutrality Act, Roosevelt had declared in 1936 that the United States was prepared to defend itself and its neighbourhood against aggression; and had become more explicit in 1938, when he said at Kingston: 'The Dominion of Canada is part of the sisterhood of the British Empire. I give you assurance that the people of the United States will not stand idly by if domination of Canadian soil is threatened by any other empire.'

To this, Mackenzie King had responded a few days later in a speech at Woodbridge, Ontario, when he said:

The people of Canada deeply appreciate all that is implied by the President's visit. At the same time they know that they have their own responsibilities for maintaining Canadian soil as a homeland for free men in the western hemisphere. We, too, have our obligations as a good friendly neighbour, and one of them is to see that, should the occasion ever arise, enemy forces should not be able to pursue their way, either by land, sea, or air, to the United States, across Canadian territory.

In that same year an arrangement was made between Canada and the United Kingdom under which British pilots might come to Canada for long-distance flying and other advanced training. The British authorities had in mind that the necessary training establishments would be under their own control, but King insisted that they must be entirely Canadian. He was criticized as being narrowly nationalist, but he stuck to his point, and parliament appropriated $6,000,000 to cover the cost.

Canadians forgot their fears for a few weeks early in 1939 when, for the first time, they entertained their sovereigns, King George VI and Queen Elizabeth, who, attended by the Prime Minister, toured the country from coast to coast.

Although King at first believed Europe's troubles could be settled without war, each year from 1936 parliament was asked for increasing military appropriations, and other preparations were made for eventualities. Various boards and commissions, necessary in the event of war, were organized, ready to be proclaimed when needed.

When war seemed imminent, a state of 'apprehended war' was proclaimed under the War Measures Act, 1914, still on the Statute Books.

After Hitler marched into Poland, parliament met in special session on September 7. The Speech from the Throne, consisting of only 33 lines in *Hansard*, was one of the shortest on record, and according to opposition critics, one of the most ambiguous. Parliament was summoned 'in order that the government may seek authority for the measures necessary for the defence of Canada, and for co-operation in the determined effort which is being made to resist further aggression, and to prevent the appeal to force instead of to pacific means in the settlement of international disputes'. Nothing was said in the Speech about going to war.

In the Commons, the procedure was no different from the opening of any other session. Tributes were paid to deceased members, reports and orders-in-council were tabled, and Mr. King announced changes in the cabinet that had occurred since the House prorogued, most important of which was the acceptance of Dunning's resignation, the day previously, and the appointment of Colonel James L. Ralston as Minister of Finance. Ralston had been defeated in 1935 and, in the interval, had resumed his Montreal law-practice. That was all for the day; the House adjourned at 4.10 p.m.

Next day, according to custom, the Address in Reply to the Speech from the Throne was moved, in a speech of about forty minutes, by one Liberal backbencher, and seconded by another, after which the leader of the opposition, Dr. R. J. Manion, who had been chosen at a convention in Ottawa the previous year to succeed R. B. Bennett, pledged his party's support, if war was meant, but he was somewhat at a loss to determine just what the government had in mind.

Doubt was dispelled when Mackenzie King's turn came to speak. In a long, rambling speech, he made it clear that Canada was going into the war as a principal, on its own volition. He outlined measures being considered. First among these was the defence of Canada and Canadian trade; next, economic aid to those engaged in the same crusade; but he left under the heading of matters to be considered when the time came, the question of an expeditionary force. It was not ruled out, but it was not discussed. And he stated that a declaration of war would follow the adoption of the Address.

On one thing, he was definite and specific. 'I now wish to repeat the undertaking I gave in parliament on behalf of the government on March 30, last,' he declared. 'The present government believe that conscription of men for overseas service will not be necessary or an effective step. No such measure will be introduced by the present administration.'

J. S. Woodsworth followed, and a hush descended upon the House as he rose to speak. His views were well known. He was an uncompromising pacifist, but in his eighteen years in the House his sincerity and transparent honesty had gained the respect of most of those who opposed nearly everything he stood for. And probably more than one envied him the courage which enabled him at that moment to face a hostile House and make a statement with which, not excluding members of the party he had led for six years, none would agree.

Denying that force could ever be overcome by further force, and pointing to the state of the world as evidence, he declared that 'it requires a great deal of courage to trust in moral force', and, speaking of his own boys, he said that he hoped that 'if any one, . . . not from cowardice but really through belief, is willing to take his stand on this matter and, if necessary, to face a concentration camp or a firing-squad, I shall be more proud of that boy than if he enlisted for war'.

This brought a cry of 'shame' from a Tory who had been in the House only since the 1935 election, and members on both sides blushed for him.

Woodsworth made it plain that he spoke only for himself. (The following day, M. J. Coldwell, to whom the leadership had passed, with certain reservations, pledged C.C.F. support for the war.) The ordeal through which Woodsworth had passed in the days since the world had turned again to war was too much for his frail strength. A few months later he suffered a stroke, and, on March 21, 1942, he died.

Canada could ill afford the loss of a man of Woodsworth's stature. Because he represented a point of view which is fundamental to any concept of civilization, even the great majority who disagreed with him were poorer for his death. While admitting the futility of force, Canadians believed themselves compelled to resort to it. Woodsworth, who belonged to no church, accepted literally the precept of the brotherhood of man, which, for him, precluded the killing of one's brother, even though he should be grievously in the wrong. He firmly believed that the only Christian way to ensure freedom and liberty was through a reliance upon 'the moral forces which are still resident among our people, and not by another resort to brute force'.

Many people in Canada believe as Woodsworth did, but with his death they were without a leader; their influence has counted for less than it might have done had there been someone about whom they might rally.

Two others, Maxime Raymond and Liguori Lacombe, opposed the war. Unlike Woodsworth, their opposition was not based on conscientious scruples, but on what they believed to be logical arguments. But war is not a matter of logic, its roots lie deep within the emotions, and whereas Woodsworth, whose plea was based on emotion, was listened to with respect, Raymond and Lacombe only aroused hostility. Nevertheless, in the light of what has happened since, their speeches, if the particular circumstances be overlooked, seem much more intelligent than most of the others delivered during that short session.

The Address was adopted on Saturday evening, September 9, at 10.25, and the next day Canada was at war with Germany.

In the meantime, King had been compelled to beat down the arguments of his friend and deputy-minister, Dr. O. D. Skelton, who tried to persuade him that Canada should remain neutral. Skelton's arguments, purely intellectual, were unanswerable in terms of logic. King, whose mind was not logical, but intuitive, believed that no government could remain in office, even for a day, which tried to keep Canada neutral. A certain type of Canadian of British ancestry, still numerous, would have plunged Canada into civil war to prevent such a thing.

On September 19, Norman Rogers became Minister of National Defence, and on that day a statement was issued outlining the government's plans. Canada's naval forces were already serving on both coasts. A division would be trained ready for despatch overseas when required, and a second division would be raised and kept under arms as a further measure of preparedness. In conformity with the plan already adopted, key men in industry would not be disturbed.

When, after Poland had been overrun, the supreme importance of air power was demonstrated, the British government proposed a joint air-training plan for the Commonwealth countries, the nucleus of which had already been established by arrangement with Canada in 1938. The eventual success of the scheme, which altogether cost Canada $1,281,000,000, was largely due to Canadian management and control, for which King had held out, and was a tribute to C. G. Power, Minister of National Defence for Air.

What of Quebec in this new war? As in 1914, Quebec people did not look with enthusiasm upon the prospect of war and all that it entailed. If they had been in a position to do so, they would gladly have followed the example of the United States and remained neutral. In 1936, the Liberal government of Adelard Godbout, which had succeeded the moribund Taschereau government, had been defeated by a combination of dissident Liberals and the Conservatives, now called Union Nationale, under Maurice Duplessis, the former Conservative leader. The Union Nationale government was inclined to consider the war a purely Liberal affair, and thirteen days after the declaration of war, the Quebec House was dissolved and an election called for October 23, with the war as the main issue. At that time the government held 73 seats in a House of 90.

Mr. Lapointe, who had taken his stand in a speech during the special session, in which, like his leader, he had specifically declared against conscription, with other *Canadien* members of the cabinet, including Power, immediately accepted Duplessis' challenge. Reiterating their promise not to remain in a government which adopted conscription for overseas service, they informed the people of Quebec that if the Duplessis government were returned, they would take it as a vote of want of confidence in themselves and resign from the cabinet. This would leave Quebec without representation at Ottawa. To make sure that no such contingency should occur, they threw themselves into the contest to such effect that the Liberals under Godbout carried 69 seats in a reduced House of 86.

No sooner had this attack been repelled than another came from a different quarter. In 1934, the Liberals, under Mitchell Hepburn, had gained office in Ontario, after thirty years in opposition. Hepburn, a dynamic, wise-cracking young farmer of Elgin County, had spent one term at Ottawa as an inconspicuous backbencher, but his selection as Ontario leader and his subsequent success at the polls seem to have turned his head, for his administration was characterized by a series of irresponsible acts. For some reason, he had developed an intense antipathy to Mackenzie King. He now caused a resolution to be carried in the legislature criticizing the Ottawa government's conduct of the war.

Since Hepburn's popularity was still great throughout the province, King's Ontario ministers did not dare challenge him in the same manner as Lapointe and his colleagues had challenged Duplessis; but the time had come for a federal election, and this Mr. King called for March 26, 1940.

In the campaign, the Conservatives, under Dr. Manion, criticized the government's conduct of the war in terms similar to those employed by Hepburn, and called for a national government. The Conservatives, however, did not differ, at least, officially, from the Liberals on the question of conscription.

To the demand for a national government, Mr. King replied that his government already represented every part of Canada, whereas the party led by Dr. Manion was without any representation in one-third of the provinces. He relied on the record of his government, with which the voters seemed to be satisfied, for on election day the Mackenzie King government was sustained by the largest majority in the history of Canada, having carried 183 seats out of 245. Dr. Manion himself was among the defeated candidates. Since first taking office in 1921, Mackenzie King had driven three Conservative leaders into retirement.

CHAPTER XXIV

THE END OF THE ROAD

THOSE who begrudge Mackenzie King his share of credit are inclined to talk of his luck; at every juncture in his career they discern the element of luck. And so it was with the manner in which he fell heir to Bennett's reform policies. Ignoring or discounting the constitutional issues involved, and having resisted all previous attempts to deal with such matters, Bennett, at the last moment, had rushed in with a variety of hastily-considered measures, most of which were later declared unconstitutional. One of these was an unemployment insurance scheme.

Mackenzie King, when his turn came, wrote to the provincial premiers, asking whether they would agree to an amendment of the British North America Act giving the federal government power to enact and administer unemployment legislation. Not till June 1940 had all the provinces agreed to the proposal, after which appropriate legislation was introduced (August 7) and passed. The measure, as subsequently amended, covers men and women working for a daily or weekly wage and on salary up to $4,800 a year. Minimum benefits in 1950 were, for a single man, $16.20 a week, and for a man with one dependant, $21.00.

During the 'phony' war, and for some time afterward, despite Canada's enormous industrial effort, the demand for fighting men did not strain the country's resources. From the landing of the first contingent in December 1939, the army had been concentrating in England under command of General McNaughton.

Highly trained in specialized warfare, it had been held in readiness for the expected invasion of Britain. Some sections had taken part in an expedition to Spitzbergen late in 1941; and on August 19, 1942, picked detachments 5,000 strong had led the van up the beaches at Dieppe, when 3,350 were killed, wounded or taken prisoner, in a vain attempt to gain a foothold in France.

In June 1940, the government had proclaimed the National Resources Mobilization Act, under which every person over 16 years of age was required to register, stating, among other things, whether or not he or she possessed any particular skills, and providing for the calling-up of any person for military or other service within Canada.

Fears were at once aroused in Quebec that this was the thin edge of the conscription wedge, but the Quebec members of the cabinet assured their compatriots that it was not so, again promising to resign should conscription be imposed. This, however, was not enough for Camillien Houde, mayor of Montreal, who urged people not to register. He was whisked away to an internment camp.

In October, the first men were drafted for service under the N.R.M.A. Contemptuously referred to as 'zombies', they were never taken seriously by the military authorities, and when, later on, they were needed overseas, they were found to be inadequately trained.

The United States government, in spite of the Neutrality Act, was as friendly to the cause of the Allies as the circumstances would permit; and from the first President Roosevelt was a participant in spirit. In a radio address the day war broke out, he said: 'This nation will remain a neutral nation. But I cannot ask that every American remain neutral in thought as well. Even a neutral has a right to take account of facts. Even a neutral cannot be asked to close his mind and his conscience.' Thereafter, Roosevelt closed neither.

In the ten days previous to Canada's declaration of war, which closed the border to war supplies, stores and equipment, to the value of many millions of dollars, were rushed to Canada.

On August 18, 1940, the Ogdensburg agreement between the United States and Canada established a Permanent Joint Board on Defence; and shortly after, the 'lend-lease' arrangement, in which King had a prominent part, became effective. It was a transparent device to allow 'conscience' free play.

The Hyde Park agreement of April 20, 1941, arrived at in the course of a friendly visit by King to Roosevelt's Hyde Park home, after the failure of more formal efforts at the official level, further extended the collaboration of the two countries to make possible the securing for Canada of badly-needed supplies and equipment without too greatly depleting its store of vital dollars.

Then, with the entry of the United States into the war on December 7, the shattered remnants of neutrality were thrown aside and the two countries worked together with a common aim. One result of this was the construction of the Alaska Highway, between

Edmonton and Fairbanks, pushed through the wilderness by the United States army in 1943. And if the Japanese had not been so promptly driven from the Aleutians, there would also have been a railway, for which plans and surveys had already been completed.

In the meantime, Canada had been advancing on every front. On April 9, 1940, the Department of Munitions and Supply had been organized under Clarence D. Howe, who proceeded to mobilize the resources of the country, producing a steady stream of war equipment and supplies out of all proportion to Canada's limited population.

While on a flight, in a military plane, from Ottawa to Toronto, on June 10, Norman Rogers died in a crash, and Ralston was transferred from Finance to National Defence, Ilsley going to Finance. In the light of later events, and in view of talk about King's luck, it is interesting to reflect upon the consequences of that airplane crash in 1940.

Another turn of inscrutable fate was the death, on November 26, 1941, of Ernest Lapointe, King's faithful lieutenant, respected and trusted by his compatriots in Quebec as no other had been trusted and respected in the history of Canada. Laurier and La Fontaine both had their admiring and devoted followers, but also had opponents, bitter and uncompromising. Lapointe was not without opponents, for a politician without opponents would be an anomaly, but even his opponents respected him and were reasonably friendly.

To King, and to the cause of national unity, likely to become strained at any moment, this was one of the hardest blows imaginable. No one was in sight to take Lapointe's place. Here again it might be said that King's luck came to the rescue. Returning from Lapointe's funeral, King, in a quandary, asked Power if he could suggest a successor, and Power suggested Louis St. Laurent, a Quebec corporation lawyer, little more than a name to King. Having a high regard for Power's opinion, King invited St. Laurent to Ottawa, and within a matter of days he had been appointed Minister of Justice, and in due course won Lapointe's former seat in Quebec East.

The most important event in the economic sphere during these days was the imposition by the Wartime Prices and Trade Board of an overall price ceiling. The Board had been instituted at the beginning of the war, and in the interval had placed controls upon certain commodities already in short supply; but in the autumn of 1941 Donald Gordon, Deputy-Governor of the Bank of Canada, had been transferred to the Board as chairman; and on December 1, for the first time in any democratic country an attempt was made, across the entire economy, to arrest the tide of rising prices. Better than its corresponding agencies in the United Kingdom and the United States, the Board succeeded in holding the cost of living during the entire period of the war.

From the outbreak of war there had been a considerable demand for conscription. This issue cut across parties and came from all parts of Canada—except French-speaking Quebec. The situation was different from that which obtained during World War I, because now there were large numbers of veterans of the first war who felt especially entitled to express an opinion. Also, Canadian military authorities were now largely recruited from the ranks of professional or semi-professional soldiers, most of whom were in favour of conscription. To them, the military side of the war was the most important, and they were in a strategic position to make their prejudices effective.

Sooner or later, conscription becomes an issue whenever a country is at war. Previous to World War I, British countries looked with contempt upon the conscript armies of continental Europe, insisting upon the superiority, on every ground, of their own volunteer forces. But necessity has a way of overcoming conviction, and one by one most of those formerly opposed to conscription changed their views. In Canada, the country was almost torn asunder in the process. Not many thoughtful people wanted to see the process repeated.

Canada's situation with respect to war differs from that of most countries. The people are divided into the two principal groups, those whose ancestors were French, and those of other derivations. The latter group is divided again into those of British origin, and those of non-British origins.

If Canada were being attacked, there is little doubt that people in all these groups would rally to its defence in equal proportions. But Canada, since the days of the Fenians, has never been attacked, nor, in the opinion of most Canadians, has ever been in much danger of attack. Canada's involvement in war has been chiefly because the United Kingdom was already involved, and almost entirely due to the emotional attitude of those whose ancestry was British, and whose emotional attachment to the ancestral homeland was greater than to Canada.

The United States, having probably a greater actual concern with the issues involved in each case, remained neutral during the first two years of World War I and World War II, despite the fact that it has a greater percentage of people of British ancestry than Canada. Sometimes Canadians of British descent are inclined to look down upon the 'isolationism' of the United States, and to take credit for a larger loyalty and a broader appreciation of world events, when, as a matter of fact, they are merely responding to different loyalties.

And so it goes in the matter of conscription. With many important exceptions, those who favour conscription put the war, the fighting war, ahead of everything else. This has been further complicated by the fact that people of British descent have for almost 200 years believed in their superior right to determine such policies; and they also unconsciously feel that *Canadiens*, who generally are opposed to, or indifferent to, what they consider British wars, are, as a people, inferior to themselves. This, of course, is not peculiar to British-Canadians; it is a universal human trait, and one that has probably brought more grief to the world than any other. In ordinary circumstances, these feelings are more or less submerged; only in times of emotional strain, such as wartime, do they come to the surface.

Another factor is involved. In wartime the military authorities, in any country, tend more or less to become a state within a state, largely autonomous, making its own rules and imposing its own judgments. To the military mind, winning a war by military means is naturally the most important consideration; anything else is looked upon as poltroonery. Yet history is filled with evidences of their error.

During the elections of 1940, while Manion had hoped to gain some support in Quebec by taking an anti-conscriptionist stand, the Conservatives had suppressed their militant wing; but when that gesture toward Quebec failed, and Manion had gone his way, Arthur Meighen again resumed the leadership, hoisting the flag of conscription to the Tory masthead.

Meighen resigned from the Senate and, to provide a safe seat, arranged for the resignation of Colonel Alan Cockeram, Conservative member for South York, then on active service. South York had never elected anyone but a Conservative; and, as an act of courtesy, the Liberals in that riding agreed not to oppose Meighen. When the C.C.F. nominated a candidate, a number of prominent Liberals distributed a circular asking their fellow-Liberals to vote for Meighen. The C.C.F. candidate was Joseph Noseworthy, for many years a high school teacher in the riding, and popular among the younger generation; but with the Liberals supporting Meighen, Noseworthy, who, in 1940, had polled only 5,372 votes, seemed to have little chance.

Mackenzie King was not looking forward with any pleasure to the prospect of Meighen's return to the House. He felt that Meighen would be a disturbing influence, one certainly not calculated to promote the unity of Canada, as he saw it. Then, King's luck, or Meighen's ineptitude, turned what seemed a certain success into defeat. 'Mitch' Hepburn, still pursuing his vendetta against King, had joyfully joined forces with Meighen, and his attacks on King so incensed the Liberals of South York that they reversed their decision and threw their support to Noseworthy. Substantial contributions from Liberal sources found their way by indirect channels into the Noseworthy election fund. The vote on the night of February 9, 1942, stood: Noseworthy, 16,408; Meighen, 11,952.

Although Meighen did not get the chance to lead the assault in the House, the conscriptionists had their fifth column in the cabinet itself. Following Norman Rogers' death, King had chosen Ralston as Minister of National Defence. Ralston, born in 1881 at Amherst, N.S., graduate of the Dalhousie Law School, had served with distinction in World War I, but, unlike most former soldiers, had continued his connection with military affairs. He believed in conscription, and with him it was a matter of principle. Well aware, when he joined the ministry, that the government was committed to voluntary enlistment, he did not believe that such a policy could be maintained.

The possibility that, at an unfavourable moment, he might be forced to accede to the pressure for conscription became almost an obsession with King. To the steady pressure of Ralston was added that of J. L. Ilsley and Angus L. Macdonald, former Premier of Nova Scotia, who had become Minister of Defence for Naval Service, both Maritimers, and that of T. A. Crerar, a conscriptionist from Union government days.

King now decided to take another step which could lead to conscription if absolutely necessary, but which, depending upon circumstances, need never go so far. This was a plebiscite designed to relieve the government of its repeated pledges concerning conscription, giving it a free hand to meet any situation that might arise. Accordingly, on April 27, 1942, the people were asked to vote on the question: 'Are you in favour of releasing the government from any obligation arising out of any past commitments respecting the methods of raising men for military services?'

The answer, on the basis of majority vote, was 'yes'. Sixty-four per cent of those who participated voted to free the government of its promise; but, in Quebec, 76 per cent voted 'no', and of those who voted 'yes', the majority were in English-speaking-districts. The government, if not all of its members, was free of its pledges, but it would still need to coerce Quebec if conscription were resorted to.

When Bill No. 80 was introduced for the purpose of annulling Clause 3 of the N.M.R.A., which restricted the area of service permitted under the Act, Cardin, who had supported the plebiscite because he believed it to be but a formality so far as Quebec was concerned, resigned. This could mean the beginning of the end for the government, which King was determined to prevent at all costs. Many anxious moments were still ahead of him.

General McNaughton, who described his army as 'a dagger pointed at the heart of Berlin', had hoped to lead his men into action as a unit in the expected invasion of Europe across the English Channel. But when the invasion went through Sicily instead, his command, broken into sections, was despatched to join the British Eighth Army in Italy; and, in the following year, when the 3rd Canadian Division fought as a unit in France, McNaughton found himself a general without an army.

This brought to a head differences of opinion becoming increasingly frequent between McNaughton and Ralston; and in December 1943, McNaughton resigned and was succeeded by General H. D. G. Crerar.

Meantime, under C. D. Howe's guidance and direction, Canada's factories had increased enormously in productivity; and if there is one feature more than another of Canada's war effort which may be referred to in superlatives, it is the manner in which the industrial resources of the nation were mobilized. Considering its small population, and the number of men and women drawn into the army, air force and navy, Canada's exploit in this regard has never been equalled. While successive manpower 'crises' occurred, it can still be said that Howe's feat was outstanding.

The war marked the final collapse of the traditional political economy of Adam Smith. According to Smith, if you haven't a dollar, you can't spend it; but, according to the new economy, you should then spend two dollars. Government budgets were mounting beyond all previous experience, and so were taxes. Yet most people had more money than ever. Instead of planning ways to save money, economists devised schemes for greater spending; that is to say, spending in compensatory ways. And thus it was that economists, not politicians, least of all a bachelor Prime Minister, thought up a scheme to subsidize the mothers of Canada.

King was not slow, however, to see the political implications, once he was assured the project could be financed. In it he achieved a bloodless victory. The C.C.F. had been advocating some such measure since Woodsworth's earliest days; and while it did not entirely meet Social Credit ideas of the national dividend, Social Crediters could not oppose it. The Conservatives were trapped; it was contrary to their beliefs, but they dare not vote against it. In this way, since 1945, every child under sixteen has received a monthly payment, usually through its mother. Furthermore, payments go to the children of both rich and poor, to the papoose in the tented encampment and the Eskimo tot in its mother's *artigi*.

Women had come forward in increasing numbers to handle jobs previously considered suitable only for men; and in some cases they did so well that they were kept on after the war.

In the armed services, the air force and the navy were never short of recruits; only for infantry units, never so popular, was there fear of a shortage; and, in this regard, as in the previous war, the ambitions of military men, with their disregard for other aspects of the national economy, led to plans, despite the announced intention of the government, that could only result in a manpower shortage.

With the invasion of Europe, the need for infantry recruits increased, and the demand for conscription grew more insistent. As Borden had done in 1917, Ralston, in the fall of 1944, made a trip overseas, returning on October 18 in a great state of alarm concerning the imminent failure of replacements, and demanding the immediate conscription of men in the home defence army. To this, King would not agree, arguing that further men could be secured by the voluntary method. Ralston, unconvinced, agreed to make a further attempt, but, on November 1, declared his efforts were unavailing. King then accepted a resignation that Ralston had given him two years before in a disagreement over conscription. The following day, General McNaughton, who still believed in voluntary recruiting, was sworn in as Minister of National Defence.

McNaughton assured King that he could raise the needed men, but soon found it impossible to overcome the resistance, amounting almost to sabotage, of a military organization determined to discredit the voluntary system. Parliament had been called for November 22, and it was on that day that McNaughton is said to have informed the Prime Minister that four senior officers of the headquarters staff had threatened to resign, and that a general breakdown in the military organization seemed imminent.

In the face of this threat, King was forced to change his policy, and in this was supported by Louis St. Laurent, who had never made any pledge concerning conscription. St. Laurent was able to hold other Quebec cabinet members in line (except Power, who resigned). An order-in-council authorized the transfer of 16,000 men from the N.R.M.A., and this was confirmed by parliament early in the morning of December 8.

This clash of opinion, which convulsed the cabinet, nearly wrecked the government, and rocked official Ottawa, caused scarcely a ripple throughout the country. One writer has since referred to it as 'bordering on mutiny', and another as a 'revolt'. Whether either term was justified must await publication of diaries and other records still unavailable; but there is no doubt that the government failed to receive the support it had a right to expect from its top military personnel.

Looking back on the event, from the vantage of even a few years, it is obvious that those who were willing to risk the disruption of Canada for what, in reality, had little effect upon the war, were taking themselves too seriously. Even then the war was converging to its close; and certainly, in the light of what has since occurred— with the 'victors' at each others' throats, and armaments piling up for a third war—considerable hardihood is required to contend that the conscription of a single Canadian was justified.[1]

While this struggle was in progress in Ottawa, a group of Canadians were making history in the Arctic. Sailing from Halifax in July, with Vancouver as its destination, the R.C.M.P. 80-ton schooner *St. Roch*, under command of Sergeant (now Sub-Inspector) Henry A. Larsen, with a crew of 11, left Pond Inlet, Baffin Island, on August 17, 1944, and proceeded westward along Lancaster Sound, Barrow Strait and Melville Sound, then turned southward

[1] For a different point of view concerning this incident, see Hutchison, Bruce: *The Incredible Canadian*, Toronto, 1952.

through Prince of Wales Strait to reach the R.C.M.P. post at Holman
Island, off the west coast of Victoria Island, on September 4, thus
making the famed Northwest Passage in eighteen days!

Germany surrendered on May 7, 1945, while spokesmen for the
victorious nations gathered at San Francisco to plan the successor
to the League of Nations. Mr. King headed a deputation from
Canada which included representatives of the opposition parties.
Since then, Canada has been an active member of the United
Nations, and Canadians, generally, have continued, despite its
defects, to give it their support.

With the European war at an end, but with yet no easing of
restrictions and controls, Canadians might have turned for relief to
a new government. This, Mr. King gave them a chance to do on
June 11, 1945, but apparently they preferred him to John Bracken,
who now led the (Progressive) Conservatives, or Mr. Coldwell.
The Liberals carried 125 seats, the Conservatives, 67, the C.C.F., 28,
Social Credit, 13, with a dozen assorted independents, including one
communist (Labour-Progressive), later put in gaol. Mr. King lost
his own seat in Prince Albert to the C.C.F., which carried 18 of the
21 Saskatchewan seats, but was later elected in Glengarry.

Having played a large part in bringing about Canada's status as
an independent member of the Commonwealth, Mackenzie King
wished also to have a hand in rounding out Confederation by bringing Newfoundland into the Union. This was a long-held ambition,
and, at last, in 1948, it seemed attainable. Representatives of Canada
and Newfoundland met at Ottawa in October to settle the final
details, and on the following March 31, Newfoundland became the
tenth province of Canada.

King had shattered the hopes of four Conservative leaders in a
row, and having held office for a longer period than any other British
Prime Minister, he began to think of the party which, to a large
extent, was the product of his own political genius; and, of course,
it was natural for him to believe that if the future of his party was
assured, the future of Canada would be secure. A true representative
of his time, while admitting some of its defects, he believed to the
end of his days in the two-party system.

King resigned as leader of the party on August 5, 1948. Although
it was known that Louis St. Laurent was King's choice as his successor, several others were in the running, but the convention was
strong for St. Laurent. For the moment, King retained his place as
Prime Minister, but on November 15 this office, too, was passed on

to St. Laurent. That King's work was well done was amply demonstrated on June 27, 1949, when the people of Newfoundland joined with those of every other province (except, perhaps, Alberta!) in voting the St. Laurent government back into office with the greatest majority ever given any government.

Irrespective of politics or party, such unanimity was, in the circumstances, a good sign. It showed that the work of Macdonald, Laurier and King had not been in vain. Canadians had come through the strain of war and could unite in support of a government headed by a *Canadien*. The chances were good that at last the two cultures had merged into a common citizenship.

In December 1949, parliament passed a statutory amendment giving the Supreme Court of Canada final authority (in place of the Judicial Committee of the Privy Council, in England) in all judicial cases; and, on December 31, an act was proclaimed granting parliament the right to amend the Constitution of Canada in federal matters.

These final fruits of his efforts, Mackenzie King lived to see. He died at Kingsmere, his country place in the Gatineau hills, near Ottawa, on July 22, 1950.

And, on February 28, 1952, Vincent Massey became governor-general, the first Canadian ever to assume that post, marking the end of the long road from colonialism to nationhood.

CHAPTER XXV

NORTH AMERICAN NATION

WHEN Moses led the Jews out of Egypt to seek the 'Promised Land', it was grass they went in search of. And, ever since, people on the move have sought grass for flocks and herds, or fertile fields for the growing of crops.

That is one of the reasons why Canada's vast northern hinterland has been either overlooked or discounted. Most people have a traditional predilection for arable land; land that would not produce crops could not provide an enduring basis for society. Not till recently has it been fully appreciated, and then not by all, that in this mechanized age, metals might provide an even more enduring basis for society.

Sir Wilfrid Laurier had an abiding faith in the future of Canada, yet he died without realizing the real basis of its greatness. Mackenzie King did much to make Canada an autonomous nation, but he was only slightly less unaware of the importance of the Canadian Shield in the working out of its destiny.

During Laurier's day, and well into King's, Canada was generally believed to be a narrow strip of disconnected communities separated by permanent wasteland barriers. And this narrow strip must remain so by the presence, across the north, from the Atlantic to the Rockies, of a vast expanse of barren rock, covered by stretches of muskeg, or dense growths of trees, too small for sawlogs. Outside of trapping or hunting, this region, comprising two-thirds of Canada, had very little to commend it.

As late as 1951, the Royal Commission on National Development in the Arts, Letters and Sciences, commonly called the Massey Commission, had this to say in its report: 'Our population stretches in a narrow and not even continuous ribbon along our frontier—fourteen millions along a five thousand mile front. In meeting influences from across the border . . . we have not even the advantage of what soldiers call defence in depth.'

Defence in depth! It is true that during most of its history Canada has consisted of the narrow strip already mentioned. And so long as this was true, it might never expect to be a great country—or even remain an independent one.

But that is no longer true. During the years since World War II, the picture has changed. Canadians have learned the value of the rocks that constitute the Canadian Shield. And ever since then the northern frontier has been rapidly receding. Canada has already largely attained that 'defence in depth', lack of which was so deplored by the Massey Commission.

Mining developments, stretching across the continent, from Labrador to the Yukon, provide a zone from 400 to 1,000 miles wide. For example, the iron ranges of Labrador and New Quebec are from 800 to 1,000 miles north of Halifax, St. John and Montreal; the goldfields of Porcupine and Kirkland Lake are 500 miles north of Toronto; the copper-gold deposits of Flin Flon are 500 miles north of Winnipeg, and the nickel of Lynn Lake, another 120 miles, as the airplane flies; the goldfields of Yellowknife are 1,000 miles north of the international boundary; while the silver-lead of Mayo is even farther north.

The intervening territory may not support as dense a population as other parts of Canada; but, in time, because of the richness of its resources, it will probably maintain as many people as Canada has had up to the middle of the twentieth century; and certainly many more than any country depending mainly upon agriculture, lumbering or fishing could ever support.

Not only has Canada the metals, but it also has the power necessary to convert them into things people need. Next to the inexhaustible power that its rivers can produce, the greatest power-source is the oil and natural gas that have accumulated through geologic ages beneath the western plains. These oilfields, now only at their beginning, will eventually extend down the Mackenzie valley to the Arctic. And then there is uranium, which makes it possible to tap the energy that binds the earth together.

Next to oil, or perhaps of equal value, is iron ore. Till recently, Canada seemed likely to remain an iron-importing country. Now, with immense deposits in Labrador and New Quebec, together with those of northwestern Ontario, Canada moves into the category of an iron-exporting country. Either of these essential commodities would be enough to make a country important, industrially, but the presence of both in unlimited supply makes Canada one of the most fortunate of countries.

When Laurier, in a moment of sublime faith, declared that the twentieth century would be Canada's he was much nearer the truth than he realized, for not till that century could Canada ever have been of much consequence. Even with its wealth of minerals, Canada could not have been important before the age of machines; and not till the invention and general use of the internal combustion engine could the oilfields of the plains have justified the immense cost of discovery and development.

Even so, Canada would have had to wait till the age of aviation really to come into its own. Without the airplane, the new mining regions could never have been opened up as they have (materials for the railways into Labrador and Lynn Lake have been transported by air).

But the airplane has done much more than that. Occupying the northern half of the North American continent, Canada is in a strategic position to benefit from the commerce of the airways. Not only are the shortest routes from important points in North America to important points in Europe across Canada, but also between New Zealand, Australia, China and Japan and European points.

All this, of course, while indicating that Canada might become a rich country, need not necessarily mean that Canada possesses real elements of greatness. The Royal Commission on National Development in the Arts, Letters and Sciences presented a pessimistic picture concerning Canada's cultural accomplishments up to the middle of the twentieth century.

If the Commission's assumption that Canada lacked geographic depth was correct, and could never be corrected, then its pessimism was fully justified; for, in that event, Canada could never hope to improve its lot. But assuming this to be but a temporary matter, rapidly being corrected, and taking into account men and women whom Canada has produced who have risen to eminence in the United States, such pessimism is not so defensible.

With the incorporation of the new north into the Canadian community, the eyes of Canada must increasingly turn northward. No longer will books and magazines, radio and television programs produced in the United States entirely satisfy the people of this new land, who will have developed their own ways of living and will desire their own interpreters. In the future, while even more greatly interested in what goes on in the rest of the world, Canadians will more and more want to know about their own country.

Despite their limited field, the production of Canadian writers, painters, sculptors, musicians, actors and other artists compares very favourably with that produced elsewhere; but if Canada had been able to retain all who have emigrated to other countries, principally the United States, this would be much more evident.

In support of this, it is only necessary to give a few examples. For many years, the general manager of the Metropolitan Opera, New York, a singer in his own right, was a Canadian. 'America's Sweetheart', of the silent films, was born in Toronto, as were the two actors who best impersonated Abraham Lincoln on the stage. Editors, writers, architects, educators, doctors, engineers, and, in fact, persons in all walks of life, passing as Americans, were born in Canada. The pages of *Who's Who* are filled with former Canadians.

All that is needed to keep the coming generations of Canadians in Canada is the opportunity to make a living at home, and it would seem that the time has about arrived. Despite intense pressure on the part of those who would confine the functions of radio and television more and more to commercial uses, successive governments have adhered to the policy adopted in 1932 that broadcasting should be essentially a national monopoly. The Canadian Broadcasting Corporation has been one of the chief promoters of music and the drama and undoubtedly has made it possible for many artists in these fields to remain at home.

With the passing of time, Canada's traditional problems, one after another, have been solved or greatly alleviated. The oldest and most serious, the clash of loyalties, has become less intense with the development of Canadian national sentiment; the struggle against colonialism has ended; the railways have become docile servants rather than corrupting influences; and the flow of Canada's brightest youth to the United States has not only declined, but is being reversed.

One ancient problem remains. Through all of Canada's history, the control of liquor has presented problems that have baffled solution. Now, with greatly increased social acceptance of the use of liquor, and with an increasingly mechanized society, Canada, in common with other countries, finds the problem becoming more serious. Although not yet generally so considered, it is undoubtedly Canada's most serious social problem.

As Canada occupies a strategic position with respect to air traffic, so does it occupy a similar position in economic matters. Bound by ties of sentiment, as well as self-interest, to the United Kingdom and other countries of the sterling group, and, by the dollar-partnership, closely linked to the economy of the United States, Canada has a vital interest in the economic welfare of both groups.

Canadians are well aware of how much their prosperity depends upon that of other countries. The possession of vast mineral riches and illimitable power resources are of little avail if their products cannot be economically marketed. Since the end of the depression, Canadian producers have found a ready market in providing for war or in anticipation of war. When that stimulus is removed, the experiences of the thirties might easily be repeated.

During World War II, the government, not expecting the prospect of another war to arise so soon, appointed a Royal Commission under the chairmanship of Dr. Cyril James, principal of McGill University, himself a noted economist, to study reconstruction problems.

The commission recommended that:

If Canada is going to sell goods abroad either it must take payment in goods or services produced in other countries, or it must frankly express its willingness to supply such goods as a long-term capital investment to be paid either by principal and interest in traditional fashion or to be paid intangibly by better relations and a better orderd world.

Hitherto Canada has been an importer of capital, and will continue to be for some time to come; but when the oilfields are developed to the point where they produce in excess of domestic requirements, when the iron ranges are likewise, and when outside capital for mining development is no longer needed, Canada should be in a position to extend much more of the credit suggested by the James Commission. Then its position midway between the two currency groups should be an advantage. Nevertheless, the problem of finding markets for both processed and raw materials at the same time will not be an easy one.

During the nineteenth century, the United Kingdom was the world's banker. It provided a market for countries having an excess of raw materials, and invested its surplus in countries needing capital for development. At least within the immediate future, the United Kingdom will not be able to resume this position.

The United States, on the other hand, while financially able to move into the United Kingdom's vacated position, is not likely, by reason of its traditional tendency toward autarchy, to fill such a position.

It is not to be supposed that Canada can fill the gap, but, to the extent of its financial resources, it can probably play a much larger part in this field than its rather modest demeanour might suggest. Canada is ideally situated, both geographically and industrially, to secure a large share of Asiatic trade, but this must be cultivated. And in order to cultivate it, Canada will have to formulate its own foreign policy, and not continue, as in the immediate past, to follow the lead of the United States.

For more than a century and a half, Canadians were engaged in extricating themselves from the trammels of colonialism. But they must now exercise all their astuteness to avoid coming under the unconscious domination of the United States. Although Canadians have no more reason now to fear aggressive action on the part of their southern neighbour than at any time previously, it is a fact that almost every American implicitly believes that Canada's ultimate destiny is within the United States. To them, it seems illogical that a people having so much in common with them should not wish to merge its identity with theirs.

That sort of domination Canadians need not fear. And they have no reason to fear domination by the American capital being poured into Canadian developments, for capital has a way of becoming nationalized.

Now that the last subservient link has been snapped, Canada can turn to the United Kingdom with a freedom from restraint not formerly possible. In the past, that restraint has been felt more generally by *Canadiens* than by English-speaking Canadians, but, in future, this should be much less evident. Although monarchy has become an anachronism in most of the countries of the world, it is not so considered in Canada; and the fact that the final bond is embodied in the person of the gracious young woman who won all Canadian hearts in 1951 is the strongest guarantee that Canada, while in all other respects a North American nation, will proudly continue in association with the other members of the British Commonwealth of Nations.

BIBLIOGRAPHY

BIGGAR, E. B.: *The Canadian Railway Problem*, Toronto, 1917.
BORDEN, HENRY (ed.): *Robert Laird Borden: His Memoirs*, 2 vols., Toronto, 1938.
BRACQ, JEAN C.: *The Evolution of French Canada*, New York, 1924.
BREBNER, J. B.: *The Neutral Yankees of Nova Scotia*, New York, 1937.
BROWN, G. W.: *Building the Canadian Nation*, Toronto, 1942.
BRUCHESI, JEAN: *A History of Canada*, Toronto, 1950.
BURPEE, LAWRENCE J.: *Sandford Fleming*, London, 1915.
CAMPBELL, GEORGE G.: *The History of Nova Scotia*, Toronto, 1948.
CARTWRIGHT, RICHARD J.: *Reminiscences*, Toronto, 1912.
CLARK, S. D.: *The Social Development of Canada*, Toronto, 1942.
CREIGHTON, DONALD G.: *Dominion of the North*, Toronto, 1944.
—— *John A. Macdonald, The Young Politician*, Toronto, 1952.
DAFOE, JOHN W.: *Laurier, A Study in Canadian Politics*, Toronto, 1922.
—— *Clifford Sifton in Relation to His Times*, Toronto, 1931.
DAWSON, C. M. (ed.): *The New North-West*, Toronto, 1947
DAWSON, R. M.: *Constitutional Issues in Canada, 1900-1931*, Oxford, 1933.
DAY, S. P.: *English America, or Pictures of Canadian Places and People*, London, 1864.
DORLAND, ARTHUR G.: *Our Canada*, Toronto, 1949.
EWART, JOHN S.: *The Kingdom of Canada*, etc., Toronto, 1908.
—— *The Kingdom Papers*, vol. 1, Ottawa, 1912.
—— *The Kingdom Papers*, vol. 2, Toronto, n.d.
FINNIE, RICHARD: *Canada Moves North*, Toronto, 1942.
FLEMING, SANDFIELD: *The Intercolonial Railway*, etc., Montreal, 1876.
GARRATT, GEOFFREY: *What has Happened to Europe*, New York, 1940.
GIBBON, JOHN M.: *Canadian Mosaic*, Toronto, 1938.
GLAZEBROOK, G. P. DE T.: *History of Transportation in Canada*, New Haven, 1928.
—— *Canadian External Relations, an Historical Study to 1914*, Toronto, 1942.
GUILLET, EDWIN C.: *Early Life in Upper Canada*, Toronto, 1933.
HARDY, H. REGINALD: *Mackenzie King of Canada*, Toronto, 1949.
HODGINS, THOMAS: *British and American Diplomacy Affecting Canada, 1872-1899*, Toronto, 1900.
HOWARD, JOSEPH KINSEY: *Strange Empire*, New York, 1952.
HUGHES, E. C.: *French Canada in Transition*, Chicago, 1943.
HUTCHISON, BRUCE: *The Incredible Canadian*, Toronto, 1952.
INNIS, H. A.: *History of the Canadian Pacific Railway*, London, 1923.
INNIS, H. A., and LOWER, A. R. M. (ed.): *Select Documents in Canadian Economic History, 1783-1885*, Toronto, 1933.
INNIS, M. Q.: *An Economic History of Canada*, Toronto, 1935.
KEENLEYSIDE, H. L., and BROWN, G. S.: *Canada and the United States*, New York, 1952.
LEACOCK, STEPHEN: *Canada, the Foundations of its Future*, Montreal, 1941.
LE BOURDAIS, D. M.: *Canada's Century*, Toronto, 1951.
LEWIS, JOHN: *George Brown* (Makers of Canada Series), Toronto, 1926.

LOWER, A. R. M.: *Colony to Nation. A History of Canada*, Toronto, 1946.

—— *Canada, Nation and Neighbour*, Toronto, 1952.

MACKAY, DOUGLAS: *The Honourable Company, A History of The Hudson's Bay Company*, Indianapolis, 1936.

MACKAY, R. A. (ed.): *Newfoundland, Economic, Diplomatic, and Strategic Studies*, Toronto, 1946.

MARTIN, CHESTER: *Empire and Commonwealth*, Oxford, 1929.

McHENRY, D. E.: *The Third Force in Canada, the Cooperative Commonwealth Federation, 1932-1948*, Toronto, 1950.

McINNIS, EDGAR W.: *The Unguarded Frontier*, New York, 1942.

—— *Canada, A Political and Social History*, New York, 1947.

MEIGHEN, ARTHUR: *Unrevised and Unrepented*, Toronto, 1949.

MOORHOUSE, HOPKINS: *Deep Furrows*, Toronto, 1918.

MORTON, A. S.: *History of the Canadian West to 1870-71*, London, n.d.

MORTON, W. L.: *The Progressive Party in Canada*, Toronto, 1950.

PARKIN, GEORGE R.: *Sir John A. Macdonald* (Makers of Canada Series), Toronto, 1926.

POPE, JOSEPH (SIR): *Memoirs of Sir John Alexander Macdonald*, 2 vols., London, n.d.

RIDDELL, W. A.: *World Security by Conference*, Toronto, 1947.

ROLPH, WILLIAM KIRBY: *Henry Wise Wood of Alberta*, Toronto, 1950.

SIEGFRIED, A.: *The Race Question in Canada*, London, 1907.

SKELTON, O. D.: *The Railway Builders*, Toronto, 1916.

—— *The Life and Times of Sir Alexander Tilloch Galt*, Toronto, 1920.

—— *Life and Letters of Sir Wilfrid Laurier*, 2 vols., Toronto, 1921.

SMITH, GOLDWIN: *The Treaty of Washington, 1871*, Ithica, 1941.

STACEY, C. P.: *Canada and the British Army, 1846-1871*, New York, 1938.

STEFANSSON, V.: *The Northward Course of Empire*, Toronto, 1922.

TROTTER, R. G.: *Canadian Federation, Its Origins and Achievement*, Toronto, 1924.

TUPPER, CHARLES (SIR): *Recollections of Sixty Years in Canada*, London, 1914.

UNDERHILL, F. H.: 'The Development of National Political Parties in Canada', *Canadian Historical Review*, Dec. 1935.

WADE, MASON: *The French-Canadian Outlook, A Brief Account of the Unknown North Americans*, New York, 1946.

WEATHERBE, R. L.: *The Acadian Boundary Disputes and the Ashburton Treaty*, Halifax (Collections of the Nova Scotia Historical Society, 1887-88), 1888.

WILLISON, JOHN S.: *Sir Wilfrid Laurier and the Liberal Party, a Political History*, Toronto, 1903.

WILSON, GEORGE E.: *The Life of Robert Baldwin*, Toronto, 1933.

WOOD, A. L.: *History of Farmers' Movements in Canada*, Toronto, 1924.

WOODSWORTH, J. S.: *Strangers Within Our Gates*, Toronto, 1909.

WRONG, GEORGE M.: *The Canadians, The Story of a People*, Toronto, 1938.

ZIEGLER, OLIVE: *Woodsworth, Social Pioneer*, Toronto, 1934.

INDEX

Due